The Shifting Scales of Justice

The Shifting Scales of Justice

The Supreme Court in Neo-liberal India

Edited by

MAYUR SURESH

and

SIDDHARTH NARRAIN

With a Preface by

UPENDRA BAXI

Orient BlackSwan

THE SHIFTING SCALES OF JUSTICE: THE SUPREME COURT IN NEO-LIBERAL INDIA

ORIENT BLACKSWAN PRIVATE LIMITED

Registered Office
3-6-752 Himayatnagar, Hyderabad 500 029, Telangana, India
E-mail: centraloffice@orientblackswan.com

Other Offices
Bengaluru, Bhopal, Chennai, Guwahati, Hyderabad, Jaipur,
Kolkata, Lucknow, Mumbai, New Delhi, Noida, Patna, Visakhapatnam

First Published 2014

Reprinted 2019

ISBN 978-93-5287-582-5

Typeset in Arno Pro 11/13 by
Jojy Philip, New Delhi 110 015

Printed in India at
Glorious Printers
Delhi

Published by
Orient Blackswan Private Limited
3-6-752 Himayatnagar, Hyderabad 500 029, Telangana, India
E-mail: info@orientblackswan.com

In memory of K. Balagopal (1952–2009), who through the remarkable breadth and vision of his work blurred the boundaries between legal practice, research and activism, and symbolised hope to so many of us.

Contents

Figures and Tables

FIGURES

TABLES

Abbreviations

ADR	Association for Democratic Reforms
AFSPA	Armed Forces (Special Powers) Act
ALF	Alternative Law Forum
BIS	Bureau of Indian Standards
BJP	Bharatiya Janata Party
CAD	Constituent Assembly Debate
CBI	Central Bureau of Investigation
CEC	Central Empowered Committee
CETP	Common Effluent Treatment Plants
CJM	chief judicial magistrate
CJS	Criminal Justice System
CLRA	Contract Labour (Regulation and Abolition) Act
CNG	compressed natural gas
CPI	Communist Party of India
CSCS	Centre for the Study of Culture and Society
CSLG	Centre for the Study of Law and Governance
JN	Judicial Nineties
MCOCA	Maharashtra Control of Organised Crime Act
MDMK	Marumalarchi Dravida Munnetra Kazhagam
MISA	Maintenance of Internal Security Act
NBA	Narmada Bachao Andolan
NDA	National Democratic Alliance
NGO	non-governmental organisation
NTPC	National Thermal Power Corporation
OMC	Orissa Mining Corporation
PCB	pollution control board

PDS	Preventive Detention System
PIL	public interest litigation
POTA	Prevention of Terrorism Act
PUCL	People's Union for Civil Liberties
PUDR	People's Union for Democratic Reforms
RSS	Rashtriya Swayamsevak Sangh
SAL	social action litigation
SIT	special investigation team
SSP	Sardar Sarovar Project
TADA	Terrorist and Disruptive Activities (Prevention) Act
UAPA	Unlawful Activities (Prevention) Act
UCIL	Union Carbide India Limited
UPA	United Progressive Alliance
WTO	World Trade Organization

Acknowledgements

The main themes of this book began with a feeling that the Supreme Court was moving towards the right, and were developed over a series of conversations at the Alternative Law Forum (ALF), the Centre for the Study of Culture and Society (CSCS), Centre for the Study of Law and Governance (CSLG), Jawaharlal Nehru University (JNU) and the Christ College of Law. Some of the essays in this volume were presented at a panel titled 'Assessing the "Conservative Shift" in the Indian Supreme Court's PIL Jurisprudence' at the inaugural Law and Social Sciences Research Network (LASS*net*) Conference at the CSLG, Jawaharlal Nehru University, Delhi, in January 2009.

We would like to thank our friends and comrades at ALF, CSLG, CSCS, Christ College of Law and the dispersed worlds of Bhagwan Nagar without whose generous conversations and light spirit, this book would not have been possible.

We would also like to thank Abhishek Anand, Aditi Ramesh, Amit Kiran, Megan Hjelle, Manish, Sudev Chaudhury, Stuti Subbaiah, Sahana Keshav, Ishita Gupta, Gautam Sundaresh and Poorvi Satija, who in their capacity as interns at the ALF helped us with research and transcriptions and unburdened us of the tedious task of editing and proofing.

Thanks are also due to Mimi Choudhury, Seema Sreenivas and Roopa Sharma for their patience and persevering with this book. Lastly, yet most importantly, we thank our families who have always provided the space and warmth that nurtured our intellectual endeavours.

Preface

The Alternative Law Forum (ALF)—a new tribe or 'commune' of non-campus-based thinkers and movement actors—continues remarkably even today to sustain a decade-plus promise of thinking through the 'alternatives'. The ALF labours suggest the importance of grasping the ubiquity of Indian law in Indian development; law stands imagined both as a source of domination and as a site of resistance. ALF further addresses law as a *politics of desire*; in this way, it brings to us not merely a grasp of antinomic relationships between legal *cultures* and *law as culture* but also represents law in all its complex formations of desire: thus, and to say the least here, ALF also strives to construct reflexive relationship between law and literature, visual and performing arts, theatre, film and media studies.

Overall, the ALF in a little over decade-plus existence has accomplished new forms of fellowship of critical juristic learning. Understanding 'law' is central but only when 'law' is thought to belong to the realms of both humanities and social sciences. The ALF calls towards a blending of disciplinarities in our ways of comprehending the ubiquity of law. It would be no overstatement on my part to say that ALF may be best viewed as a daring attempt at constituting an itinerant (*chalti firti*) though not a *gumrah* (pathless/directionless) multiversity.

The work in your hands reflects the 'spirit' of ALF. It began with a conference on 'Judicial Nineties' (JN, hereafter) convened by the intrepid ALF duo (Lawrence Liang and Arvind Narrain, enabled as well by other significant ALF others); it owes its monographic existence to the caring labours of Siddharth Narrain and Mayur Suresh. Their wisely crafted introduction to this volume liberates this Preface to address some wider concerns.

This volume speaks to us about 'judicial activism' generally and about social action litigation (SAL) specifically. It offers a rich fare: some contributors provide an ideological critique of SAL, many others suggest that SAL may not be understood except via scrupulous exploration of the jurisprudence of the Supreme Court of India: some maintain that the labels 'conservative' and 'progressive' are too facile and fail to reveal the institutional self-understanding of our apex justices at work. Indeed, what adds value to this work is the fact that some contributors here urge an institutional perspective—codes of constraints and opportunities—within which justices function.

I remain deeply honoured by some generous re-visitation of my writing regarding SAL, and judicial activism generally. Some contributors offer elements of critique faulting me for: (i) a penchant for qualitative over quantitative frames of analysis; (ii) deploying shifting meanings of 'judicial activism'; (iii) elevating (and to here adapt a fecund phrase-regime of Lon Fuller [1969: 5, 28]) the rather robust SAL ethic of judicial aspiration over the fragility of adjudicative performance; (iv) under-valuing the importance of legitimacy of co-equal institutors of national governance; and (v) over-privileging adjudicatory leadership without fully responding to the 'democratic deficit' of adjudicative overreach (howsoever, in turn, described).

I welcome this 'friendly fire'. I must defer the obligations of response to a future date, if only because of the space constraints of this Preface. I also think that addressing four distinct but related concerns remains more important in the context of the present work: understanding judicial activism, the notions of constitutional time, adjudicatory leadership of the Supreme Court of India and 'demosprudence'.

UNDERSTANDING 'JUDICIAL ACTIVISM'

This is never an easy task for several reasons.

First, denied life-tenures, and existing within the turnstiles of judicial elevation, most of our apex justices remain disabled from articulating any coherent adjudicatory ideology; and this is further aggravated by a roulette-wheel-type of contingent presence on fragmented Bench structure. The Supreme Court of India functions, then, more as an *assembly* of empanelled justices, rather than as any *cohesive* institution.

Second, one may seek in vain a degree of ideological or narrative coherence in adjudicative performance at the apex court level; not merely do the interpretive styles vary enormously, but so do the conflicting role conceptions about judicial role and function.

Third, judicial 'activism' is a coat of many colours; as far as I know, no Indian Supreme Court judge has been a self-consistent 'activist' being; put another way, activist justices in one sphere turn out to be quite 'reticent' in questioning the errant ways of sovereign power and function in other spheres. Thus, not all justices who consider themselves as 'activists' remain equally so in regard to all matters (cases and controversies) coming before them. Only a few justices can thus said to be self-consistent across spheres so divergent as relating to the protection of human rights of organised/disorganised labour; women's rights as human rights; patterns of human rights-oriented administration of criminal justice, specifically concerning protection of residual human rights of 'terror suspects' under the auspices of the draconian security legislation; and the rights of the urban and rural impoverished.

Fourth, SAL jurisprudence presents *many* stories, not any *singular* one. Without a will to judicial power, the remarkable expansion of judicial review process may not *at all* have occurred; yet the SAL may not be read merely as an act of 'usurpation' of powers of governance invested elsewhere. Nor does the institutional competence of the Court remain duly commensurate with wide-ranging policy formulation it undertakes.[1] SAL justices raise more expectations than they may fulfil, thus raising concerns about the legitimacy of judicial activism generally. Even so, social movement and human rights folks continue to invoke SAL jurisdiction. These very general observations would have to suffice here to reinforce a simple point: SAL has many histories/avatars, and not all its votaries and critics may speak to these in any single accent or voice.

Fifth, even as JN critics here bring a variety of perspectives concerning the SAL promise and its betrayal, those who would judge the judges also remain a house divided. The critics comprise legal professionals (lawyers and law teachers), other academics from diverse disciplines, the 24/7 mass media anchors and their reiterated guests, social movement and human rights activists, retired bureaucrats and justices, and other political actors. Like their critics, our justices come from and embody diverse social, cultural and ideological backgrounds. And if SAL justices may be said to lack narrative coherence and even integrity, justices in turn may extend a similar compliment to their critics. Recognising this mutuality, I suggest, provides a safe guide for reading the book in your hands.

UNDERSTANDING CONSTITUTIONAL AND ADJUDICATIVE TIME

This volume may perhaps best be read as suggesting distinctions between constitutional and adjudicatory time. These are not easy-at-hand categories; and all that I may do in some brief remarks is to suggest some ways ahead.

Constitutional time may be understood via some critical distinctions marking the difference between *constituent* and *constituted* time—that is the time of constitutional founding and the time of putting constitution to work, or to sleep. Most SAL critics are not as sharply imbued with the time of constitutional founding; however, SAL or activist justices are constantly reminded about the textuality of Constituent Assembly Debates (CADs); the reiterated juridical recourse to CADs brings back live the otherwise frozen moments of constitutional time into tasks of adjudication.

Constituted time is the time of everyday work of the basic institutions established by the Constitution, such as legislative, executive/administrative and adjudicative institutions as also of political parties; it is also the time of other mediating institutions such as the learned professions, mass media, and processes of participation initiated by social movement and human rights activism(s).

Constituted time, then, is the time of the 'normal' at least as contrasted with the 'extraordinary time' of the making of constitutions. 'Extraordinary' because that constituent moment births the founding of a new political and social order. Its 'new "politics" is always extraconstitutional' (as adjudged by extant constitutional orders and regimes); it 'aims either at core constitutional matters or at central social imaginary significations, cultural meanings, and economic issues, with the goal of transforming the basic structures of society and resignifying social reality'.[2] Extraordinary politics characterises what we today name as transformative constitutionalism.[3]

In this way, and to adapt Max Weber's categories, constituent time is a charismatic time legitimating a new social, political and economic order which in turn routinises itself as the time of 'normal'/ordinary politics.

Adjudicative time is an aspect of constituted time—the time of interpretation of public decisions by other branches of governance. Adjudicative time may not be, on conventional narratives of judicial role and function, invested with concerns about *legitimacy* of such decisions; rather, the constitution is said to 'command' that justices and courts should use their time wisely and well only to decide their *legality* and *constitutionality*. This means that adjudicative time and energy remain best justifiably dedicated to the tasks of demarcation of the zones of legality/constitutionality (as violative of Part III of the Constitution on fundamental rights or the federal design and detail).

We are *schooled* to think about constitutional *space* rather than adjudicative *time*. For example, much debate about 'judicial activism' and SAL remains mired in the doctrine of separation of powers which distributes spaces (jurisdiction/competence) *of* and *for* governance. My reading of this work in your hands suggests different readings of adjudicative time in ways which disrupt spatial imageries. Pithily put, 'Judicial Nineties', or the ways of Indian judicial activism, may scarcely be read with William Dicey in one hand and Ronald Dworkin in another.

The Indian constitutional experience and development presents singular difficulties in understanding adjudicative time. This is, in the main so, because the Supreme Court of India presents itself as *a sole residuary legatee of the originary constituent moment*; thus it ordains a doctrine of basic structure and essential features of the Indian Constitution. Originally strictly confined to adjudging the validity of constitutional amendments, the basic structure doctrine now extends widely and vastly to all manner of public decisions.[4] Further, the horizons of adjudicative time constantly expand with the invention of SAL jurisdictional and jurisprudential practices.

This *fusion* of constitutional and adjudicative time defines some typical (even paradigmatic) ways of Indian adjudicatory leadership. The routinisation of the exceptional moment of the enunciation of the basic structure doctrine now offers almost limitless scope for judicial action. Indeed, I have always suggested that *Keshavananda Bharati* and its normative progeny begin a process of judicial *rewriting* of the *already heavily written* Indian Constitution. The SAL processes further develop these scripts in versatile, yet complex, and often contradictory ways.

Leaving aside the rather crucial question concerning how the *Keshavananda Bharati* fusion of two orders of time may have gestated forms of inaugural SAL time in the Judicial Eighties, it is clear enough that in some remarkable ways, the SAL adjudicative time disrupts conventional understanding of this as an 'eternal yesterday' (borrowing here a phrase from Max Weber [Weber 1946]). Put starkly, SAL writes, as it were, on a clean adjudicative slate, generating in turn its very own distinctive normative/doctrinal past times.

In so doing, SAL also re-democratises investments of adjudicative time. In this way, and here extending Roland Barthes (Barthes 1975), SAL converts '*authorly*' text of the Indian Constitution almost fully into a '*readerly*' text. This means, here very simply put, that the task of production of constitutional social meaning belongs to *us all*, even when some 'imagined communities' may continue to insist that the production of legal/juridical meanings of constitutional texts may/must still remain a dominant function of the privileged community of citizen justices and lawyers.

'JN' as represented in this work questions, variously, the routinisation of the charismatic moment of SAL. The importance of this JN critique lies less in judging our justices from digital, and mimetic, wisdoms borrowed from the Euro-American circuits; rather it importantly derives form from indigenously-based normative evaluation (judgement). In this way, JN thus makes a singular statement.

Granting this, JN still falls short of grasping the adjudicative moments of SAL. Adjudicative time needs to be understood variously. Anthropologists of time speak to us of 'enduring time', 'trickle-down time', and *deceptive* time, *erratic* time, *cyclical* time, *retarded* time, time in *advance, alternating* time and *explosive* time.[5] This volume needs to be read with a full advertence to these different temporalities. In any event, reading SAL, with and beyond this volume, invites grasping a memorable statement of Julia Kristeva: '*There is meaning, and I am supposed to know it to the extent that escapes me*' (Lechte and Zournazi 2003: 310).

PERIODISATION

Periodisation of SAL adjudicative time is necessary for any meaningful grasp of its variegated itineraries; clearly the unity of constitutional time emerges only in its moments or fragments. If a 'history' archiving the narratives of adjudicative time were at all to emerge, the difficulties of the periodisation of adjudicative time will also more fully emerge.

Rather venturesomely, I have run many a narrative hazard ever since *The Indian Supreme Court and Politics* (1980)[6] till quite recently even suggesting that while nominally India has only one single constitution, in reality it has had as many as seven constitutions, and still counting.[7] Even so, a decennial comparative frame here suggested needs, at least in my view, more than a single-minded 'before-and-after' type engagement, if only because this may misrecognise the role of intervening critical events. For example, Judicial Seventies is nominally a unit of a decade; yet it marks very heterogeneous moments—the invention of the doctrine of the basic structure, the Habeas Corpus Case, and post-Emergency judicial populisms. The SAL Eighties, likewise, speak to us differently to the changing constituted times of Indian political development, among these for example, the emergence of coalitional governance at a national level. The profiles of SAL actors and of responsive justices also vary: the Narmada Dam adjudicative feats provided more scope for engagement than for the Bhopal-violated in times of Judicial Eighties (Baxi 2010a). So do some narratives concerning the constitutionality of national dragnet security legislations.

ADJUDICATORY LEADERSHIP

New conceptual frameworks are needed to study the coalescence of constitutional and adjudicative time: judicial activism, restraintivism and eclecticism are labels that justices and their critics deploy. These labels are of course important but primarily as articulations of judicial style or approach. More capacious categories are needed which bear the weight of comparative constitutionalism: for example, Ran Hirschl's (2004) enunciations of 'juristocracy'. Marking a gentle distance from Hirschl, I now begin to name 'adjudicative leadership' as at least more apt for the Indian contexts. My notion leans more towards Antonio Gramsci's phrase-regimes concerning the 'intellectual and moral leadership' of the power blocs that fashion hegemonic rule/governance. In India from the Judicial Seventies onwards, the Supreme Court has articulated itself as a Gramscian 'Modern Prince'.[8]

Summarily put, adjudicatory leadership concept designates at least three sites. First, hermeneutic adjudicative leadership concerns the production of the enduring time of the constitution via the doctrine of the basic structure and the institutionalisation of the SAL, and their several avatars. Second, this is different from adjudicative leadership directed to repairing and innovating governance institutions. SAL thus addresses micro-level adjudicatory leadership (oversight over prisons and other custodial detention sites/regimes, monitoring executive/administrative discretion, for example); and yet its ways also extend to macro level (where the Supreme Court initiates new governance policy regimes—so staggeringly diverse in range as the reform of India police system, efficient management of storage and distribution of food grain responding to minimal basic needs and rights of the impoverished Indians, interlinking India's rivers, and prevention and punishment of sexual harassment at workplaces). Third, organisational adjudicative leadership occurs via feats of interpretation that divest the supreme executive of the terminal power over judicial appointment/elevation) and its transference to a judicial collegium.

How these styles/patterns of adjudicatory leadership may interact and what impact this may have on the tasks of periodising adjudicative time generally, and SAL specifically, are concerns worthy of a fuller pursuit.

DEMOSPRUDENCE

'Demosprudence' is what the Indian Supreme Court has been practising, though the term is of recent origin engaging the studies of the US Supreme Court, now also extended to the South African Constitutional Court (Guinier 2007; Ray 2010). Of course, had the US constitutional/comparative jurisprudence specialists the time and inclination to study the ways of Indian adjudicatory leadership, they may have readily acknowledged the Indian Supreme Court's originary contribution to this concept-formation.

Indian 'demosprudence' emerges with acute and often anguished concern with popular (as distinct from legal) sovereignty. *Keshavananda*

Bharati is an inaugural feat of Indian demosprudence.[9] This hallmark of hermeneutic judicial leadership finds sustained articulation in the post-Emergency moment of 'judicial populism' (Baxi 1980, 1985, 2010b) and further in the manifold charismatic founding moment of SAL, which mark a decisive transformation of the Supreme Court *of* India towards a court for the deprived and disadvantaged *worst-off* Indian citizens.

The SAL adjudicatory leadership, I have maintained, articulates and for the most part also sustains the emergence of a *fiduciary* conception of adjudicative leadership, function and power. Put in one-sentence formulation, this means that courts and justices may not take human rights at all seriously without also taking human/social *suffering coequally seriously*. SAL practices fully suggest (in the immortal words of Justice Goswami) that the Supreme Court remains the '*last refuge of the oppressed and bewildered*'.[10]

The maturation of the Indian demosprudence entails further reconstruction and repair of this 'last refuge'.[11] The apex justices (as well the Indian High Court justices, whose specific contributions remain even today under-studied) have converted the idea of *jurisdiction* into spaces/sites of civic *conversation* about acts of remaking/transforming *constitutional cultures*. Notably, they have accomplished this conversion via fostering ways of dialogue between social movement and human rights activists, and related learned professions. New techniques of justicing have contributed to the establishment and consolidation of a creative jurisprudence of human rights. All this, and more, has resulted in manifestations of adjudicative leadership hard at work towards re-democratising India, indeed to a point where the Supreme Court itself assumes the visage of a new social movement.

Yet, one may never lose sight of the fact that at the end of the day courts and justices remain apparatuses of sovereign state power. This volume further reminds us of this brute fact; it also suggests a reading that our apex justices have failed, after all, to fulfil the SAL 'original intention'. If some of our eminent justices have all too readily proceeded to the imperatives of the structural adjustment of Indian ways of demosprudence in an era of hyper-globalising Indian development, other brethren also continue to nourish the founding inspiration of demosprudence.

In sum, this work compels us to grasp the forms of adjudicative time as '*deceptive*', '*erratic*', '*cyclical*', '*retarded*' time, 'time in *advance*', *alternating* time and *explosive* time'. It leaves each reader of this work with a sobering thought as well: our own ways of judging the judges also remain encased/ framed within these conflicted temporalities.

Upendra Baxi

Bonn, November 2012 Institute of Law as Culture

NOTES

1. For example, in matters concerning environmental rights and policy, the procedures for allocation of 'natural' resources in an era of privatisation, safety at work, systematic governance corruption, human rights monitoring over large-scale irrigation and nuclear power projects.
2. See Kalvyas (2008: 7). See further Negri (1999).
3. For this notion in the contexts of Brazil, South Africa and India, see Baxi (2009).
4. See, for a recent analysis, Krishnaswamy (2009).
5. I adapt here the phrase-regime of Gell (2001; emphases added).
6. See also Baxi (1985).
7. (Baxi 2010b). I narrate *seven* constitutions/constitutionalisms as follows: (i) the text adopted in 1950; (ii) the Nehruvian constitution, demanding a compelling respect by the Supreme Court of India for parliamentary sovereignty; (iii) the 1973 *Keshavananda Bharati* constitution which confers constituent power on the SCI, including the power to annul a constitutional amendment otherwise duly made by Parliament; (iv) the state finance capitalist constitution presaged by the Indira Gandhi constitution, via the nationalisation of banks and insurance industries and the abolition of the privy purses; (v) the Emergency constitution of 1975–77; (vi) the post-Emergency constitution which marks both judicial populism as well as the emergence of expansive judicial activism; and (vii) the neo-liberal constitution which redefines India as a vast global market fully at odds with the first, second, third, fourth and the sixth constitutions.
8. See Baxi (2011).
9. Especially in the opinions of Justices M. H. Beg, S. N. Dwivedi, K. K. Mathew and Y. V. Chandrachud.
10. *State of Rajasthan* vs *Union of India* (1977) 3 S.C.C. 634 at Para 70 (emphasis added).
11. See, for example, Fredman (2008); Sathe (2002); Baxi (2001).

REFERENCES

Baxi, Upendra. 1980. *The Indian Supreme Court and Politics*. Lucknow: Eastern Book Company.

———. 1985. *Courage Craft and Contention: The Supreme Court in Mid-Eighties*. Bombay: N. M. Tripathi (republished by Delhi: Lexis-Nexis Butterworth).

———. 2001. 'The Avatars of Judicial Activism: Explorations in the Geography of (In)Justice'. In *Fifty Years of the Supreme Court of India: Its Grasp and Reach*, eds S. K. Verma and Kusum, 156–209. New Delhi: Oxford University Press and Indian Law Institute.

———. 2009. 'Preliminary Notes on Transformative Constitutionalism'. BISA (Brazil, India, South Africa) Conference, Courting Justice-11, 27–29 April. Delhi.

———. 2010a. 'Writing about Impunity and Environment: The "Silver Jubilee" of the Bhopal Catastrophe'. *Journal of Human Rights and the Environment*, 1(1): 23–44.

———. 2010b. 'Judiciary as a Resource for Indian Democracy'. *We the People: A Symposium on the Constitution of India after 60 Years, 1950–2010*, October. *Seminar* 615. November.

———. 2011. 'Public and Insurgent Reason—Adjudicatory Leadership in a Hyper-globalizing World'. In *The Crisis of Global Leadership*, ed. S. Gill, 161–78. Cambridge, UK: Cambridge University Press.

Barthes, Roland. 1975. *An Essay*. trans. Richard Miller. New York: Hill and Wang.

Fredman, Sandra. 2008. *Human Rights Transformed: Positive Rights and Positive Duties*. New York: Oxford University Press.

Fuller, Lon. 1969. *The Morality of Law*, revised edition. New Haven, Conn.: Yale University Press.

Gell, Alfred. 2001. *The Anthropology of Time: Cultural Constructions of Temporal Maps and Images (Explorations in Anthropology)*. Oxford: Berg.

Guinier, Lani. 2007. 'The Supreme Court 2007: Foreword: Demosprudence through Dissent'. *Harvard Law Review*, 22: 4–138.

Hirschl, Ran. 2004. *Towards Juristocracy: The Origins and Consequences of the New Constitutionalism*. Cambridge, MA: Harvard University Press.

Kalvyas, Andrea. 2008. *Democracy and the Politics of the Extraordinary: Max Weber, Carl Schmitt, and Hannah Arendt*. New York: Cambridge University Press.

Krishnaswamy, Sudhir. 2009. *Democracy and Constitutionalism*. New Delhi: Oxford University Press.

Lechte, John, and Mary Zournazi, eds. 2003. *The Kristeva Critical Reader.* Edinburgh, UK: Edinburgh University Press.

Negri, Antonio. 1999. *Insurgencies: Constituent Power and the Modern State.* Minneapolis: University of Minnesota Press.

Ray, Brian. 2010. 'Demosprudence in Comparative Perspective'. Available at http://works.bepress.com/brian_ray/5 (accessed on 6 November 2010).

Sathe, S. P. 2002. *Judicial Activism in India: Transgressing Borders and Enforcing Limits.* New Delhi: Oxford University Press.

Weber, Max. 1946. 'Politics as a Vocation'. In *Essays in Sociology,* eds. H. H. Garth and C. Wright Mills, 26–45. New York: Macmillan.

Introduction

MAYUR SURESH and SIDDHARTH NARRAIN

Legal interpretation takes place in a field of pain and death.
– Robert Cover, 'Violence and the Word'

I

On 27 February 2012, the Supreme Court of India passed an order in a case titled *In Re: Networking of Rivers*,[1] by which it directed the Union government to implement a project that envisioned the interlinking of India's rivers, from the 'Ganga to the Cape Kumari'. The Court declared that there was 'a unanimity of views' that the interlinking of rivers was in 'national interest'. The Court further set up a committee to oversee this project. The committee is to submit its reports to the Union cabinet, which was to take all final and appropriate decisions within thirty days. The Court granted 'liberty to the learned amicus curiae to file contempt petition in this court, in the event of default or non-compliance of the directions contained in this order'. The interlinking project involves the construction of 200 large dams (by one estimate), reservoirs and a complex canal system. The aim of this mammoth project, the Supreme Court reasons, is to ensure that water from water-surplus, flood-affected states reaches areas of the country which are drought-prone and face water scarcity, 'thus saving the people living in drought-prone zones from hunger and people living in flood-prone areas from the destruction caused by floods'. In its imagination of this extravagant national project, the Court harnesses the equally grand idea of national progress:

> There shall be greater growth in agricultural and allied sectors, prosperity and stimulus to the economy potentially causing increase in per capita income, in addition to the short and long term benefits likely to accrue by such implementation...there shall be hardly any financial strain on the economy... such implementation would help advancement of India's GDP and bring greater wealth and prosperity to the nation as a whole. Besides actual benefits accruing to the common man, the Governments also benefit from the definite possibility of saving the States from drought on the one hand and floods on the other. This project, when it becomes a reality, will provide immeasurable benefits...

While the idea of interlinking rivers was backed by several people, most notably former president Abdul Kalam and former Union home minister L. K. Advani, the Court's order directing the interlinking of rivers was met with two major criticisms. First, the project was criticised on socio-economic grounds: that the Supreme Court had failed to foresee the catastrophic human and environmental effects of the project, if ever implemented. As one editorial put it, 'The higher judiciary should desist from the temptation to play god' (*Economic and Political Weekly* 2012). The fact that the order only summarily refers to people who would be displaced as a result of the project, for some, could indicate the ideological direction that the Court has leaned over the past two decades, away from the rights of the people and towards free market-led development and economic exploitation at great human cost.

Second, the order directing the interlinking of rivers was criticised as it was felt that the Court was reaching beyond its constitutionally defined role. Some accused the Court of failing to respect the separation of powers by stepping outside its institutional role in ordering the executive to implement its policy (Upadhyay 2012). Further, by setting up a bureaucracy to oversee the interlinking of rivers, some have criticised the Court for riding roughshod over pre-existing structures and processes by which such projects are given clearance (Iyer 2012). Institutional criticisms have not been confined to this case alone and have had echoes through the judiciary's history. Mehta (2007) points out that during the first seventeen years of the Supreme Court's existence, when it was supposedly in its restrained period, it struck down 128 pieces of legislation, and about half of the first forty-five constitutional amendments were aimed at curbing judicial power. More recently, the Supreme Court, sitting in its Writ jurisdiction, passed an order in *Ram Jethmalani v. Union of India*,[2] which dealt with the issue of 'black' money that some Indians had allegedly stashed away in foreign banks. In this case, the judges reconstituted the government's committee as a special investigation team (SIT) and entrusted it with wide-ranging functions. Apart from concerns about it violating the separation of powers (Mukhopadhyay 2011), the order was criticised for failing to explain what fundamental rights were violated and how its Article 32 jurisdiction was triggered (Khaitan 2011). The Court has in the past two decades sought to manage India's forests and define their use, has determined the fuel to be used by urban transport vehicles, taken over appointments to the higher judiciary and has even claimed the power to declare constitutional amendments invalid. How did the Supreme Court come to consider itself competent to virtually take over the administration of such a diverse set of areas?

Professor Baxi in *Supreme Court and Politics* has pointed out that judges effectively exercise political power while maintaining the illusion that they are only interpreting the law or the constitution (Baxi 1980). Baxi says about the Court: 'The question is no longer whether or not judges make law. Rather the questions are: what *kind* of law, how *much* of it, in what *manner*, within which self-imposed *limits* and to what *willed results* and with what tolerable accumulation of unintended results, may the judge make law?' (Baxi 1985a: 3). More than looking at the textual origins for the sweeping powers the Court has claimed for itself, we are concerned with the rhetorical devices, the discursive method that the Court has adopted to claim such wide authority.

Robert Cover, in his essay 'Violence and the Word', argues that judicial decisions cannot be evaluated in the same manner as traditional forms of interpretation in literature, arts and the humanities. Cover states that we need to move from looking at judiciary as the voice of reason and embodiment of principle to examining the judiciary and its pronouncements as a site that is productive of discourse (Cover 1986). At the heart of our enterprise in this volume is to move away from an account of the Supreme Court that focuses solely on the legal meaning or the technical correctness of its decisions. Instead, we seek a way of understanding the judiciary politically—not only to examine the judiciary in its avatar as the creator and arbiter of social and economic policy, but also to examine the links between the judiciary, politics and discursive power.

The essays in this book have attempted to provide an account of this shift within a larger political economy narrative that seeks to locate the precise manners in which these changes are taking place via the emergence of a judicial sovereignty that does not merely adjudicate any longer but actually creates law and produces notions of legality and illegality. Whether it is the sealing of commercial establishments in Delhi, or evicting slum-dwellers or banishing people who live on river banks, the Supreme Court's orders are not only marked by a brutal physical reordering of everyday life, but are also accompanied by a violent reconstruction of the ideas of the social and citizenship. Far from being discrete and pre-existing categories, ideas of legality and illegality, citizenship and social space are actively constructed through the orders of the Supreme Court. The Supreme Court imagines what an ideal city should look like or how proper citizens should behave. Which categories of citizens have the most legitimate claim upon the city and who are the 'encroachers'? What discourses does the judiciary mobilise in order to rewrite the idea of the social? If, as Pratap Bhanu Mehta suggests, the Supreme Court's primary concern has been in maintaining its own authority at the cost of laying down clear and consistent 'constitutional vision' (Mehta 2007: 70–83), what implications does this have on the idea of law itself?

II

Like many public institutions in India, there is a public memory, a common lore about the Supreme Court. Many authors provide three periods of the history of the Supreme Court.

The first occurs soon after Independence. At its foundational moment, the Supreme Court jostled with Parliament for control over the Constitution, but remained within the confines of English positivist tradition (Sathe 2002: 6). Thus, whenever the Supreme Court interpreted the Constitution in a manner that Parliament took issue with, Parliament merely amended the Constitution to reflect its reading of the Constitution and to narrow the scope of judicial review by the Supreme Court.[3] Given that during this first period of the Supreme Court's history many major controversies that arose between the legislative and judicial branches centred around the right to property, this period has been characterised as one marked by Supreme Court's resistance to the Congress party's brand of nationalist socialism, marked by principles of state ownership, regulation and control over key sectors of the economy in order to improve productivity and curb economic concentration.[4]

Soon after Independence in 1947, several state governments had enacted legislation in order to effect a redistribution of land. This involved appropriating the land held by zamindars and other persons who had been conferred title to large estates by the British Raj. Parliament had by the Constitution (First Amendment) Act, 1951, inserted Articles 31A and 31B, which limited the power of the judiciary to review these land reform laws.[5] In *Shankari Prasad*,[6] the First Amendment was called into question and numerous landowners from around the country challenged its validity. A five-judge bench of the Supreme Court held that it had no authority to review the amending power of Parliament and held that Parliament, by amendment, could take away or abridge fundamental rights.

The conflict between Parliament and the Supreme Court again arose in 1967 with the *Golaknath*[7] decision. Parliament had again amended the Constitution in order to protect several land reform legislations from judicial review. The question here again was of the limits of Parliament's power to amend the Constitution and, concomitantly, the power of the Supreme Court to review those amendments. The Supreme Court on this occasion swung away from its decision in *Shankari Prasad* and in a six-to-five decision held that Parliament could not amend the Constitution so as to take away or abridge fundamental rights. According to S. P. Sathe (2002), the *Golaknath* decision was a watershed moment in the Supreme Court's evolution from a positivist court to an activist court. The Court at this moment took away Parliament's hitherto unbridled power to amend the Constitution and thus held itself to be the primary oracle of the constitutional text.

In July 1969, purportedly in pursuance of its socialist policies, Indira Gandhi's government passed the Banking Companies (Acquisition and Transfer of Undertaking) Bill by which fourteen banks were nationalised by the government, and later in September the next year her government issued an executive order de-recognising the Indian princes and former rulers of the princely states.[8] Both these actions by the government were successfully challenged in the Supreme Court. The protection of private property formed the underlying logic of both these decisions. In the former case, the Supreme Court held that the banking institutions which were nationalised were legal persons and hence their right to property could not be taken away without providing 'just and equivalent compensation',[9] and in the latter case held that the privy purses provided to the rulers of the Indian states was a property interest which accrued to these rulers and could not be taken away by executive fiat.[10] While the Central government worked around the Supreme Court's objections in the bank nationalisation case by enacting a new ordinance and Bank Nationalisation Bill, the ruling reopened the question of the individual's right to adequate compensation and imposed prohibitive financial obligations on the state in its plans to acquire large properties and enterprises (Frankel 2004: 440–41).

In the parliamentary elections of 1971, the faction of the Congress party under Indira Gandhi fought largely based on the prime minister's personal image and her commitment to renew economic and social reform. Mrs Gandhi's campaign was exemplified by the slogan 'garibi hatao' ('get rid of poverty'). She promised her electorate that, given a mandate, she would go ahead with a programme of radical social change that included basic changes to the Constitution (Ibid.: 454–57). The Congress party won a landslide victory and secured a two-thirds majority in the Lok Sabha—more than enough seats to ensure that constitutional amendments were passed without much opposition. Soon after her election as prime minister, Parliament passed the Constitution (Twenty-Fourth Amendment) Act, 1971, with the purpose of restoring to Parliament the unhindered power of constitutional amendment it had possessed until the *Golaknath* decision. The same bills specified that ordinary procedures provided for amending the Constitution were sufficient to confer constituent powers on Parliament extending to those of amending any provision of the Constitution. Parliament thereafter passed the Twenty-Fifth Amendment which further restricted the right to property and established the supremacy of Parliament over the judiciary as the arbiter of fundamental rights. This was followed by the Twenty-Sixth Amendment, which abolished privileges and privy purses of the erstwhile rulers of the princely states.

These constitutional changes went beyond their purported aims of social justice and affected the heart of the existing constitutional order including the right to equality before the law and equal protection of the law, and the freedom of speech, association and movement including the freedom of the press (Ibid.: 467–69). Matters came to a head when in 1973 a thirteen-member bench of the Supreme Court, acting on writ petitions challenging the validity of the Twenty-Fourth and Twenty-Fifth Amendments, took up this issue in the famous *Keshavananda Bharati*[11] case. The main question facing the court was that if according to *Golaknath's* decision Parliament did not have the power to amend the Constitution so as to take away or abridge fundamental rights, then how could it empower itself to do so through a constitutional amendment? In the *Keshavananda Bharati* decision, eleven of the thirteen justices on the bench held that *Golaknath* had been wrongly decided. While the Supreme Court ceded the power to amend all parts of the Constitution to Parliament, the Court, by a seven-to-six majority held that the amending power could not be used to destroy the basic structure of the Constitution. This ensured that the judiciary would have the final say in deciding which amendments to the Constitution would be permissible and which would fail. The judgement was widely seen as a personal loss of face for Indira Gandhi, and led to the supercession of three of the most senior judges of the Supreme Court, Justices J. M. Shelat, K. S. Hegde and A. N. Grover, in the Cabinet's recommendation on who would be appointed the next chief justice. This in turn galvanised opposition to Mrs Gandhi's policies with the Opposition parties charging her with appointing a 'committed' judiciary.

These disputes in the first period of the Supreme Court's history reflect a deep concern over who controls the rules of constitutional governance. At another level they also represent the Supreme Court's tripping up of the social revolution that the Constitution was to engender. One common narrative of this period is that Supreme Court's seemingly consistent defence of the right to property stood in the way of the socialist vision that Nehru, Indira Gandhi and the Congress party held for India (Sathe 2002: 68). However, it was clear that the Congress party, which was by then dominated by Indira Gandhi and her coterie of advisors at the expense of organisational strength, was in no position to deliver on its promised of radical economic reform within a democratic framework, a promise that formed the basis of many of the policy and legal changes that Mrs Gandhi was attempting at the time.

The second period in the Supreme Court's history coincides with the Emergency declared by Indira Gandhi on 25 June 1975 after a political and economic impasse that resulted from Mrs Gandhi's policies. In November 1976, the Congress government, through the Forty-Second Constitutional Amendment, institutionalised the expanded powers of Parliament and the Central government at the expense of all the other autonomous centres of authority in the Centre, administration, opposition parties and the courts. These changes were justified on the pretext of enabling radical social change (Frankel 2004: 555–66).

Critics of the Supreme Court, who accuse it of capitulating to executive dominance during the Emergency, point to its decision in *Additional District Magistrate, Jabalpur v. Shiv Kant Shukla*.[12] In exercise of the emergency powers granted to it under the Constitution, the Government of India suspended the right of citizens to approach the courts for a writ of habeas corpus in the event that they were detained or arrested by government officials. Furthermore, Indira Gandhi's government enacted the Maintenance of Internal Security Act—commonly known as MISA—a preventive detention law. People who were detained under the Act challenged their detentions before various high courts and broadly argued that their detentions under the Act were *mala fide* and were hence entitled to a writ of habeas corpus. Seven high courts agreed with the detainees and ordered their release, and states came in appeal to the Supreme Court. By a four-to-one majority the Supreme Court held that in light of the order of the Government of India suspending the writ of habeas corpus, the judiciary could not examine actions of the executive detaining persons. Four justices agreed that no citizen had locus standi to move for a writ of habeas corpus or to challenge the orders of detention on any other ground.

Thus, the Court virtually held that no one had an inherent right to life and liberty and that these rights were dependent on the largesse of the state. As a former judge of the Supreme Court puts it, the result of this judgement was that 'the Court ceased to be a bulwark of a citizen's life and liberty and it looked as if the very reason for the existence of the Supreme Court as the protector of the people against despotic injustice also ceased to exist' (Reddy 2008: 69). Justice H. R. Khanna was punished for his dissent when he was superseded for the appointment to the post of chief justice.

The third period in the history of the Supreme Court is often described as one of atonement. The Court, facing public condemnation for its capitulation during the Emergency, embarked on an effort to reclaim its stature as the pre-eminent bulwark against curtailment of citizens' rights by the state. One of the ways it went about this was to refashion its approach towards the role of Directive Principles of State Policy, enshrined in Part IV of the Constitution. The Court reasoned that just because the Directive Principles were not enforceable, it did not mean that the Court could not use this part of the Constitution to refashion its approach towards discharging its duties and in the manner it interpreted the Constitution and laws (Ibid.: 78–84).

III

The post-Emergency Supreme Court, through a series of decisions, radically rearticulated the relationship between the citizen and the state by introducing procedural and substantive 'due process',[13] and expanded the right to life and personal liberty to include the right to education,[14] the right to housing,[15] the right to information[16] amongst other rights. The Court was hailed as *the* protector of the rights of the people. The Supreme Court described itself in 1977 as 'the last resort of the oppressed and bewildered'.[17] The post-Emergency Supreme Court has been variously described not just as the Supreme Court of India, but 'the Supreme Court for Indians' (Baxi 1985a: 107), and as the 'main educator in constitutional values and democratic culture' (Sathe 2002: 284).

An important procedural aspect of the Court's approach post-Emergency was the evolution of public interest litigation (PIL), or as Baxi (1997) prefers, social action litigation (SAL), with its liberalised rules of locus standi, in making the Supreme Court more participatory and democratic. PILs or SALs have not only been used to establish and enunciate newer fundamental rights for the 'weaker sections of society' but also to challenge administrative actions of the government.[18] Hence, as Sathe notes, '*the concept of justiciability underwent a metamorphosis, thereby including within the Court's purview several matters of governance that would not have been the Court's concern under traditional notions of justiciability*' (Sathe 2002: 17).

The judge-led alterations in the rules of locus standi and justiciability in the creation of PILs were accompanied by the discursive production and invocation of 'the people'. Justice Chandrachud, writing in 1973, was prescient of the role that the Court would claim for itself after the Emergency. Speaking on behalf of the 'teeming millions—half-clad, half-starved, half-educated', he stated, 'It is really the poor, starved and mindless millions who need the court's protection for securing themselves the enjoyment of human rights.'[19]

By relaxing the requirements of locus standi, by employing PILs and by acting, on occasion, without any formal complaint of rights-violations being presented to it, the Supreme Court carved out an expansive role for itself (Austin 2000: 10). The Court has extended its jurisdiction to areas beyond the domain of rights to include the scrutiny of constitutional amendments, executive proclamations of national and state emergencies, and areas traditionally considered to be in the realm of policy (Krishnaswamy 2009: xv–xvi). It not only multiplied the rights available to citizens, but also claimed the sole prerogative to interpret the Constitution and in enunciating the basic structure doctrine. The Court even claimed the right to strike down constitutional amendments (Mehta 2007: 70–83). The Court became the 'bastion of the Constitution' (Austin 2000: 13). Writing in 1997 on the Supreme Court of the 1980s and 1990s, Baxi says that 'the judiciary has become a prime instrumentality of re-democratizing the processes of governance and practices of politics. The contemporary patterns of judicial behaviour of the judiciary has transformed it from a mere apparatus of governance into an institutionalised social movement' (Baxi 1997: 351).

IV

Yet, writing a decade later, Baxi notes that there has been a 'structural adjustment of the distinctively Indian judicial power, process, and activism' (Baxi 2006). There has been a sense that the Supreme Court in the era of the new economic policies commenced in the 1990s has betrayed a lack of sensitivity towards the 'rights of the poor and disadvantaged sections of society' (Bhushan 2004: 1770). The Supreme Court is now sealing the source of livelihood and employment for thousands of those very 'people' on whose behalf it claims to speak (Delhi Janwadi Adhikar Manch 1997). It tells us that in the era of global capital, the right to strike, the right held dearest by labour and a right claimed by sustained struggle, does not actually exist.[20] In 2006, in holding that contract workers, some of whom had been employed via a contract for periods up to ten years, had no right to be regularised, five justices of the Supreme Court overruled its own previous decisions and noted that their predecessors had laboured under the misapprehension that India was a socialist republic.[21]

Supreme Court lawyer Prashant Bhushan, an outspoken critic of the Supreme Court's role in the post-liberalisation era, points to how the Supreme Court has been solicitous towards large corporates such as Vedanta and Posco in allowing them mining leases in large tracts of forest land despite the resulting displacement of thousands of tribal families (Bhushan 2009: 35). The Supreme Court has stated that allowing people who build their homes over generations on public land—encroachers—to remain on land is akin to giving money to a pickpocket,[22] the right to shelter notwithstanding. The violent reordering of cities in India driven by the judiciary to remove slums is a practice that not only violates legal protection to slum-dwellers but also denies the legal obligation of the state to provide resettlement alternatives to the evicted families. As Baxi (2006) notes, demolitions, which were once seen as excesses perpetrated during the Emergency, now come to be seen as the badges of good governance.

In a 2010 decision, in a rare reflexive moment, the judges of the Supreme Court, while deciding a matter related to the retrenchment of a worker, refer to the shift in the approach of the judiciary that has resulted in the whittling down of the Court's existing jurisprudence that protected the rights of those protected by the constitutional vision of social welfare.

> Of late, there has been a visible shift in the courts' approach in dealing with the cases involving the interpretation of social welfare legislations. The attractive mantras of globalisation and liberalisation are fast becoming the raison d'etre of the judicial process and an impression has been created that the constitutional courts are no longer sympathetic

> towards the plight of industrial and unorganised workers. In large number of cases like the present one, relief has been denied to the employees falling under the category of workmen, who are illegally retrenched from service by creating by-lanes and side-lanes in the jurisprudence developed by this Court in three decades.[23]

Ironically, it is the Supreme Court that has recently in the *Salwa Judum* judgement,[24] while striking down the use of special police officers and other paramilitary forces in Chhattisgarh in the state's operations against the Naxalites, eloquently described the political economy of India today. Delving into the reasons behind these violent times, the Court argued that people were taking up arms against the state because of the increasing inequalities spurred by the 'amoral political economies' and unfettered 'extractive industries'. Comparing the logic of mineral extraction in Chhattisgarh to that of early colonial expansion in Africa through Joseph Conrad's description of colonialism in Congo, the Court said that the Maoist violence in Chhattisgarh, and other parts of the country, is the violent outcome of an equally violent economic logic.

In Partha Chatterjee's (2001) formulation of the relationship of the state to modernity and democracy, he makes a distinction between political society and civil society. Civil society for him is the domain of modernising, bourgeois elite, and political society is the place of the messy politics of democracy. The judiciary plays an important role in the domain of civil society marked by notions of the rule of law and an investment in the idea of the legal and adherence to the principles of a constitutional state.

The demands by political society on the state, in Chatterjee's words:

> are founded on a violation of the law. They may be associations of squatters, encroachers on public property, ticketless travellers on public transport.... It is not that they are associations of citizens who merely happen to have violated the law; the collective form in which they appear before the state authorities implies that they are not proper citizens, but rather population groups who survive by sidestepping the law (Chatterjee 2001: 177).

Chatterjee's idea of political society is reflected in works of others like Solomon Benjamin, who puts forward the notion of porous bureaucracies where there was an acknowledgement of the porous spaces between the legal/illegal that allowed people to participate in democratic politics (Benjamin 2005).

Baxi (1980) suggests that the post-Emergency Supreme Court cultivated a constituency by reaching out to, what was in Partha Chatterjee's formulation, political society. In contrast, the Court in the 1990s has played an important role in the emergence of a new political consensus and socio-economic vision pushed by a globalising and increasingly assertive Indian middle class, and the creation of a new and distinctive model of consumer-citizenship marked by a shift from workers' rights to the rights of a consumer (Fernandes 2007: 82). The Supreme Court's 'conservative turn' is exemplified by a newfound romance of the idea of the legal. In this new phase there is very little room for the kind of negotiations that characterised the ways in which large sections of the population accessed basic services. This space is effectively being whittled down by the judiciary along with its compact with political society.

We are seeking to provide a history of the contemporary moment that the Supreme Court finds itself in. The periodisation that we provided could suggest that we think of the '1990s' as a distinct time, bound off from the court's 'liberal' 1980s. Instead, we think of the 1990s as a conceptual period. Our aim is to understand the *longue durée* of history of the contemporary moment in which the Supreme Court finds itself. Hence, we look at the '1990s' not as a bounded decade but, as Ramanathan in her contribution to this volume does, we are also interested in exploring the origins of the judicial power that is now wielded by the Supreme Court.

V

The essays in this volume examine the nature, origins and implications of this shift in the Supreme Court's politics. Most of the chapters contained in this volume were presented at a conference on the 'Judicial Nineties' held in Bangalore in 2008, and at a panel at the inaugural LASS*net* conference held in Delhi in 2009 titled 'Assessing the Conservative Shift in the Supreme Court's PIL Jurisprudence'. The note for the 2008 conference was provocatively posed. The concept note considered whether the judiciary had abandoned its commitment to social and economic equity and instead chose to use its accretion of power in favour of global capital. It noted that it was usually argued that the law and the judiciary are complicit with the neo-liberal project. It was argued that this maybe too generous a reading, and instead suggested that the law and the judiciary *are* indeed the neo-liberal project. It concluded by questioning whether the judiciary ought to remain a site of engagement and struggle. Several of the chapters are responding to these provocations.

Aditya Nigam argues that the first phase of PILs in the Supreme Court was marked by a commitment to the various groups that Chatterjee describes as political society. As political society was marked by its illegality, the Supreme Court's commitment to political society during this phase was thus marked by a setting aside of the strict letter of the law and an acknowledgement of 'claims that would never have been acknowledged in any other context'. The second phase of PIL is marked by the turn away from political society to civil society. Through a discussion of case law pertaining to contract labour and slums, Nigam shows how the Supreme Court of the conceptual 1990s rolled back many of the progressive pronouncements of the earlier era. He argues that the Supreme Court's shift away from 'governmentality (political society) to the "rule of law" (civil society, rights)' is symptomatic of deeper realignments of India's political economy, where political society ceases to be politically relevant and is now seen as a drag on the progress and economic growth of civil society.

Usha Ramanathan's chapter provides us with a historical context for the powers that are now claimed by the Supreme Court. She argues that in its quest to atone for its surrender to Indira Gandhi's Emergency dictatorship, the Supreme Court sought to reinvent itself and in the process claimed greater and wider powers. The power to do 'complete justice' which renders the Court's conservative turn immune from legal and doctrinal criticisms, she argues, once provided the justification for many innovative and progressive judgements in the 1980s.

The post-Emergency Supreme Court's activism has come under criticism from several quarters—including justices of the Supreme Court—for overstepping institutional limits set by the doctrine of separation of powers. Nivedita Menon, through a discussion of environmental cases in the Supreme Court, argues that the debate of judicial activism versus judicial restraint elides what the Supreme Court is actually doing. She argues that the judiciary's invocation or criticism of judicial activism is actually a crutch upon which it justifies its ultimate decision. In examining the judiciary's approach to environmental cases she argues that the 'environment' emerges as a crucial issue in two circumstances—the leisure and lifestyle of the urban middle classes; development projects and the accompanying contestations over natural resources. She argues that the general formula—environment trumps people, development trumps environment—emerges out of these cases. Menon then suggests that the judiciary's turn away from political society requires us to rethink foundational ideas of the state and civil society. She argues that the state is not distinct from civil and political society, but as interpenetrating the two. 'The judiciary in India since the 1990s', she argues, 'is an exemplary instance of civil society in Chatterjee's sense, in action—shaped by the normative ideals of Western modernity and adopting a "pedagogical mission of enlightenment" towards the vast mass of the population'.

Varun Gauri's chapter parses through the two major criticisms of PILs—questions regarding the separation of powers and queries about judicial attitudes. While these criticisms are presented as normative claims on the role of the court, they are, Gauri argues, based on factual claims. To date, Gauri argues, PILs have been debated largely in abstract. Hence, related to the criticisms are factual questions relating to the institutional capacity of the Court to handle these complex 'polycentric disputes', whether the PILs make a difference or whether PILs still play their 'proper' role of protecting the rights of the poor and underprivileged sections of society. Gauri thus argues that the charge that PIL undermines policy formulation and implementation of the legislature and executive is 'dressed up' as a separation of powers argument. Gauri suggests that this concern involves an assessment of the impact of PILs on governance, which is an empirical assessment rather than a doctrinal one. Gauri then undertakes an analysis of around 3,000 cases decided by the Supreme Court between 1988 and 2007 which were designated by the Court as PILs or cases involving women, children, Scheduled Castes or Scheduled Tribes. The chapter arrives at the conclusion that until the late 1980s the average annual win-rate for claimants from advantaged classes was below the win-rate of claimants who were not from advantaged classes.

Now, according to Gauri, claimants from advantaged classes have higher win-rates than claimants not from advantaged classes.

In this book, the dominant narrative of the Supreme Court in the 1990s is one where the Court turned away from its progressive vision soon after the Emergency. In this volume, Krishnaswamy and Khosla disagree with the hypothesis that the Supreme Court has reneged on its commitment to socio-economic rights and argue that in order to sustain such a claim, we must have evidence to suggest that the 1990s' Supreme Court chose not to enforce a right which, under similar facts and circumstances, the 1980s' Supreme Court would have. They argue that there is nothing to suggest that the judiciary has become doctrinally conservative, and they suggest, instead, that in order to test whether the judiciary has become more conservative, one needs to look at the remedy fashioned by the courts in response to a claim of a violation of socio-economic rights. One also has to examine, they argue, whether this response of the judiciary resulted in a social transformation measured through empirically verifiable social and economic indicators.

In his chapter, Arun K. Thiruvengadam first disputes Krishnaswamy and Khosla's claim that the Supreme Court has not become more conservative, while at the same time reiterating their call for more comprehensive and empirically rigorous research to be undertaken to facilitate a firmer grasp on the actual practice of contemporary PIL. Thiruvengadam urges progressives to increase—rather than abandon—engagement with the law and the courts. He says that some of the criticisms of the court relate to the vast powers claimed by the Court, which is viewed with great suspicion, while others have urged a return to the Court's progressive era of the 1980s. Thiruvengadam suggests that the problem does not lie with PILs but with the expansive powers themselves and that the expansive powers forged in the 1980s have allowed for the present predicament. Instead, he argues that Court should abandon what he terms as the 'command and control' approach to PILs, where judges, not the litigants, control the process, and instead embark on forging a facilitative approach to the adjudication of public interest matters, where the emphasis is on enabling all possible stakeholders to contribute meaningful inputs. He further argues that if PILs are to have any significance for the marginalised sections of Indian society, the focus should be on building a network of organisations and adopting a bottom-up approach to litigation.

Philippe Cullet's essay examines the judiciary's treatment of water. Broadly, he argues that water in law has two avatars. In one form, water emerges as a property right and in the other as a fundamental human right. The first avatar of water, i.e., water as property, has occupied most judicial attention. He states that courts have devoted most of their attention to water issues in the context of disputes related to real property rights and inter-state issues, which have emerged out of common law principles. With regard to water as a fundamental right, Cullet argues that over the past two decades, while high courts around the country and the Supreme Court have confirmed and restated the existence of the right to water, they have done little more. Courts have not focussed on the scope and content of that right and have failed to enunciate a consistent policy with regard to the fundamental right to water. He further argues that while there has been the recognition of the human right to water, little has been done to translate this into the actual instruments that make a difference to people's lives. While discussing the *Narmada Dam case* and the *Yamuna Pushta case,* Cullet argues that the Supreme Court has used rhetorical invocations of the right to water in order to justify the eviction of hundreds of thousands of people from the banks of the Narmada and the Yamuna.

Ujjwal Kumar Singh examines the implications of the 'judicialisation of politics' in the 1980s and 1990s, whereby the judiciary became a surrogate for political engagements between the state and the 'people' and also participated in the legitimation practices of the neo-liberal security state. Singh examines and compares two sites on which the Supreme Court mediates disputes between the state and the 'people'. First, the Supreme Court's pronouncements on electoral reform—where the Court held that electoral candidates must declare their income, assets and criminal antecedents; second, in the Court's approval of extraordinary security legislation. By comparing the Court's differential treatment of these two domains, he suggests that the Supreme Court understands politics primarily in procedural terms. And unlike its intervention in the electoral domain, the Supreme Court's judgements on extraordinary laws, he argues, 'clearly takes up a position of legal-formalism, and a notion of politics where political rights and civil liberties may be dispensed with in the face of what it considers more pressing concerns of security of the state'. For political groups and social movements that fall outside the site of electoral democracy, Singh suggests that the Court has failed to acknowledge the place of social movements and ideological pluralism—often the target of special security legislations—and has instead becoming complicit with the state in its neo-liberal nationalist project.

The essays in this volume have been written at a point where the role of the Supreme Court has come under enormous scrutiny from both within the institution and outside. While there are differing opinions within these essays, almost all of the authors agree that there is a definite shift in the politics of the Court in the last two decades. The Court of the 1990s has gradually dismantled the procedural and jurisprudential changes made by the post-Emergency Court, helping refashion citizenship and creating a political consensus around global capital. This volume brings together a range of scholarship on the role of the Supreme Court in the 1990s that attempts to capture some of the nuances of the reasons behind the shift in the Court's politics. It focuses on what accounts for this shift and what this says about the nature of law and its institutions. We hope that through these enquiries this volume will generate both answers to these questions and greater critical engagement with these issues.

NOTES

1. WP(C) 512/2002.
2. 2011 (8) SCC 1.
3. First, Fourth and Seventeenth Amendment Acts.
4. Frankel (2004: 71–112). Frankel points out that the socialist policies endorsed by the Congress party were set off by contradictory tendencies within the party which pressed for liberal economic policies and incentives to private investment justified by the sole criterion of achieving maximum economic production.
5. The First Amendment also amended the fundamental right to freedom of speech and expression, narrowing down the scope of the right, by widening the terms of Article 19(2) that dealt with exceptions to the right to free speech. The two cases that prompted Nehru to do this were the *Romesh Thapar* case (AIR 1950 SC 124), in which the Madras government, after declaring the Communist party illegal, banned the left-leaning magazine *Crossroads* as it was very critical of the Nehru government. The court held that banning a publication because it would endanger public safety or public order was not supported by the constitutional scheme since the exceptions to 19(1) were much more specific and had to entail

a danger to the security of the state. The second case related to an order passed by the chief commissioner, Delhi, asking the Rashtriya Swayamsevak Sangh (RSS) mouthpiece *Organiser* to submit all communal matter and material related to Pakistan to scrutiny (*Brij Bhushan and Anr. v. The State of Delhi* 1950 SuppSCR 245). Nehru's government decided to amend the Constitution by inserting the words 'public order' and 'relations with friendly states' into Article 19(2) and the word 'reasonable' before 'restrictions', which was meant to provide a safeguard against misuse by the government.

6. *Shankari Prasad v. Union of India*, AIR 1951 SC 458.
7. AIR 1967 SC 1643.
8. These actions coincided with Mrs Gandhi's efforts to take control of the power struggle within the Congress that eventually resulted in its split into Contress(R), loyal to Mrs Gandhi and the Congress(O) that comprised the old guard within the Congress (the Syndicate) and their supporters (Frankel 2004: 388–433).
9. *Rustom Cavasjee Cooper v. Union of India*, AIR 1970 SC 564.
10. *His Highness Madhav Rao Jivaji Rao Scindia v. Union of India*, AIR 1971 SC 530.
11. AIR 1973 SC 1461.
12. AIR 1976 SC 1207.
13. *Maneka Gandhi v. Union of India*, AIR 1978 SC 597.
14. *Unnikrishnan PJ & Others v. Union of India* (1993) 4 SCC 111.
15. *Olga Tellis v. Bombay Municipal Corporation & Others*, AIR 1986 SC 180.
16. *Union of India v. Association for Democratic Reforms* (2002) 5 SCC 294.
17. *State of Rajasthan v. Union of India* (1977) 3 SCC 592.
18. For example, in *D. C. Wadhwa v. State of Bihar* AIR 1987 SC 579, the continuous re-promulgation of ordinances was successfully challenged, and in *S. P. Gupta v. President of India* AIR 1982 SC 149, the Supreme Court entertained a petition challenging the appointment and transfer of judges of the high courts and the Supreme Court.
19. *Keshavananda Bharati v. State of Kerala*, AIR 1973 SC 1461.
20. *T. K. Rangarajan v. Government of Tamil Nadu*, AIR 2003 SC 3032.
21. *Secretary, State of Karnataka v. Uma Devi & Others* (2006) 4 SCC 1.
22. *Almitra H. Patel v. Union of India* (2000) 8 SCC 19.
23. Justice G. S. Singhvi, *Harjinder Singh v. Punjab Warehousing Corporation* (2010) 3 SCC 192.
24. *Nandini Sundar and Ors v. State of Chhattisgarh* (2011) 7 SCC 547.

REFERENCES

Austin, Granville. 2000. 'The Supreme Court and the Struggle for Custody of the Constitution'. In *Supreme but not Infallible: Essays in Honour of the Supreme Court of India*, eds B. N. Kirpal, Ashok H. Desai, Rajeev Dhavan and Raju Ramachandran. New Delhi: Oxford University Press.

Baxi, Upendra. 1980. *The Indian Supreme Court and Politics*. Lucknow: Eastern Book Company.

———. 1985a. *Courage, Craft and Contention: The Indian Supreme Court in the Eighties*. Bombay: N. M. Tripathi Ltd.

———. 1985b. 'Taking Suffering Seriously: Social Action Litigation in the Supreme Court of India'. *Third World Legal Studies,* 107–32.

———. 1997. 'Judicial Activism: Usurpation or Re-democratization?' *Social Action,* 47: 341–57. (Oct.–Nov.).

———. 2006. 'Access to Justice in a Globalized Economy'. ILI Golden Jubilee Conference. New Delhi. 5 August.

———. 2006a. 'Access to Justice in a Globalised Economy'. *Combat Law,* 6 (6): 57–64.

Benjamin, Solomon. 2005. 'Touts, Pirates and Ghosts'. In *Sarai Reader 2005: Bare Acts,* eds Monica Narula, Shuddhabrata Sengupta, Jeebesh Bagchi and Geert Lovink, 252–54. Delhi: Sarai Media Lab.

Bhushan, Prashant. 2004. 'Supreme Court and PIL: Changing Perspectives under Liberalisation'. *Economic and Political Weekly,* 39 (18): 1770–74.

———. 2009. 'Misplaced Priorities and the Class Bias of the Judiciary'. *Economic and Political Weekly,* 44(14): 32–37. 4 April.

Chatterjee, Partha. 2001. 'On Civil and Political Democracies in Post-Colonial Democracies'. In *Civil Societies: History and Possibilities,* eds Sunil Khilnani and Sudipta Kaviraj, 177. Delhi: Foundation Books.

Cover, Robert. 1986. 'Violence and the Word'. 95 *Yale Law Journal,* 1601 (July).

Delhi Janwadi Adhikar Manch. 1997. 'Aftermath of Supreme Court Order: Workers Hounded Out of the City'. *Economic and Political Weekly,* 32 (33–34): 2098–2100. 16 August.

Economic and Political Weekly. 2012. 'Editorial, Supreme Folly'. *Economic and Political Weekly,* 47 (11): 8.

Fernandes, Leela. 2007. *India's New Middle Class: Democratic Politics in an Era of Economic Reform*. New Delhi: Oxford University Press.

Frankel, Francine. 2004. *India's Political Economy: 1947–2004,* 2nd edition. New Delhi: Oxford University Press.

Iyer, Ramaswamy. 2012. 'River Linking Project: A Disquieting Judgment'. *Economic and Political Weekly,* 47 (14): 33–40.

Khaitan, Tarunabh. 2011. 'A Six Pack Judiciary'. *Times of India,* 10 July.

Krishnaswamy, Sudhir. 2009. *Democracy and Constitutionalism in India: A Study of the Basic Structure Doctrine*. New Delhi: Oxford University Press.

Mehta, Pratap Bhanu. 2007. 'The Rise of Judicial Sovereignty'. *Journal of Democracy,* 18 (2): 70–83.

Mukhopadhyay, Sukumar. 2011. 'Power of Supreme Court to Intervene in Executive Policy'. *Economic and Political Weekly*, 46 (32): 17–19.

Reddy O. Chinnappa. 2008. *The Court and the Constitution of India: Summits and Shallows*. New Delhi: Oxford University Press.

Sathe, S. P. 2002. *Judicial Activism in India: Transgressing Borders and Enforcing Limits*. New Delhi: Oxford University Press.

Upadhyay, Videh. 2012. 'Judicial Control of Policy Making, and Implementation: Interlinking Rivers'. *Economic and Political Weekly*, 47 (13): 10–12.

1

Embedded Judiciary

Or the Judicial State of Exception?

ADITYA NIGAM

PIL MARK 1: SUPREME COURT IN POLITICAL SOCIETY

In a series of well-known essays, Partha Chatterjee has proposed the concept of 'political society' as a domain that is marked by the singular absence of the language of rights. As opposed to the more theoretically visible domain of civil society, where claims are made and settled on the basis of legally and constitutionally sanctioned rights, claims in political society are never settled on the ground of rights—even though the rhetoric may continue to frame the language of claim-making. We can see, says Chatterjee, a whole range of decisions of governments being taken with regard to the inhabitants of this domain, in an entirely different language of 'policy'—of a certain responsibility that attaches to the government, simply by virtue of its being government. This happens primarily because the mobilisations and claim-making by populations that inhabit political society are 'founded on a violation of the law' (Chatterjee 2002: 177). Among the various kinds of groups that Chatterjee envisages as characterising political society, he lists squatters, encroachers on public property, ticketless travellers on public transport, habitual defaulters of civic taxes, unauthorised users of water, electricity and other public utilities (Ibid.).

Paradoxically, rights rhetoric *is* deployed here quite often while making claims but these are collective—not individual—'rights' that have no legal backing. We might say, taking a cue from Michel Foucault, that these represent what could be called 'rights of the governed' as opposed to either the rights of 'man' or rights of 'citizen' (Gordon 2000: xxxvii). These claims arise from the fact that any government is supposed to have a minimal responsibility towards the population it governs.

It was this ground that the judiciary, especially the Supreme Court, entered in the late 1970s, waving the flag of democracy. As proof of its commitment, it emblazoned on its banner three magic words: Public Interest Litigation (PIL). This was the period after the twenty-one dark months of Emergency (June 1975–March 1977). The end of the Emergency had left the entire society in a mood of collective reflection and remorse at having allowed things to come to such a pass where all democratic rights and civil liberties could be abrogated at the whims of a single dictator. The judiciary was no exception to this. After all, at one level, the judiciary had been central to the drama that had led to the imposition of Emergency, given that it was the courageous judgement by the Allahabad High Court judge, Justice Jagmohanlal Sinha, that had set aside Prime Minister Indira Gandhi's election on grounds of corruption. The image of the judiciary was truly heroic at that time. It is important to remember that the judiciary's conflict with the legislature/executive has been a long one and almost half of the first forty-five constitutional amendments were aimed at curtailing the power of the former (Mehta 2005: 168; Beller 1983: 525), even though much of the initial conflict centred on the more conservative impulses within it. We know that many of those conflicts had to do with what came to be known as the 'basic structure of the Constitution' and the place of the 'right to property' within it. Irrespective of which side one wants to be in the conflict between Parliament and the Supreme Court during that era, the point really is that that conflict too points to the very same tension between political imperatives and the Law. At the heart of the struggles were the questions of land reforms and the abolition of privy purses for instance—and at some level these were the actualisation of the radical political impulse of the anti-colonial struggle. They could only be given material form by placing the strict letter of the law under suspension. This is not the place to go into a more detailed discussion of the actual merits and demerits of the different sides to the conflict. What is important, however, is that in the prelude and the immediate aftermath of the Emergency, it was the judiciary that was on the radical side of the spectrum, giving voice to the widespread feeling against the abuse of power that the country had just witnessed.

So, when the Emergency was lifted and the country entered into a period of collective introspection, the judiciary naturally assumed the role of the 'vanguard'. Its role was crucial to dismantling the entire legal-juridical structure erected during the Emergency. Judges and senior lawyers, in their official as well as individual capacities, took the lead in evolving constitutional and legal safeguards against any possible repetition of such an eventuality in the future.

There is a strong opinion among some scholars that the judiciary's decision to open out Law to PILs was an attempt to 'recast itself in a more populist mode', taking the cue from 'Indira Gandhi's populism' (Mehta 2005: 167). Some others do not see this populism as inherent in this turn towards PILs and the specific forms that it adopted but do see it as a serious potential danger that eventually did not fail to materialise (Sathe 2002; Baxi 1997, 2006). While there is enough reason to share this general disquiet over the populist manifestations of the PILs, to see it as simply populist misses, in my view, the significance of this moment of the immediate post-Emergency era. It misses the significance of a new discursive configuration that had emerged where the abrogation of democratic rights had been held to be coterminous with the previous regime's anti-popular, authoritarian character. The centrality of the 'common man' to the project of democracy in this discursive environment was assumed to be almost self-evident. In fact, most stories about the excesses of the regime had to do with the travails of the 'common man'—forced sterilisations, forcible demolitions of colonies and relocation from the city, and so on. This is the environment that produced the new judicial instrument of the PIL as a way of the Law itself reaching out to the ordinary person, cutting out the cumbersome formalities that made it so unapproachable.

To the extent that it opened itself out to the 'popular', one could say it was populist. What such an understanding misses is that this was a creative, if short-lived attempt to deal with a constitutive split at the heart of Law, as I shall try to argue: the split between the normative spirit of the law and the letter of the law, especially its 'procedural' dimension. For, it was the normative spirit that drove the judiciary in this period into taking account of the larger environment within which the letter of the law had to be implemented. Thus, it was that Justice Bhagwati could comment in *Bandhua Mukti Morcha v. Union of India*[1] that:

> It must be remembered that the problems of the poor which are now coming before the Court are qualitatively different from those which have hitherto occupied the attention of the Court and *they need a different kind of lawyering skill and a different kind of judicial approach*. If we blindly follow the adversarial procedure in their case, they would never be able to enforce their fundamental rights (cited in Sathe 2002: 210).

As S. P. Sathe underlines, the pre-Emergency 'clientele' of the Court 'consisted essentially of landlords whose lands were about to be taken away under the land reform legislation, industrialists whose businesses were about to be nationalised, higher caste applicants opposing reservations in educational institutions or civil services ...' (Ibid.). Given that background, this was a new experience and despite all the dangers that were to play themselves out, it was a brief period of innovation and creativity. As has been remarked, prior to this there was no case law that could be referred to when dealing with cases other than property disputes, not especially when dealing with issues of human rights.

To that extent it was a bold new imagination that needs to be acknowledged as such. I am aware that some recent scholarship has drawn attention to the way in which this phase of judicial activism has led to practices that subvert or transform the judicial process itself in crucial ways but I would see that too as an effect that was not a necessary consequence of the exercise.

This novelty of PILs is underlined by Justice Ruma Pal, one of the most vigorous advocates of the power of judicial review, which has been the primary justification for judicial activism. It is interesting that in a recent paper Justice Pal seeks to draw as seamless and unbroken a connection between this period of judicial activism through PILs and the subsequent period as is done by the critics of PILs. She justifies her argument in favour of PILs precisely in terms of the experience of the Emergency. She refers to the 'specific case' (*Keshavananda Bharati*[2]) that 'gave an expansive meaning to the phrase "procedure established by law" in Article 21' and introduced the idea of 'substantive due process' (Pal 2008: 19). This case was triggered, she says, by 'an unprecedented attempt by the executive to firmly entrench itself as the sovereign power under the Constitution suppressing any form of dissent' (Ibid.). She traces the developments since the judgement of the Allahabad High Court setting aside the prime minister's election on grounds of corrupt electoral practices. In what she considers one of the darkest chapters of the Supreme Court's history, the Supreme Court

> granted a stay on the operation of the decision, but injuncted her from voting in Parliament till the appeal was heard. The next day a state of internal emergency was declared. Two days later, in exercise of powers conferred by Clause (1) of Article 359, the President suspended the right of any person including a foreigner to move any Court for the enforcement of fundamental rights ... (Ibid.: 20).

Detailing the role of the judiciary in this instance, Pal goes on to observe: 'This shameful instance of judicial deference to and abdication of its powers of judicial review in favour of the executive has remained a blot on the reputation of the Supreme Court as a protector of the citizen from executive excesses' (Ibid.: 22). She continues:

> Emergency was ultimately withdrawn in 1977 immediately before elections were held when the ruling political party was defeated. *Public condemnation (which was as severe as it was widespread) of the Supreme Court's role in supporting the executive during the period of the emergency, was the empirical context in which the construction of Articles 14 and 21 was revisited* in two seminal decisions of the Supreme Court (Ibid.: 22, emphasis added).

It was in this context, in a case (one of the two mentioned by Pal earlier) filed by the Bandhua Mukti Morcha relating to the release of bonded labourers working in stone-quarries, that the foundations of the PIL were laid, according to Pal. The Supreme Court negated the state government's claim that 'no fundamental rights of the workers had been infringed', according to her, by 'reading into the concept of "life" in Article 21, the Directive Principles which *inter alia require the State as a matter of policy to ensure adequacy of livelihood* and "just and humane conditions of work"' (Ibid.: 23).

The activist phase of the judiciary was then, of a piece with its overall preoccupation of defining the contours of Indian democracy, indeed, of substantive democracy. Thus we have, during this phase, a whole range of judgements upholding claims that would never have been acknowledged in any other context; though it is probably the case that the overall values merely built on what was the common sense of that 'epoch'.

Thus, in a series of judgements related to the employment of contract labour the Supreme Court had spoken against the practice in no uncertain terms. In a well-known case relating to the Central Public Works Department workers, it had even directed in 1986 that if workers are employed on any job for a continuous period of over 180 days, then the work shall be deemed to be of perennial nature and the worker will have to be regularised. The Supreme Court was especially concerned that the government, which should function as a model employer, had been resorting to this practice of keeping workers temporary and on contract for years. Thus, in *Catering Cleaners of Southern Railway etc v. Union of India and Ors*[3] it had expressed surprise that 'employment of contract labour is steadily on the increase including the public sector which one expects to function as the model employer'. In 1989, the Supreme Court once again observed that 'the contract system was nothing but an improved version of bonded labour'.[4] In *Gujarat State Electricity Board Thermal Power Station, Ukai v. Hind Mazdoor Panchayat Sabha and Ors*,[5] the Court observed: 'The only ostensible purpose in engaging contract labour instead of direct employees is the monetary advantage (accrued) by reducing the expenditure.' It then went on to add in its characteristic style: 'Economic growth is not to be measured only in terms of production and profits. *Man has to be the focal point of development*.' In fact, as late as in 1996, in connection with the *Air India Statutory Corporation v. United Labour Union and Ors*,[6] the apex court had directed that with the abolition of contract labour under Section 10 of the Contract Labour Regulation Act (CLRA), the workers concerned should automatically become permanent workers of the principal employer.

We might also remember the most important and almost emblematic judgement relating to housing rights, the *Olga Tellis v. Bombay Municipal Corporation*,[7] delivered in 1985. In delivering that judgement, Justice Chandrachud had observed:

> Today, India is still grappling with unmet basic housing needs of hundreds of thousands of its citizens. While we represent the world's largest democracy and have a truly remarkable Constitution, *millions of people are still living in sub-human conditions on pavements, in squatter*

> *settlements, bastis, jhuggies, or unauthorized slums and are under constant threat of being evicted...* (cited in Kothari 2002, emphasis added).

Notice here the reference to the 'millions of people living in sub-human conditions' and the assertion in the earlier labour judgement that 'Man has to be the focal point of development.' These are not, strictly speaking, concerns of the law. The highest court in this instance at least, acknowledges that there are people living in *unauthorised* habitations, that is to say, they are based on some kind of violations of the law. However difficult this be for the law to recognise—and the text of the judgement gives enough evidence of this—the law had to take into cognisance the larger environment within which it functions. The operative part of its judgement, therefore, was based then not on the legality or constitutionality of the position of the pavement-dwellers but on a classically 'governmental' concern. It is the business of the government, of which the Court presumably sees itself as an arm, to provide for the basic conditions of livelihood of the 'millions of people'. It thus 'expanded the right to life guaranteed under Article 21 of the Constitution to include within its scope, the right to livelihood, which in this context, translated into the right to be allowed to remain on the pavements' (Kothari 2002). The important point here is that even though 'the final orders in the Olga Tellis case found that the BMC Act was valid and that pavement dwellers should be evicted, the Supreme Court also laid down that *this could be done only after arranging alternative accommodation for them*' (Ibid.). The legality of the law is thus maintained but the Court underlines that the government has a moral duty to provide for livelihoods and habitat—a task in which it has failed; it must therefore first fulfil its duty towards 'the people' before it can start evicting them.

This clearly is the logic of political society in which the judiciary in its early PIL-related judgements participated. The judiciary did not, in other words, for a brief while, see itself as an independent power—the new sovereign that it was to become in the decade to follow.

It is worth underlining here, however, that Justice Ruma Pal considers this (Olga Tellis), along with the *Bandhua Mukti Morcha* case[8], to be among the important landmarks in the judiciary's assertion of independence and of its power of judicial review. In her rendition, the second phase, which we are about to discuss, is actually of a piece with this first one:

> By construing the negative right not to be deprived of life under Article 21 *as a positive right to life* and *by redefining 'life'* to include the right to live with dignity, the charge [of the critics] is that judges have created new fundamental rights like rights to livelihood and shelter, education, privacy, legal aid, a clean and pollution free environment and the right of women to freedom from sexual harassment at work, to name a few (Pal 2008: 15).

PIL MARK 2: THE BRASS BAND OF NEO-LIBERALISM

By the turn of the decade, things were to change considerably. From flag-bearers of democracy, the judiciary was to now emerge as the champion of the new order. Thus, Justices Ruma Pal and Markandeya Katju, in connection with the demolition of Nangla Maachi slums, can opine that 'whatever the case may be, "occupation of land without legal authority cannot be allowed. Even people whose lands have legal rights have been relocated" for projects' (Sarda 2006). Further:

> On the question of the difficulty of being on the streets in this intense heat, the hon'ble bench stated that it is "never comfortable to live out", that there will always be intense heat, or cold, or rainfall in the city. *The hon'ble bench suggested that people need not come to Delhi, unless they can afford to live in the city* (Ibid.).

Other versions of the remarks by the honourable judges are more stark: 'If you are occupying public land, *you have no legal right, what to talk of fundamental right,* to stay there a minute longer' (cited in Ramanathan 2006: 3197, emphasis added). Further: 'Nobody forced you to come to Delhi ... If encroachments on public land are to be allowed, there will be anarchy' (Ibid.).

It is worth remembering that these are seen by Justice Ruma Pal *as a continuation* of the initial impulse. In a purely formal sense, it might be. But in another sense, it is a reversal to the old role that the courts played in relation to Parliament—the courts now became the upholders of the banner of conservatism and the power of the powerful.

It was in this new spirit that in August 2001, in relation to the *Steel Authority of India Ltd v. National Union Water Front Workers and Ors,*[9] 'a constitutional bench of the Supreme Court clubbed together several cases and overturned the earlier landmark *Air India* judgment'[10] and stated that 'Neither S. 10 of the Contract Labour (Regulation and Abolition) Act 1970 nor any other provision in the Act, whether expressly or by necessary implication, provides for automatic absorption of the contract labour working in the concerned establishment.' In an instance of what Upendra Baxi has befittingly called the 'structural adjustment of judicial activism', he refers to a 2006 decision of the Supreme Court that 'goes so far as to "overrule" without specific naming all prior judicial decisions [with respect to labour jurisprudence]'. Baxi goes on to observe that 'the learned Justice who writes the principal opinion even goes so far as to suggest that his predecessors *laboured under a misimpression that ours was a socialist constitution*' (Baxi 2006: 6, emphasis added).

Though the pronouncements of the judges in the Nangla Maachi case are diametrically opposed to those of Justice Chandrachud in the Olga Tellis case, how exactly does Justice Ruma Pal see a straight line of continuity between them? Her narrative continuously rhetorically pits 'the Judiciary' as the saviour and the voice of justice and sanity against the corruption, populism and non-performance of 'the Executive'. The straight line that she draws between judicial activism 'then' (Mark 1) and judicial activism 'now' (Mark 2) is underwritten by a deep contempt for the political processes of democracy, elections, parties, coalitions, alliances, and so on. In a way, this contempt parallels the contempt that we witness especially strongly in the 1990s, among the urban middle classes to all such politics.[11]

For the moment, let me return to the remarks made by Pal and Katju in the Nangla Maachi case referred to earlier: 'If you are occupying public land, you have no legal right, leave alone fundamental right to be there for a single minute longer.' This remark insists, let us underline here, on the *pure legality* of the matter. And this is no isolated judgement. Six years before this, in the *Almitra Patel* case,[12] the Supreme Court was already reiterating this new principle: 'Rewarding an encroacher on public land with an alternative free site is like giving a reward to a pickpocket.' In fact, as Usha Ramanathan (2005) reminds us, *Almitra Patel* was not a case about slums and slum settlements at all but about garbage disposal and was dexterously turned into a case about slum clearance by the court. It had, in other words, strayed far away from the logic of governmental rationality that governs political society, and started asserting the non-negotiability of the 'rule of law'.

As a matter of fact, as Ramanathan shows, even in the best of times, even at the time of the Olga Tellis judgement, the law was unequivocally stated by the judiciary: 'no person had the right to encroach... on footpaths, pavements or any other place marked for a public purpose' and if it did happen, the municipal corporation was obliged to remove it (Ramanathan 2006: 3193). It was only through a long and painful back and forth, weighing the pros and cons, as it were, that the matter was decided in favour of the pavement-dwellers. The logic of governmentality won the day over the logic of the 'rule of law'. Ramanathan identifies the *Almitra Patel* judgement (2000) as the judicial moment when: (i) illegality was singled out as the trait of the slum-dweller, and (ii) 'cleaning up of the city' was declared to be the primary task in which governmental agencies needed to be engaged (Ibid.: 3195). Thenceforth, the judiciary was to also increasingly set itself up as the virtual sovereign power, continuously supervising governmental functions and ensuring that 'rule of law' was not violated.

Elsewhere, in the domain of forests and forest-dwellers, this change was probably initiated much earlier. The *TN Godavarman v. Union of India*[13] case, where a writ petition had been filed in 1995 to protest illegal timber-felling in a part of the Nilgiri forests, the Supreme Court transformed this into a composite case (clubbing with all other forest-related ones) into something entirely different. Its scope was expanded 'from ceasing illegal operations in particular forests into a reformation of the entire country's forest governance and management' (Rosencranz and Lele 2008: 11).

This shift from the logic of governmentality (political society) to the 'rule of law' (civil society, rights) represents, it seems, a deeper transformation. It would certainly be simplistic to see the functioning of the judiciary in this period as though it is a simple instrument of neo-liberalism. However, there seems to be little doubt that the new atmosphere of neo-liberal reforms provides the backdrop of the vast and rapid change in common sense about a range of things, at least among the urban middle classes and the intelligentsia. But this shift is not simply a shift towards neo-liberalism and as the case of the Hindutva judgements[14] shows, there is also a decisive turn away from the prevailing secular wisdom in this period. We must also not forget that it is precisely in this period that the judiciary emerges as the champion of the post-

Mandal discourse of 'merit' and 'efficiency' and as the most powerful force against reservations.

I have argued elsewhere (Nigam 2006) that the turn of the decade (i.e., the end of the 1980s and the beginning of the 1990s) sees the convergence of three distinct discursive currents into a single master discourse. First, the discourse of neo-liberalism that launches a full-fledged attack on the presuppositions of the former, supposedly 'socialist' welfare state for its rigid labour laws, the absence of the right to 'hire and fire' that is so essential for development and economic growth. This goes hand in hand with the attack on the licence-permit raj and the protection provided, legally speaking, to small-scale industry and an argument is made about the need to unshackle the economy for taking the big plunge. Second, discourse of Hindutva that made an analogous argument against the 'pseudo-secularism' of the Nehruvian state by claiming that this state had deviated from 'true secularism' and made it into a kind of 'minorityism'—that provided the same kind of protection to the religious/Muslim minority as it did with labour and small-scale industry. Third, the anti-reservation discourse that made an almost identical argument about unfettering 'merit' and 'efficiency', equating all kinds of affirmative action with encouraging mediocrity. The coming together of these three currents into a single discursive constellation was expressed most starkly through two institutions—the judiciary and the media.

As it happens, however, the logic of politics was driving in an altogether different direction. 'Mandalisation' had come to stay and new forces emerged at the helm of government, forces that owed their success directly to the churning initiated by post-Mandal politics. This changed the terrain of politics so decisively that eventually even the Bharatiya Janata Party (BJP) and the Hindu Right decided to go along with this change—at least, it found itself unable to challenge it openly. The flip side of this is that, at least in words, all political parties seemed to accept the idea of neo-liberal reforms just as they did post-Mandal politics. Nonetheless, the logic of politics had diverged decisively from the logic of the economy. Judicial activism Mark 1, which started with concerns for the 'people' and the 'popular', the poor and the disadvantaged, had by now taken on a different dimension: We were in a different world now and India had to prepare to enter that world. In that hypermodern

MacWorld, India too had to enter as a modern entity. India had to be made worthy of being inserted into the grid of the global economy (Baxi 2006; Bhushan 2004). This certainly seems to be an important imperative and in some peculiar, perverse way, the corporate sector began to be seen to be the engine powering this journey into the hypermodern. There is therefore certain urgency to the way in which the judiciary, in particular, has thrown its full weight behind the corporate-capitalism-driven agenda of spatio-temporal transformation of India.

It is the urgency, the sense that in some way we will 'miss the bus' yet again if we miss out on this hypermodern revolution, as we did the first time round, that seems to have become the driving common sense of the new era. The recognition that we have all been brought up with, that we ended up being colonised because we were 'backward', is a key force that propels this new 'revolution'. In a sense, this also means that we have no control over our own time; we must run and keep running and anything that seems even remotely like a drag, something that might hold us back, must be excised from the body politic/social.

THE NEW SOVEREIGN AND POLITICAL SOCIETY

That is what lends this situation its extreme *violence*: The violence of the Law, in defence of modernity. And this violence is all-pervasive and threatening, with the judiciary installing itself as the new sovereign and using its power to charge even the elected government and executive with 'contempt of court'. This has led to a situation where the elected governments themselves often seem to have been forced to give up on their governmental functions—in the name of Law. This has been repeatedly demonstrated over the past decade and just two instances from Delhi will suffice here. The first instance is that of the relocation of hazardous/polluting industries from the city. On a PIL filed in 1985 by M. C. Mehta, regarding the pollution of Yamuna River, the hearings continued for over eleven years, and in December 1996 the Supreme Court ordered the relocation of these industries. In the first round only 168 hazardous ones were to be moved out, to be followed by another 9,000 polluting units and then another 30,000 odd in other categories like 'non-conforming industries' (i.e., not conforming to the Delhi Master Plan). In the eleven years that the case went on, at no point were the workers employed in these units made party to the case. They were not even called to state their position. Some attempts were made to find intermediate solutions like installation of common effluent treatment plants (CETP) but it was left to the owners to install them. Installation and running costs being expensive, the owners were not really interested in installing them. The units had to eventually move out and even though some attempt was made to raise these issues through a coalition of citizens and some smaller trade unions, the political class by and large remained untouched by these developments. Unlike Parliament of an earlier era which would have confronted the judiciary, Parliament and the political parties silently approved of the Court's order. It needs to be remembered that this was when the United Front government was in power and the Left parties were in a fairly influential position. The maximum that was done was that the home ministry, under Communist Party of India (CPI) leader Indrajit Gupta, moved an interlocutory petition through which the blow was somewhat lessened as it made downright closure of the units a little more difficult and increased the compensation amount to be paid to workers who opted not to move. This apart, all the classic mechanisms of political society seemed to have completely failed in appealing to any notion of governmental responsibility. This continued through the next five years or more, as more and more units were shut down causing loss of livelihoods to workers in their thousands.

As a second instance, we could take the spate of *jhuggi jhonpri* (squatter settlements) demolitions in the city that have been intermittently going on while the industries were being closed down. The most dramatic and violent demolitions took place in 2005–06, when the settlements in the Yamuna Pushta and the Nangla Maachi for instance were demolished and thrown to the peripheries of the city. Some alternative sites were provided for resettlement but these were entirely insufficient open lands with nothing around. In none of these cases, however, could any of the mobilisational forms of political society be of any use. The virtually absolute judicial power made it impossible for any such mechanism to work.

Largely because of this, and because of the particular way in which Chatterjee defines political society as a place of resolution, critics have often commented that the model of political society has now become largely irrelevant. These critics see political society, therefore, as a model that belongs to the era of a more responsive welfare state, where the state would respond in some positive fashion to popular demands. In the era of the relatively more malignant neo-liberal dispensation, the idea of political society loses its significance. In my opinion, the idea of 'governmentality' should not be linked to 'welfare' in the welfare-state sense, but to a particular kind of modern form of power that 'takes charge of the population' in the sense that an empire or a monarch does not: ensuring public health, its concern with mortality rate, death and birth rates, ensuring that the population does not die of hunger and destitution, educational and literacy levels, and so on. In this sense, the colonial state too was no less a governmental state.

I would further suggest that at least a part of the difficulty in thinking about political society at this juncture arises from Chatterjee's own rendering, which ties it up too closely with the 'welfare' aspect of governmentality. We need to think of governmentality itself in more complicated ways that has to do not only with providing food and clothing for the population but also with the task of collecting its revenues and taxes and managing its finances in a manner that makes it possible to 'govern'. This involves a twofold understanding of governing in the longer term sense. First, good government must also be predicated upon 'managing' the economy, ensuring growth rates (the idea of which will vary from time to time) and/or redistribution; enlarging, continuously, its revenue base as well as shifting its priorities of expenditure and investments and such other activities. Second, in a longer term sense, this can only be ensured by producing the 'ideal citizen'—a citizen who pays taxes conscientiously, abides by the law, etc. Looked at from this point of view, it seems that the onset of neo-liberalism has underlined this other function or aspect of governmentality. Rather than abdicate its concern for the poor, it would seem, the new ideological dispensation is undergirded by the belief that the only way poverty can really be removed and the fruits of 'development' reached to all is by rapid growth and a relentless battle against 'corruption'—both of which suffer from the deficit in the ideal of citizenship which is further seen to be compromised by the susceptibility of the legislature and executive to populism. At least this is the belief that the best representatives of the judiciary would seem to be basing their arguments on. In that sense, the judicial interventions of the 1990s could be seen *not as an abdication* of the initial impulse but its re-tuning in accordance with the new 'zeitgeist'. This makes the domain of political society a highly uncertain one defined by just one criterion: its illegality and the fact that its claims can never be addressed as 'rights' of 'citizenship'. To that extent, the judiciary in its pursuit of hypermodernity seems to have taken on the task of producing the ideal citizen—a task that is continuously compromised by the logic of political society.[15]

We must also take seriously the claim made by Justice Ruma Pal referred to earlier , while responding to the critics of judicial activism. She agrees that by redefining the negative right not to be deprived of life under Article 21 *as a positive right to life* and *by redefining 'life'* the Supreme Court has created new fundamental rights like rights to livelihood and shelter, education, a clean environment and the right of women to freedom from sexual harassment at work.

Pal accepts the charge of the critics and justifies this role of the judiciary:

> The fact is that the framers [of the Constitution] did not define such concepts like equality, liberty or freedom. They did not lay down the standards of 'reasonableness' of the restrictions which the Constitution allows on the freedom of speech, the rights of peaceable assembly, to form associations, to move freely and settle anywhere in the country... None of the rights have a fixed content. Most of them are 'empty vessels' as Justice Billings Learned Hand said, *into which each generation pours its content by judicial interpretation in the light of its experience* (Pal 2008: 16, 17, emphasis added).

Law and Rights as empty vessels that have to be imbued with content in keeping with the spirit of the times: this is what Pal ultimately argues for. And what may be the spirit of the times but the embedding of judicial discourse within a new discourse of power, even if occasionally subverted by the emergence of counter power/s in society? As lawyers and scholars of law alike have noted, not a word in the statutes had to be changed and yet, between PIL Mark 1 and PIL Mark 2 a whole world changed.

We might need to reckon here with the fact that this moment of 'taking charge of life' by the judiciary, the precise moment when it redefined 'life' and the 'right to life' to include everything that 'governmentality' should be concerned with, is also the moment when the basis of judicial activism was laid. This is the moment when the imperatives of the 'right to life' can seamlessly invite the intervention of the judiciary now for right to livelihood, and now for the right to a clean and pollution-free environment. Since the framers of the Constitution have not fixed any hierarchy between these different 'rights', the logic of which dominates at which point is endlessly open to the play of judicial interpretation.

NOTES

1. *Bandhua Mukti Morcha v. Union of India* (1985) 3 SCC 161, 182.
2. *Keshavananda Bharati v. State of Kerala,* AIR 1973 SC 1461.
3. (1987) 2 SCR 164.
4. *Sankar Mukherjee and Others v Union of India and Others,* AIR 1990 SC 532 at 534 at para 6
5. AIR 1995 SC 1893.
6. AIR 1997 SC 645.
7. AIR 1986 SC 180.
8. *Bandhua Mukti Morcha v. Union of India* (1985) 3 SCC 161, 182.
9. AIR 2001 SC 3527.
10. *Air India Statutory Corporation and Ors v. United Labour Union and Ors* AIR 1997 SC 645.
11. It is necessary to point out at this stage that the immense democratic possibilities realised through the electoral process in the 1990s primarily through the rise of Dalit and backward caste parties culturally located in the 'vernacular' world seemed to have run out of steam in the subsequent decade. At any rate, in terms of raising issues of poverty and redistribution, these parties have been no different from other parties. As a consequence, the nature of alienation and disgust with politics in the second half of 2000s took on a very different character, some of which was evident in more recent mobilisations against corruption in 2011.
12. *Almitra Patel v. Union of India* (2000) 2 SCC 679.
13. WP (Civil) No. 202 of 1995.
14. *Ramesh Yeshwant Prabhoo v. P. V. Kunte,* AIR 1996 SC 1113, *Ramakant Mayekar v. Celine S'Souza,* AIR 1996 SC 826 and *Manoj Joshi v. Nitin Bhaurao Parikh and Anr,* AIR 1996 SC 796.
15. There have been newer developments in the latter half of the decade of 2000 with the judiciary perhaps marking yet another phase—moving away from this spirit of the 1990s, but that is another story and we cannot possibly go into it here.

REFERENCES

Baxi, Upendra. 1997. 'Judicial Activism: Usurpation or Re-democratization'. *Social Action*, 47: 341–57 (October–December).

———. 2006. 'Access to Justice in a Globalized Economy'. Indian Law Institute Golden Jubilee Conference Address, mimeo.

Beller, Gerald E. 1983. 'Benevolent Illusions in a Developing Society: The Assertion of Supreme Court Authority in Democratic India'. *The Western Quarterlym* 36 (4): 513–32.

Bhushan, Prashant. 2004. 'Supreme Court and PIL: Changing Perspectives under Liberalization'. *Economic and Political Weekly*, 39 (18): 1770–74. 1 May.

Chatterjee, Partha. 2002. 'On Civil and Political Society in Postcolonial Democracies'. In *Civil Society: History and Possibilities*, eds Sudipta Kaviraj and Sunil Khilnani, 165–78. New Delhi: Cambridge University Press.

Gordon, Colin. 2000. 'Introduction'. In *Power: Essential Works of Foucault, 1954–1984*. Vol. 3, ed. James D. Fabion. England: Penguin Books.

Kothari, Jayna. 2002. 'A Right to Housing?' Available at http://www.indiatogether.org/opinions/rhousing02.htm. (accessed on 25 July 2013).

Mehta, Pratap Bhanu. 2005. 'India's Judiciary: The Promise of Uncertainty'. In *Public Institutions in India: Performance and Design*, eds Devesh Kapur and Pratap Bhanu Mehta, 158–93. New Delhi: Oxford University Press.

Nigam, Aditya. 2006. *The Insurrection of Little Selves: The Crisis of Secular-Nationalism in India*. New Delhi: Oxford University Press.

Pal, Ruma. 2008. 'Judicial Oversight of Overreach: The Role of the Judiciary in Modern India'. Center for the Advanced Study of India, University of Pennsylvania, CASI Working Paper Series, Number 08-03, March 2008.

Ramanathan, Usha. 2005. 'Demolition Drive'. *Economic and Political Weekly*, 40 (27): 2908–12. 2 July.

———. 2006. 'Illegality and the Urban Poor'. *Economic and Political Weekly*, 41 (29): 3193–97. 22 July.

Rosencranz, Armin, and Sharachchandra Lele. 2008. 'Supreme Court and India's Forests'. *Economic and Political Weekly*, 43 (5): 11–14. 2 February.

Sarda, Shveta. 2006. 'Notes on Supreme Court Hearing on Nangla Maanchi'. May 9. posted at http://osdir.com/ml/culture.india.sarai.reader/2006-05/msg00053.html. (accessed on 11 September 2013).

Sathe, S. P. 2002. *Judicial Activism in India: Transgressing Borders and Enforcing Limits*. New Delhi: Oxford University Press.

2

In the Name of the People
The Expansion of Judicial Power

USHA RAMANATHAN

The Supreme Court reinvented itself in the fading years of the 1970s and the early years of the 1980s.[1] A once conservative institution was changed by judicial activism and the judicial process was introduced to people and problems that it may never have encountered if the old order had persisted unchanged. Credible lore has it that the reputational slough into which the Supreme Court had declined after its infamous judgement in the Emergency-era *Habeas Corpus* case[2] produced the moment when differences among judges about judicial orthodoxy could be buried in a bid to recover from institutional embarrassment. This was the case where a five-judge bench of the Supreme Court heard cases pertaining to the right of the citizens who were detained by the state to sue for their release by filing for writs of habeas corpus. Four of the five judges, faced with a constitutional challenge in the midst of mass detention and the exercise of extraordinary state power, had abdicated their role as bulwarks against absolute power. They justified the 'sweeping power' of the state as 'extraordinary powers (necessary to be vested in the government) in order to enable it to overcome such crisis situations and restore normal conditions'.[3] They did not know then that the Emergency would end while the judgement was still within public memory. Political expediency had inscribed in the pages of law reports a judge's words:[4] 'Furthermore, we understand that the care and concern bestowed by the state authority upon the welfare of the detenus who are well-housed, well-fed and well-treated is almost maternal. Even parents have to take appropriate preventive action against their children who may threaten to burn down the house they live in.' The need to erase indelible memory is understandable.

The court grasped the opportunity to recreate its reputation when some of its activist judges brought matters of severe deprivation, vulnerability, rightlessness and apathetic neglect to the court. Two judges who had reflected long and hard on legal aid and access to justice[5] had made a case for what was to become public interest litigation (PIL) in their judgements. Expressions that were to acquire a familiarity when juristic activism was in its heyday had been rehearsed in the unlikely site of the *Habeas Corpus* case. 'Even a postcard written by a detenu from jail has been sufficient to activise this court into examining the legality of the detention (sic.)', P. N. Bhagwati had said,[6] and continued:

> this practice... has been adopted by this court in view of the peculiar socio-economic conditions prevailing in the country. Where large masses of people are poor, illiterate and ignorant and access to court is not easy on account of lack of financial resources, it would be most unreasonable to insist that the petitioners should set out clearly and specifically the grounds...

This dramatic reconstitution of the judicial imagination in its PIL jurisdiction, and of the court's constituency, was not without its doubters. There was unease about the implications of the near-demise of procedure in approaching the court, the dilution of locus standi, throwing the court open to strangers to the case and discomfort with the constituency of extreme deprivation whose cause the court was expected to adopt.[7] Yet, the court had to recover its reputation. The constituency of the illiterate, indigent and ignorant and the rightless not only gave the court a chance to regain relevance, but also sculpted a morality that could be displayed within constitutional contours without having to refer, at all, to its embarrassing capitulation during the Emergency. This involved a striking departure from traditional rules of standing, and was, at that time, beyond the court's experience. Judicial prose and juristic activism were deployed to explain the constitutional and pragmatic logic of this enterprise.[8]

Hussainara Khatoon,[9] the Bhagalpur blindings,[10] bonded labour,[11] inter-state migrant workmen,[12] women in what is euphemistically termed 'protective' custody,[13] children in state institutions[14]— all of it demonstrated that poverty and rightlessness were plainly inseparable companions. The notion of the bona fide petitioner whose impulse was altruistic; the responsibility of the court stretching to seek and find the existence, cause and response to deprivation and vulnerability; the involvement of uncompensated court commissioners in the enterprise of taking constitutional justice to those who would not even know to ask for it; the thought that the court's concern was not limited to ensuring access to the court, but to reaching justice to the deprived, and the elevating idea that the court could banish hopelessness, replacing it with justice and rights—this was the stuff of the court's 'compassionate jurisdiction'.

Judicial activism that intervened in situations of extreme poverty brought the judiciary to public and press notice in ways that were flattering. The courts became newsworthy and judges of the Supreme Court became household names. The times in which they were so written about gradually, but surely, obliterated the unenviable reputation that the court had earned during the Emergency. PIL inaugurated collaboration, even complicity, between the Court, the press, social activists and academics which, in turn, aided to inter memory and foster forgetting.

TAKING THE PUBLIC OUT OF 'PUBLIC INTEREST'

The shift in the Supreme Court's jurisprudence began even before the end of the 1980s. When did the signs of this change begin to show? How did it happen? A part of the explanation may lie in the eclipse of a generation of judges who did not have to tote the weight of the Emergency's guilt and shame. Perhaps the answer lies, in some considerable measure, with a new public morality that was engineered into the system by structural adjustment, liberalisation, privatisation and globalisation. A corollary of the new economic order was that the poor and those with skills irrelevant to the economy were a drag on the system and that those resisting the forces sweeping a nation on the way to achieving development were barriers to progress.

While in the 1980s 'life' was infused with a meaning that was wide and brought many rights, including dignity, health, livelihood and shelter, into the constitutional fold, in later years, these very terms were recreated to accommodate the imperatives of growth and development.

In the welter of reasons why 'public interest' became the adversary of the poor and the vulnerable, the expansive power of the court, which PIL facilitated, is significant. Several cases suggest how this power was chiselled out of its PIL jurisdiction.

In 1988, Sheela Barse, a journalist and a public interest petitioner before the Supreme Court, protested that the Court had become 'dysfunctional' in the case of constitutional and statutory violations of children in custodial institutions. She charged the Court with liberally granting 'unjustified adjournments' and being besieged by 'functional deficiencies'. The court had not been able to 'exact prompt compliance' with its orders and directions. She had initiated the proceeding as 'voluntary action on the part of a citizen' and as such, she was 'entitled to withdraw them'. The petition, she asserted, could not be continued against her wishes and without her participation.[15]

The Court's response contained early indications of the structures of control and power made possible in the benign enterprise of PIL. The Court reacted with asperity, casting itself as 'not merely a passive, disinterested umpire or onlooker' in matters that had been brought before it in the public interest. It spoke of a 'more dynamic and positive role' while shouldering a responsibility that required it to order the proceedings, mould relief and monitor implementation. 'This wide range of responsibilities necessarily implies correspondingly *higher measure of control over the parties, the subject matter and the procedure*.'[16]

This assumption of control was accompanied by the fading significance of the person who recognised the cause and took it to the Court. 'The lowering of *locus standii* threshold,' the court said, 'does not involve the recognition or creation of any vested rights on the part of those who initiate the proceedings ....'[17]

In its act of denuding the petitioner of relevance to the proceedings, the Court drew a distinction with disputes between private parties, 'with the result there is no recognition of the status of a *dominus litis* for any individual or group of individuals to determine the cause or destination of proceedings, except to the extent recognised or permitted by the Court'.[18] This was justified by suggesting that this was the inevitable consequence of subordinating the 'rights' of those who bring the action on behalf of others whose 'interests' had been the basis for the PIL. 'Only a private litigant,' the Court would say, 'can abandon his claims.'[19] The Court then refused permission to withdraw the petition, directed that Sheela Barse be deleted from the array of parties in the proceedings and directed that the Supreme Court Legal Aid Committee replace her 'to prosecute the petition together with the aid and assistance of such persons or agencies as the court may permit or direct from time to time'.[20]

The case had been listed for final disposal in November 1986, but Justice Bhagwati's impending retirement had let it slip off the Court's docket. The Court, in 1988, controverted her accusation of tardiness and delay in dealing with this matter of children in custodial institutions by referring to orders made on 15 April 1986, 12 July 1986, 5 August 1986, 13 August 1986 and 21 November 1986, with the claim that these orders demonstrated 'that certain important and far-reaching actions were initiated and appropriate directions were issued to the states and authorities concerned'.[21] However, there was nothing to suggest that the Court had even nudged the cause forward since November 1986. The Court conceded, however, that there was no denying that a debate on judicial accountability, especially in the promptitude and despatch with which the cases are dealt, was overdue. But the Court stated that the applicant before the Court could not choose to constitute herself as a judge.[22] Criticisms of judicial functioning, as a matter of principle, are healthy aids for introspection, the Court said, but parties to judicial adjudication cannot constitute themselves as 'overseers of the judicial performance and accountability in the individual cases'.[23] According to the Court, it is the principled right of the Indian citizen to speak out his mind and the judiciary is not exempt from such criticism. But a participant in proceedings cannot 'resort to this freedom and privilege to criticise'.[24] Further, if a person who brings a matter of public interest to court were to be allowed to withdraw it, it is conceivable, the Court feared, that the PIL may be used by persons for personal ends 'resulting in prejudice to the public weal'.[25]

This case marks the moment when the Court established a hierarchy of participation and control. It is possible that 'language [which was] not conspicuous for its moderation' and 'strong expressions of remonstrance'[26] may have steered the Court to the act of 'deleting' the applicant. Yet, it is what the Court has done in asserting power, assuming control and treating as dispensable the public interest petitioner that marks this judicial moment.

IN THE NAME OF 'COMPLETE JUSTICE': THE AGGRANDISEMENT OF JUDICIAL POWER

Beginning in the early 1990s, several decisions scripted a remarkable expansion of judicial power. Article 142, with the innocuous marginal heading 'Enforcement of decrees and orders of the Supreme Court and orders as to discovery, etc.' which gave the Supreme Court the scope to 'pass such decree or make such order as is necessary for doing *complete justice* in any case or matter pending before it', was the axis around which this change rotated.

Prem Chand Garg v. Excise Commissioner, U.P.[27] was an early case that considered the scope of Article 142. At issue was a rule that required a petitioner to furnish security in the Supreme Court in a case under Article 32 which deals with constitutional remedies for violation of fundamental rights, and which itself is a fundamental right. If the case failed, the security could be directed to be paid as costs. Striking down the rule, a five-judge bench of the Supreme Court (one judge dissenting) rejected an argument that the Article 142(1) power to do complete justice allows the Supreme Court to make an order inconsistent with fundamental rights. The judges went on to say:[28] 'An order which this court can make in order to do complete justice between the parties must not only be consistent with the fundamental rights guaranteed by the court, but it cannot even be inconsistent with the substantive provisions of the relevant statutory laws.' Again:[29]

> [T]hough the powers conferred on this court by Article 142(1) are very wide, and the same can be exercised for doing complete justice in any case ... this court cannot even under Article 142(1) make an order plainly inconsistent with the express statutory provisions of substantive law, much less, inconsistent with any constitutional provisions.

A decade and a half later, Article 142 was summoned up in *M. H. Hoskot v. State of Maharashtra*[30] where a prisoner sentenced to imprisonment was 'virtually unable to exercise his constitutional and statutory right of appeal, inclusive of special leave to appeal, for want of legal assistance'. There the Court held, it

> is implicit in the court under Article 142, read with Articles 21 and 39A of the Constitution, power to assign counsel for such imprisoned individual 'for doing complete justice'. This is a necessary incident of

> the right to appeal conferred by the Code [of Criminal Procedure] and allowed by Article 136 of the Constitution.[31]

In *A. R. Antulay v. R. S. Nayak*,[32] an order of a five-judge bench of the Supreme Court in 1984 directed that Antulay's alleged corruption case be transferred to the High Court of Bombay. This was challenged as violative of Articles 21 and 14: Article 21, because it was contrary to the procedure established by law; and Article 14 because it was treated as a 'very special case among the special cases, without any guidance as to which cases required speedier justice'. The irony was that the bench in 1984 was acting to expedite the trial and obviate delay. The case gained complexity because the 1984 decision had acquired finality, with no challenge to the judgement by asking for a review. It was revived long after the possibility of a review had been exhausted by the passage of time—over two years. Yet, when called upon to decide the constitutionality of the 1984 order that had provided an extraordinary remedy, beyond the prescriptions of the law governing the subject, six of the seven judges constituting the 1988 bench were concerned that an order of the Supreme Court had been made in violation of statutory law. One of the six judges held that the transfer to the high court was improper but it should not be dislodged, among other reasons, because of delay, and because it would not in fact cause substantial injustice. The five others decided that the order could not stand. The power to give the extraordinary order in 1984 would have needed the support of Article 142(1) with its prescription of 'complete justice'. Relying on *Prem Chand Garg* that Article 142(1) would not extend to an order that is 'inconsistent with fundamental rights' and 'substantive provisions of the relevant statutory laws', they held that 'where the attention of the court is drawn, the court has always the power and the obligation to correct it *ex debito justitiae*' and use 'its inherent power as a power of review to correct the original mistake. No suitor should suffer for the wrong of the court',[33] and that sentiment guided the majority. Justice Venkatachaliah, the dissenting judge, saw things differently: that it was not an error *of* jurisdiction, but an error *in* jurisdiction. 'The authority to decide,' he said, 'embodies a privilege to bind despite error, a privilege which is inherent in and indispensable to every judicial function.'[34] His reasoning did not lead him into an encounter with Article 142(1).

The significance of *Antulay* lay in the effect of the court's decision on the finality of its decisions: an error is an error, and may be remedied whenever noticed, or challenged. Of course, a correct decision might have been erroneously identified as an error in which case it would presumably have to be remedied, again. And so on. The idea of a 'curative' petition has since taken over,[35] adding further dimensions to the possibilities of judicial error.

These were the uses of Article 142(1), and the interpretation of its scope, when in 1991 the *Nadiad* case and the *Bhopal review* were heard and decided.

Nadiad[36] was about an incident in the town of Nadiad in Gujarat in which a chief judicial magistrate (CJM) was 'tied ... with a thick rope like an animal and made a public exhibition of' by an inspector of police. He was then sent in that bound state to the hospital for medical examination 'on the alleged charge of having consumed liquor in breach of the prohibition law' in force in that state. A photographer was then called in to capture the spectacle of the CJM, bound and handcuffed, and this was published in newspapers around the country. In this, the inspector had the help and connivance of others from the service. The 'object', a commissioner who investigated the happening for the Court later said, 'was to wreak vengeance and to humiliate the CJM who had been policing the police by his judicial orders'.[37] These extreme circumstances provoked the Court to seek and find the power to respond. Even though the High Court of Gujarat had been given statutory powers to deal with contempt of the subordinate judiciary, the Supreme Court intervened. The image of a helpless Supreme Court constrained to turn away from a case such as this, citing lack of jurisdiction, could not be contemplated.

The court found the power to act in Article 129 by reading the phrase '*including the power to punish for contempt of court*' as expressing an extended and wide scope of its power. Trouble arose when Mr Fali Nariman, appearing for the police officers, argued that there was no power in the Court to quash the criminal proceedings that had been initiated against the CJM, and which were pending. The attorney general countered that there is no limitation on the power of this Court under Article 142 in quashing a criminal proceeding pending before a subordinate court.[38] The Court found the power in Articles 136, 32 and 142. 'The inherent power of this court under Article 142,' the Court was emphatic in its reiteration,

> coupled with the plenary and residuary powers under Articles 32 and 136 enhances power to quash criminal proceedings before any court to do complete justice in the matters before this court. If the court is satisfied that the proceedings in a criminal case are being utilised for oblique purposes or if the same are continued on manufactured and false evidence or if no case is made out on the admitted facts, it would meet the ends of justice to set aside or quash the criminal proceedings.[39]

Countering Mr Nariman's argument that Article 142(1) does not contemplate any order contrary to statutory powers, the Court averred: 'No enactment…can limit or reduce the power of this Court under Article 142 of this Constitution though while exercising power under Article 142 of the Constitution the court must take into consideration the statutory provisions regulating the matter in dispute.' What would be the needs of 'complete justice' would depend on the facts and circumstances of each case, but: 'Once this court has taken seisin of a case, cause or matter, it has power to pass any order or issue direction as may be necessary to do complete justice in the matter.'[40]

It is trite that hard cases make hard law. PIL had provided a storehouse of experience, which warranted extraordinary interventions by the Court. The dilution of the doctrine of locus standi and the expansion of the notion of 'public interest' made easy the passage from the occurrence of an event to the courtroom. Confronted with a difficult situation, whose enormity was impossible to ignore, the Court found itself having to fashion a remedy from within the language of the Constitution. *Nadiad* was an exploration, born of exigency, which, assisted by the flexibility and innovation of PIL, expanded the power of the Court.

THE UNCHECKED POWER OF COMPLETE JUSTICE: THE BHOPAL CASE

It was in the *Bhopal review* case[41] that the Supreme Court walked the next mile. 'It will be wholly incorrect,' the court explained, 'to say that powers under Article 142 are subject to express statutory prohibitions. That would convey the idea that statutory provisions override a constitutional provision.'[42] The Court will 'take note' of express prohibitions in a statute 'based on some fundamental principles of public policy and regulate the exercise of its power and discretion accordingly'. But this would only reflect on the 'propriety' of exercise of the power and not on the power itself. So, 'no question of lack of jurisdiction or of nullity can arise'.[43]

The existence, and exercise, of the power to do 'complete justice' grew in circumstances that became curiouser and curiouser. The fateful tale of the criminal cases that were 'settled', till reopened, took twists and turns that led to an extraordinary power being read into Article 142.

In the intervening night of 2/3 December 1984, a deadly poisonous gas was released from the Union Carbide plant in Bhopal into the working class neighbourhood, killing thousands—estimates vary between 2,800 and 8,000 in the first 24 hours, with the number crossing 20,000 as the years rolled by—and harming over 500,000 people. In March 1985, Parliament enacted the Bhopal Gas Leak Disaster (Processing of Claims) Act, 1985. The Act handed over the 'exclusive right' to represent, and act in place of, victims to the Central government, to act 'for all purposes connected with such claim in the same manner and to the same effect' as the victims.[44] The 'claimants' right to be represented by a legal practitioner' was recognised, but limited to being 'associated in the conduct of any suit or other proceedings relating to his claim'.[45]

On 14 February 1989, while an appeal relating to interim compensation was pending before it, a constitutional bench of five judges pronounced an order that set out the terms on which a settlement of the case was being effected. In a prelude to the terms they set out, the Court declared that 'this case is pre-eminently fit for an overall settlement ... covering all litigations, claims, rights and liabilities ... relating to and arising out of the disaster'. The Court 'ordered' that Union Carbide Corporation pay US$ 470 million, and, 'to enable the effectuation of the settlement', all civil proceedings would 'stand concluded in terms of the settlement', and 'all criminal proceedings related to and arising out of the disaster shall stand quashed wherever they may be pending'.[46]

On 15 February 1989, the Court referred to a memorandum that the parties had filed before it while detailing how the US$ 470 million would be recovered (Union Carbide Corporation [UCC] to pay US$ 420 million; Union Carbide India Limited [UCIL] to pay US$ 45 million; American Red Cross to deposit US$ 5 million), setting out the cast of characters who would receive the immunity that this settlement-order was investing in them in both civil and criminal matters connected with the disaster; and spelling out that any claims hereafter would have to be made to the Union of India, since it would be responsible for the amount that would be received in compensation.[47] On 15 February 1989, too, advocates for the UCC, UCIL and the Union of India filed 'Consequential Terms of Settlement', which included the clause 'and all such criminal proceedings including contempt proceedings stand quashed and accused deemed to be acquitted'.[48]

On 4 May 1989, faced with a barrage of protest led by victims' groups and their supporters, the Supreme Court explained how it had arrived at the sum of US$ 470 million. The fact that the original claim had been for US$ 3.3 billion and the settlement was for a sum that was paltry in comparison and that the extent of damage and injury had not yet been assessed and that there was no re-opening clause if the harm was more pervasive or severe than was then manifest—led to irate questioning of the settlement-order, and the Court set out an arithmetic derived from a hypothesis. About the 'part of the settlement which terminated the criminal proceedings', the court declined to speak since review petitions challenging the settlement were already in court, and it 'might tend to prejudging this issue one way or the other'.[49] In the explanation that it did offer, the Court referred to what it had done on 14/15 February as an 'order of settlement'.[50]

In 1986, the Claims Act, 1985 had been taken to court by victims who contested the power of the state to take away their right to conduct, and control, the litigation. These petitions lay dormant in the registry of the Court even as the settlement-order was passed. The petitions were resuscitated, and heard in the brooding shadow of the settlement. The judgement was delivered on 22 December 1989, before the year was out.[51]

In their rejection of the settlement, and of the power as also its exercise by the Central government, it was argued for the victims that the Claims Act did not cover criminal liability, but only civil claims, and so there could have been no absolution of criminal liability. Interestingly, the government too did not see the Claims Act as covering the criminal cases. The Court records the attorney general's argument:

> It was further submitted that the Act only authorised the government of India to represent the victims to enforce their claims of damages

> under the Act. *The government as such had nothing to do with the quashing of the criminal proceedings* and it was not representing the victims in respect of the criminal liability of the UCC or UCIL to the victims. He further submitted that quashing of criminal proceedings was done by the court in exercise of plenary powers under Article 136 and 142 of the Constitution… According to the attorney general, there is also power in the Supreme Court to suggest a settlement and give relief…[52] (emphasis added).

Time and again, the victims claim, the attorney general concedes, and the Court deciding on the Claims Act agrees, that criminal liability is not part of the Act.[53]

The attorney general is recorded as having taken one further step, and said, in relation to the settling of criminal liability:[54] 'These are not considerations which induced the parties to enter into settlement.' This is a startling statement which returns to haunt the *Bhopal review* case. For, if the criminal cases could not have been settled between the parties to the litigation, and these were 'not considerations which induced the parties to enter into the settlement', why did the court use its plenary powers to quash the criminal cases?

The *Bhopal review* court gave its decision on 3 October 1991. Two of the five judges who had constituted the original bench had moved on since the 4 May order that had been authored by Justice Venkatachaliah. Chief Justice Pathak had left to take his place on the International Court of Justice. Justice E. S. Venkataramiah had served an unanticipated stint as the chief justice of India, made possible by Chief Justice Pathak's departure, and retired. Chief Justice Mukharji had been on the bench hearing the review petitions, but his sudden demise had led to a reconstitution of the bench and a rehearing. Justices K. N. Singh and A. M. Ahmadi joined Justices Ranganath Misra, Venkatachaliah and Ojha who, having been on the original bench, carried individual and institutional memory to the review proceedings. As did Mr Nariman, counsel for UCC.

In the time that elapsed between the decision in the *Claims Act* case and the review, the government had changed, as had its position. The victims and the government were on the same side. It was to Mr Nariman that the Court turned to conjure up arguments that would help them sustain the settlement-order. Anxiety that the settlement-order should remain undisturbed can be seen to have influenced the course the court took in laying down the law, including the interpretation of its power under Article 142.[55]

The victims, and the Union of India, argued that 'stifling of the prosecution' was 'unlawful and opposed to public policy'; that non-compoundable offences could not be compounded; that 'unlawfulness of the consideration' would render the settlement invalid.[56]

It is interesting how the Court crossed this thorny path. First, the Court declared that 'the power under Article 142 is at an entirely different level and of a different quality. Prohibitions or limitations or provisions contained in ordinary laws cannot, *ipso facto*, act as prohibition or limitation on the constitutional power under Article 142.'[57] The powers of the Court under Article 136, it was said, are in the nature of special or residual powers, 'exercisable outside the purview of the ordinary laws in cases where the needs of justice demand interference by the Supreme Court'.[58] The Court had to admit that the order terminating the pending criminal proceedings is not supportable on the strict terms of Section 320 (compounding) or 321 (withdrawal) or 482 (quashing) CrPC. The Court then used the device of conjecture—'if'—to explain its settlement order. '[I]f,' as Mr Nariman had argued:

> the Union of India as *dominus litis* through its Attorney General *invited the court to quash the criminal proceedings and the court accepting the request quashed them,* the power to do so was clearly referable to Article 142(1) read with the principle of Section 321 CrPC which enables the government through its public prosecutor to withdraw a prosecution.[59] (emphasis added)

The judgement nowhere sets out if the conjecture was, in fact, fact. There was both individual memory of the judges and lawyers who had negotiated the settlement, and institutional memory as a court, a bar and a bench, which could have been drawn upon to test whether this conjecture had any basis in fact. That did not happen.

The court then began its retreat. 'It is really not so much a question of the existence of the power', the court said, 'as one of justification for its exercise'. There could be a variety of reasons why the power of the court may be exercised. But the 'government must indicate what these considerations are... In the present case, no such endeavour was made.' The stand of the UCC 'in these review petitions is not specific as to grounds justifying the exercise of the power of the court to permit a withdrawal. Even the stand of the Union of India has not been consistent…'[60]

It had been argued for the victims that the offences committed were serious and their investigation was of vital interest and 'that considerations of public interest, instead of supporting a withdrawal, indicate the very opposite'.[61] The Court followed this up with a statement of the dimensions of the disaster which it is necessary to reproduce:[62]

> The offences relate to and arise out of a terrible and ghastly tragedy. Nearly 4000 lives were lost and tens of thousands of citizens have suffered injuries in various degrees of severity. Indeed at one point of time UCC itself recognised the possibility of the accident having been the result of acts of sabotage. It is a matter of importance that offences alleged in the context of a disaster of such gravity and magnitude should not remain uninvestigated. The shifting stand of the Union of India on the point should not by itself lead to any miscarriage of justice.

This last statement may need to be deciphered. The 'miscarriage of justice' had occurred when the settlement had been ordered and recorded, by the Court. The 'shifting stand' had been to demand that the criminal cases be re-opened—and that is what the Court proceeded to do. But not before laying itself open to questions about the logic and judicious use of the power to do what could only be justified in the interest of 'complete justice'. 'We hold,' the Court said, 'that no specific ground or grounds for withdrawal of the prosecutions having been set out *at that stage,* the quashing of the prosecutions requires to be set aside.'[63]

If there were no grounds, and it was not in public interest, why were the criminal cases quashed by the Court? The existence of the power, to borrow the language of the Court, appears to have trumped the justification for its exercise.[64]

Reviving the cases could have spelt the end of the settlement. It is a basic principle of settlements that, being in the nature of contracts, illegal consideration would invalidate the agreement. The judgement suggests that the Court was keen to save the settlement. If the quashing of criminal cases was the 'consideration', however, it would not have been possible to save the settlement.

The Court turned to Mr Nariman, whose effort, like that of the Court, was not to let the settlement fall. Mr Nariman is recorded as having explained:

> that the true principle was that while non-compoundable offences which are matters of public concern cannot be subject matter of private bargains and that administration of criminal justice should not be allowed to pass from the hands of judges to private individuals, the doctrine [of stifling of prosecution] is not attracted where side by side with criminal liability there was pre-existing civil liability that was also settled and satisfied.[65]

The invalidity was based on the possibility of coercion by 'private individuals for private gains taking advantage of the threat of criminal prosecution'.[66] This would not apply where it was the Union of India which moved in the matter for that would not be a case of the administration of criminal justice being exploited by a private individual for private gains. The distinction was between 'motive' and 'consideration', and this was not consideration because no private person had taken the administration of criminal justice into their own hands;[67] because 'it is inconceivable that Union of India would, under threat of a prosecution, coerce UCC to pay US $470 million'; and, because 'in the context of the Union of India the plea lacks as much in reality as in a "sense of proportion"'.[68] What the motive could have been is nowhere explained.

It is not known if the Union of India asked the Court to quash the criminal cases. They may have had some motive for so doing, but what it was, and what would constitute a motive that could, in the circumstances, invite the Court to quash criminal cases, is not clear. In any event, 'at that stage', the Union of India had not given specific grounds why the criminal cases ought to be quashed. And the quashing of criminal cases in a serious matter that ought to be investigated was contrary to the public interest. The one reason that this error, which was caught and corrected in review, occurred was because of the expansive understanding of judicial power under Article 142. That power was reinforced, and left untamed, in the course of this case.

This perception of judicial power, and its expression in matters of 'public interest', can be seen to have had the effect of expanding the scope of discretion. Subsequently, the existence and practice of this expanded power may be seen as having allowed pragmatism and prejudice to influence the universe of 'public interest'.

AMICUS

One of the extraordinary aspects of the jurisprudence that was evolved in the 1980s was the easy equation that developed between the court and public-spirited persons. Dilution of the rule of locus standi, dispensing with complex form and procedure, and making the courtroom a forum where the well-intentioned could speak, democratised judicial engagement. *Sheela Barse* (1988) was the first assertion of hierarchy and control.

In December 1997, in a case that was to raise the pitch of the debate around judicial activism and the power of the court, the Supreme Court placed on record a practice that it had engineered and which was to affect the democratic possibilities of the judicial process. This was the institution of the *amicus curiae*. 'Even though the matter was brought to the court by certain individuals to represent the public interest,' the court said:

> yet as the case progressed, in keeping with the requirement of public interest, the procedure devised was to appoint the petitioner's counsel as the *amicus curiae* and to make such orders from time to time as were consistent with public interest. *Intervention in the proceedings by everyone else was shut out* but permission granted to all, who so desired, to render such assistance as they could, and to provide the relevant material available to them to the amicus curiae for being placed before the court for its consideration.[69] (emphasis added).

This is a procedure that has been adopted in other matters too, and the *Forest Matters* case[70] was a striking precursor. The effect this has had on the representation of 'public interest', the distance it re-introduced between the court and those willing to make the journey to the court in the public interest, the re-privileging of lawyers, and the return to exclusive conversations between lawyers and the bench with the additional dash of the power that the idea of 'public interest' has brought with it, is the amalgam that holds many explanations.

In an order dated 7 October 1996, in the *Forest Matters* case, officially titled *T. N. Godavarman Thirumulpad v. Union of India,*[71] Justices Verma and B. N. Kirpal record Mr Salve as appearing for the state of Tamil Nadu. In an order dated 24 October 1996, in *Environment Awareness Forum v. State of J&K,* W.P. (C) 171 of 1996, the judges refer to Mr Salve as '*amicus curiae*'. In an order dated 12 December 1996, relating to both W.P. (C) 202/1995 and 171/1996, the judges record Mr Harish Salve's status in the cases as '*amicus curiae*'. Mr Salve has continued over the last fourteen years as the *amicus curiae* in the forest matters. Ritwick Dutta and Bhupender Yadav's (2007) *Supreme Court on Forest Conservation* is a compilation of the orders in the *Forest matters* case which demand close scrutiny to critically assess the role, logic and impact of the *amicus curiae* in relation to public interest, policy and proceedings. The *amicus*, it may be noticed, did not dislodge the counsels for the state governments or the Central government who, along with the attorney general, have continued to address the bench.

A spectrum of circumstances influenced the pathways that the Court traversed in the 1990s. The definitive change in economic policy and its reflection in the depleting responsibility of the state in relation to its socio-economic obligations had a discernible effect on the Court. This was the era when it became commonplace to blame the poor for their poverty.[72] The burden of backlog, and the embarrassment of delays, began to be spoken about in the late 1970s and reached a crescendo in Justice Bhagwati's Law Day speech in 1985, when he famously warned that the judiciary was on the verge of collapse.[73] The 1990s, and since, have been years of introducing and consolidating practices and procedures that would relieve the congestion in the courts and restore its reputation and relevance. Lok Adalats,[74] fast track courts, 'camp courts' on jail premises for petty offences, arbitration, mediation and, more recently, plea bargaining have been adopted to ease the pressure on the judicial system. The idea of 'judicial impact assessment'[75] as meaning *not* the impact that the judiciary has on a people, but the burden that was likely to be cast on the judiciary by new legislation, is a symptom of how the problem is being ascribed. This context helps explain the emergence of pragmatism as a judicial standard.

In the ticking away of time, the court's performance in the *Habeas Corpus* case has been forgotten, with succeeding generations on the bench allowing institutional memory to fade. It has been replaced by a confidence that has grown out of the credibility and legitimacy that the compassionate jurisdiction of the court brought with it.

Compassion itself was soon overridden by considerations of pragmatism, prejudice about the poor and the possibilities offered by power that it had discovered through PIL. The court acted on opportunities offered to it to declare a right to food,[76] or recognise the existence of a right to health.[77] In the same period of legal history though, slum demolition without resettlement, dam building without rehabilitation of the displaced and a denuding of the protection for the working classes were to become systemic responses, and 'public interest' petitioners could walk into the courtroom asking for the destruction of the rights of the poor.[78]

NOTES

1. See, for example, *S. P. Gupta v. Union of India*, AIR 1982 SC 149, *Bandhua Mukti Morcha v. Union of India*, (1984) 3 SCC 161.
2. *ADM Jabalpur v. Shivkant Shukla*, (1976) 2 SCC 521.
3. Ibid.: 722 (per Justice P. N. Bhagwati).
4. Ibid.: 643 (per Justice M. H.Beg).
5. Justices P. N. Bhagwati and V. R. Krishna Iyer.
6. *ADM Jabalpur v. Shivkant Shukla*, (1976) 2 SCC 521, p. 724 (per Justice P. N. Bhagwati).
7. Justice R. S. Pathak in *Bandhua Mukti Morcha v. Union of India*, (1984) 3 SCC 161 and Justice E. S. Venkataramiah's 10 questions in *Sudipt Mazumdar v. State of Madhya Pradesh* (1983) 2 SCC 258.
8. *S. P. Gupta v. Union of India*, AIR 1982 SC 149.
9. *Hussainara Khatoon v. Home Secretary, State of Bihar*, AIR 1979 SC 1360.
10. *Khatri & Ors. v. State of Bihar & Ors.*, AIR 1981 SC 928.
11. *Bandhua Mukti Morcha v. Union of Indias* (1984) 3 SCC 161.
12. *People's Union for Democratic Rights v. Union of India*, AIR 1982 SC 1473.
13. *Upendra Baxi (Dr) v. State of U.P.*, (1983) 2 SCC 308.
14. *Sheela Barse v. The Secretary, Children's Aid Society*, (1987) 3 SCC 50.
15. *Sheela Barse v. Union of India*, (1988) 4 SCC 226, pp. 231–32.
16. Ibid. para 12.
17. Ibid.: 234.
18. Ibid.: 233.
19. Ibid.: 246.
20. Ibid.: 247.
21. Ibid.: 235.
22. Ibid.: 242.
23. Ibid.: 242.
24. Ibid.: 243.

25. Ibid.: 243.
26. Ibid.: 232.
27. *Prem Chand Garg v. Excise Commissioner, U.P.*, 1963 Supp 1 SCR 885.
28. Ibid.: 899.
29. Ibid.: 899–900.
30. *M. H. Hoskot v. State of Maharashtra*, (1978) 3 SCC 544.
31. Ibid.: 556–57.
32. *A. R. Antulay v. R. S. Nayak*, (1988) 2 SCC 602.
33. Ibid.: 656–57 (per Justice Sabyasachi Mukharji).
34. Ibid.: 701 (per Justice Venkatachaliah).
35. *Rupa Ashok Hurra v. Ashok Hurra*, AIR 2002 SC 177.
36. *Delhi Judicial Service Association v. State of Gujarat*, (1991) 4 SCC 406. Bench: Justices K. N.Singh, Kuldip Singh and N. M. Kasliwal.
37. Ibid.: 456 (per Justice K. N. Singh).
38. Ibid.: 461 (per Justice K. N. Singh).
39. Ibid.: 462 (per Justice K. N. Singh). See also p. 452, para 37; and p. 461, para 49.
40. Ibid.: 463 (per Justice K. N. Singh).
41. *Union Carbide Corporation v. Union of India*, (1991) 4 SCC 584.
42. Ibid.: 635 (per Justice Venkatachaliah).
43. Ibid.
44. Section 3(1), Bhopal Gas Leak Disaster (Processing of Claims) Act, 1985.
45. Section 4, Bhopal Gas Leak Disaster (Processing of Claims) Act 1985.
46. *Union Carbide Corporation v. Union of India*, (1989) 1 SCC 674.
47. Ibid.: 675. The switch in the role of the Union of India—standing in for the victims one day to a holder of monies to whom the victims must petition the next—was an irony that the court did not acknowledge.
48. Ibid.: 677.
49. Ibid.: 42. Bench: Chief Justice R. S. Pathak, and Justices E. S. Venkataramiah, Ranganath Misra, M. N. Venkatachaliah and N. D. Ojha.
50. Ibid.: 41.
51. *Charanlal Sahu v. Union of India* (1990) 1 SCC 613. Bench: Chief Justice Sabyasachi Mukharji, Justices K. N. Singh, S. Ranganathan, A. M. Ahmadi and K. N. Saikia.
52. Ibid.: 677.
53. See also Ibid.: 726–27, para 162, where Justices Ahmadi and Ranganathan were emphatic: 'It has been pointed out by Mukharji, CJ and we agree that the Act talks only of the civil liability of, and the proceedings against, the UCC or UCIL or others for damages caused by the gas leak. It has nothing to say about the criminal liability of any of the parties involved. Clearly, therefore, this part of the settlement comprises a term which is outside the purview of the Act.'
54. *Charanlal Sahu v. Union of India* (1990) 1 SCC 613, p. 683.
55. See, for example, 'Re Contention (F) *Supra* n. liv at 642–50.
56. *Charanlal Sahu v. Union of India* (1990) 1 SCC 613, pp. 642–46.
57. Ibid.: 635.
58. Ibid.: 625.

59. Ibid.: 634.
60. Ibid.: 637.
61. Ibid.: 638.
62. Ibid.: 638.
63. Ibid.: 638, para 91; emphasis added.
64. Ibid.: 637.
65. Ibid.: 645.
66. Ibid.: 647.
67. Ibid.: 647–48.
68. Ibid.: 650.
69. *Vineet Narain v. Union of India* (1998) 1 SCC 226, p. 234.
70. *T. N. Godavarman Thirumulpad v. Union of India*, (2006) 1 SCC 1.
71. Ibid.
72. The image of the slum-dweller as pickpocket (*Almitra Patel v. Union of India* (2000) 1 SCALE 568, para 14) was an extreme manifestation that presumed a natural correlation between poverty and criminality.
73. In his speech on the Law Day in 1985, Chief Justice Bhagwati warned: 'I am pained to observe that the judicial system in the country is almost on the verge of collapse. These are strong words I am using but it is with considerable anguish that I say so. Our judicial system is creeking under the weight of arrears.' Cited in Ashok H. Desai (1996).
74. National Legal Services Authority Act, 1987, which came into effect in 1995.
75. *Salem Advocates Bar Association v. Union of India*, AIR 2005 SC 3353.
76. *People's Union for Civil Liberties v. Union of India*, WP No. 196 of 2001.
77. *Paschim Banga Khet Mazdoor Samiti & Ors v. State of West Bengal*, AIR 1996 SC 2426.
78. *Okhla Factory Owners' Association v. Government of NCT of Delhi*, (2003) 108 DLT 517. This was a PIL dealing with the removal and relocation of slum-dwellers squatting on government land, where the Delhi High Court eventually examined 'the legality, validity and propriety' of the resettlement policy that was implemented by the Delhi government.

REFERENCES

Das, Gobind. 2000. *Supreme Court in Quest of Identity*. 2nd edition. New Delhi: Eastern Book Co.

Desai, Ashok H. 1996. 'Speech Law Day 1996—On Monday, the 26th November 1996 in the Supreme Court Premises'. Available at http://www.ebc-india.com/lawyer/articles/97v2a2.htm (accessed on 18 November 2010).

Dutta, Ritwick, and Bhupender Yadav. 2007. *Supreme Court on Forest Conservation*. 2nd edition. Universal Law Publishing Co. Ltd.

3

Environment and the Will to Rule

Supreme Court and Public Interest Litigation in the 1990s

NIVEDITA MENON

It is generally accepted among judiciary watchers that the 1990s marks a specific phase in court responses to public interest litigation (PIL). In the 1980s, PIL initiatives resulted in important judgements protecting human rights; in the 1990s, judgements privileged, in some cases, 'development' and, in others, 'environment' over people's lives and livelihood. This trend has been noted and criticised by legal scholars and activists, but while one school attributes the change to *excessive judicial activism,* with the judiciary expanding its scope and encroaching into the executive/legislative sphere, the other holds that the judiciary has *withdrawn from its activism* of the 1980s, turning anti-PIL. Both therefore, suggest mutually contradictory measures for bringing the judiciary back on track from the point of view of 'people's interests.'

This chapter examines the debate and suggests an alternative reading of the transformation.

'EXPANDED SCOPE OF JUDICIARY' ARGUMENT

Ramaswamy R. Iyer argues that the judiciary in India has expanded its scope and jurisdiction in four ways: by using the power of interpretation to virtually create new laws, by enlarging the boundaries of its human rights and environmental concerns, by bringing more and more executive action and decision-making within the purview of judicial review and by assuming the right to ask public authorities why they have not performed their statutory functions (Iyer 2006). Iyer notes that such activism need not always be 'progressive', it can be 'reactionary' (from the point of view of 'people's lives and livelihoods' we must assume, since he does not specify). He points out several instances of judicial overreach by the Supreme Court—directing the government to set up a central regulatory body for groundwater; addressing air pollution in Delhi by endorsing a particular technical solution (compressed natural gas) endorsed by the Centre for Science and Environment, the non-governmental organisation (NGO) that had filed that particular PIL; and the Supreme Court's direction to the government to accelerate action on the Interlinking of Rivers Project, when it was in its very initial stages, thus converting 'a non-project into the most important national project' (Ibid.: 2069), without hearing any interested party, including state governments, and without considering prevalent views suggesting that there are very serious ecological and human costs to such a project.

Lavanya Rajamani is approving of the Supreme Court having 'fleshed out the right to a wholesome environment by integrating into Indian environmental jurisprudence not just established, but even nascent principles of international environment law' (Rajamani 2007: 294). Some of these are the 'polluter pays' principle, the principle of 'sustainable development' and 'the state as trustee of all natural resources'. Interestingly, Rajamani cites the sustainable development principle as having been invoked in response to the PIL of Narmada Bachao Andolan (NBA) of 2000. This was the judgement, we may remind ourselves, in which the Supreme Court, dismissing all pleas of environmental costs due to the dam, held that on the contrary, 'there has been ecological *upgradation* with the construction of large dams'.[1] We will return to the question of the judiciary's environmental activism later in this essay, as well as to whether the principle of 'state as trustee of all national resources' is conducive to a 'wholesome environment', as Rajamani believes.

Despite this overall assessment, however, Rajamani comes to the conclusion through two case studies (the *Municipal Solid Waste Management* case and the *Delhi Vehicular Pollution* case) that the Court overstepped its mandate in its wide-ranging orders. Moreover, it ignored the fact that sections that had no say in court (the informal recycling sector, i.e., waste-picker communities, and those who provide/use public transport) were seriously affected by the Court's decisions, which imposed high-cost options. Rajamani concludes that the Court should evolve guidelines for 'restrained and responsible PIL' (Ibid.: 321).

As Iyer does, Rajamani too assumes that the Court has the 'best intentions', but that despite these, processes were set in motion by judicial activism that were neither participatory nor impartial.

'SEPARATION OF POWERS ONLY AN ALIBI' ARGUMENT

Mathew John, discussing the NBA judgement of 2000, holds that the supposed 'judicial restraint' was only an alibi to 'sidestep issues of entitlement and suffering', and to 'evacuate the case of its politics' (John 2001: 3031). John interprets the judgement as narrowly technical, restricting itself to questions of relief and rehabilitation, and preventing 'meaningful debate on the dam' (Ibid.).

Drawing on Upendra Baxi's analysis, John terms the 'structural adjustment of SAL' jurisprudence (social action litigation or PIL) in the era of liberalisation as a tendency towards 'measured intervention' in issues concerning civil and political rights of people while practicing 'abstinence' regarding economic rights, citing separation of powers. This 'weak interrogation' of the separation of powers has allowed the Court, John (via Baxi [1999]) holds, to 'abdicate its responsibility' to those affected by the Sardar Sarovar Project (John 2001: 3032). The NBA judgement is an instance, in this reading, of 'judicial wavering in the face of an aggressively globalizing India' (Ibid.: 3033).

Similarly, S. P. Sathe holds that there has been a trend among judges to 'despise PIL' and in the NBA judgement too, the Supreme Court had made derogatory references to PIL as 'private inquisitiveness litigation' and 'publicity interest litigation'. Sathe believes that the Court took a 'formal view' of issues like rehabilitation and environment, thus withdrawing from its larger role that it had assumed in the previous decades (Sathe 2000: 3994).

Prashant Bhushan evaluates several cases in which the Supreme Court has criticised PIL and tried to limit it; for instance, in a case in which it refused to consider the petition of a lawyer challenging the disinvestment of the public sector company BALCO, on the grounds that he was not directly affected by it.[2] In another case, the Supreme Court virtually restrained courts from granting interim orders in PILs challenging any 'development project', by decreeing that the petitioner would have to give a bank guarantee that he/she would make good the loss that may occur to government or any other person due to such interim orders, in the event of the petition being eventually dismissed.[3] Thus, Bhushan reads the judiciary's criticism of PIL as 'betraying a lack of sensitivity towards the rights of the poor and disadvantaged sections of society' (Bhushan 2004: 1774).

SO WHICH IS IT?

Judicial overreach or judicial restraint? Which of the two is responsible for the dramatic 'anti-people' shift of the 1990s? Both sets of arguments are, of course, very aware of the opposite trend in the same period. However, there is a tendency to explain this away in different ways. Iyer, who believes there has been judicial overreach, terms it as 'the zigzag on PIL and activism'. He speculates that on the one hand

> a concern for human rights, equity, social justice, protection of the environment and so on, doubtless lay behind many of these instances of judicial intervention, but we cannot rule out the possibility that at least in some cases a desire for social approval or for a place in history or for rendering a landmark judgment before retirement might have weighed with a judge (Iyer 2006: 2069–70).

Seen from this perspective, environmental activism has led to public criticism of judicial excesses, 'worried' about which, the judiciary has stepped back, resulting in a 'judicial backlash' of restraint as exemplified in the Narmada judgement (Ibid.: 2071). Iyer thus interprets the zigzag in terms of the 'predilections of individual judges' (Ibid.), but as we will see later, the 'zigzag' is in fact a fairly consistent trend.

Prashant Bhushan, who, as we saw earlier, takes the opposite position to that of Iyer, offers a less charitable explanation for what Iyer calls the zigzag. He attributes to judicial restraint and withdrawal from PIL, judgements resulting in 'anti-people' verdicts. However, there have been bold, unrestrained initiatives taken by the Supreme Court during the same period, in support of PILs seeking to protect urban environment. Addressing this, Bhushan brings to our notice the anomaly that in cases in which 'environment' was pitted against 'development projects', environment was invariably the loser (Bhushan 2004: 1772). Bhushan suggests that Supreme Court decisions arise from the Court 'frowning upon' challenges to the government's agenda of economic reforms, in pursuance of which the Court has 'diluted its interpretation of Article 21', refusing to enforce the rights implied by it. In other words, Bhushan recognises that a narrowly technical judgement, far from 'evacuating the case of politics', as John would have it, is precisely a political strategy (Ibid.: 1774).

Nevertheless, Bhushan, despite his own evidence that suggests a proactive judiciary, continues to characterise developments over the 1990s as the 'recent drawing back of the court in PIL' (Bhushan 2004: 1774). He relates this to the court's buying into the ideology of economic reforms, glorifying the market and undermining the responsibilities of the state.

A particular notion of structural adjustment is at work here, in which the state is seen to be 'in retreat'. However, we need to recognise that the 'retreat of the state' in the era of globalisation is a myth. The state is 'retreating' only from sectors in which it previously had some welfare responsibilities, such as health and education. Indeed, the 'retreat' in these spheres is a proactive step making it easier for global capital to penetrate. The state is expected, in fact, to be proactive in putting in place restrictive measures to regulate labour mobility and trade union activity, and it is the state's responsibility, in the era of corporate globalisation, to ensure a healthy climate for investment.

What a careful study of PIL in the 1990s reveals is that the Supreme Court consistently took distinctly different stands on two kinds of PIL in the 1990s, discussed in the two sections that follow.

ENVIRONMENT TRUMPS PEOPLE...

The Court was very receptive to a small number of well-known PIL petitioners who filed PILs on urban 'environment'. As Lavanya Rajamani points out, most PILs are not the result of citizens' mobilisations, but 'rather, points of entry for those with a distinct view based on particular sensibilities'. The leverage that these eminent petitioners (Magsaysay Awardee M. C. Mehta, for example) have with the court may result in 'converting one strain of opinion into policy while annihilating all others' (Rajamani 2007: 306).

In the new climate of opinion, 'environment' is invoked in two contexts. The first is the leisure and lifestyles of the urban middle classes. In cases where the government, under democratic pressure, withdrew or postponed an unpopular measure such as slum demolitions, the courts have rapped it on the knuckles for failure to protect the environment. In 1999, in response to a PIL, a court-appointed committee had recommended the demolition of *jhuggis* in a Delhi locality because of the 'unhygienic' conditions it produced.[4] The government did not move on this order because of its inability to find an alternative site for relocating the people who lived there. In 2006, the Court hauled up various government authorities for contempt of court, and demolitions were carried out forthwith (Menon and Nigam 2007: 75).

Responding to a PIL in 2000, the Supreme Court ordered the Delhi government to remove slums and unauthorised colonies from 'public land'. Denying that the government had any responsibility to find the estimated 300,000 people alternative accommodation, the judgement said:

> [T]he promise of free land at taxpayers' cost in place of a *jhuggi*... is a proposal which attracts land grabbers. Rewarding an encroacher on public land with a free alternate site is like giving a reward to a pickpocket.

Further, 'when a large number of inhabitants live in unauthorised colonies with no proper means of dealing with domestic effluents, or in slums with no care for hygiene, the problem becomes more complex'.[5]

With these two statements, the survival needs of the poor are conflated with the activities of the land mafia ('land grabbers') and the poor identified as responsible, and therefore to be punished, for living in unhygienic conditions.

In another chilling response in 2006, dismissing a PIL against the demolition of slum clusters that supposedly pollute the Yamuna River in Delhi, during the course of which lawyer Prashant Bhushan claimed the right to shelter as a fundamental right, the Supreme Court (Justices Ruma Pal and Markanday Katju) observed:

> Nobody forced you to come to Delhi. Is there a right to live in Delhi only? Stay where you can. If encroachments are to be allowed on public land, there will be anarchy (Leena 2006: 2).

The second context in which 'environment' is invoked is that of forests and wildlife, over which the state is to be the sole authority. Once an area is declared a National Park or sanctuary, forest communities that have lived in and sustained forests for generations become illegal encroachers overnight. It is in this context that we must understand the particular principle of international environment law that the Supreme Court has integrated into Indian environmental jurisprudence—that of 'the state as trustee of all natural resources'—referred to approvingly by Rajamani earlier.

Since 1996, the Supreme Court of India has assumed the role of the principal decision-maker on issues relating to forests and wildlife through its intervention in two cases, the *T. N. Godavarman Thirumalpad v. Union of India and Ors*[6] concerning the implementation of the Forest Conservation Act, 1980, and the *Centre for Environmental Law (CEL), WWF v. Union of India and Ors*[7] concerning the issue of settlement of rights in national parks and sanctuaries and other issues under the Wildlife (Protection) Act, 1972.

These cases are being heard since 1995 and are a part of what is termed as 'continuing mandamus', whereby the Court, rather than passing final judgements, passes orders and directions in order to monitor the functioning of the executive. These have led to fundamental changes in the pattern of forest administration and decision-making. As a result of such orders, no forest, national park or sanctuary can be de-reserved without the approval of the Supreme Court; no non-forest activity is permitted in any national park or sanctuary even if prior approval under the Forest (Conservation) Act, 1980, has been obtained; the removal of any dead or decaying trees, grasses, drift wood, etc., from any area comprising a national park or a sanctuary is prohibited (Dhavse 2004).

The question of who is an 'encroacher' and who is not is a very complex one given the differing histories of peoples in different parts of India, and each of these orders is a blow to the traditional livelihood practices of forest communities, in effect rendering their everyday lives illegal overnight. An Interim Order of May 2002 resulted in several state governments launching eviction drives against 'encroachers' on forest lands, fearing action for contempt by the Supreme Court against them. The Assam forest department used elephants to raze down hutments and homesteads on land recorded as forest. In Maharashtra, tribal families were evicted from farms with standing crops. Scores of houses were destroyed and hundreds were rendered homeless (*Down to Earth* 2003).

...BUT DEVELOPMENT TRUMPS ENVIRONMENT

As the logic of corporate globalisation took hold of the Indian elites, it was PIL petitions of another sort that were met unfavourably by the Supreme Court—those that challenged large infrastructure projects and urban development/'beautification' projects because of their human costs and on ecological grounds. In these instances, the Court spoke in the voice of the developmentalist rational state, valorising the voice of 'experts' and ignoring the pressures of democracy altogether. In order to achieve this end, it may be noted, different judicial strategies have been used at different times.

While dismissing petitions on environmental grounds against the Tehri Hydropower Project and the Konkan Railway in the 1990s, and the Narmada Valley Project in 2000, the Supreme Court apparently exercised judicial restraint. It claimed to be limiting its own powers by holding that it was not the Court's business to determine whether the executive had taken the right decision, but only to consider whether it had taken the decision after a consideration of all relevant aspects (Upadhyay 2000).

However, when the rights of National Thermal Power Corporation (NTPC) to set up a super thermal plant were disputed in 1992 by *adivasis* claiming customary rights to the land NTPC had acquired, the Supreme Court allowed NTPC's claim, in activist mode approving of industrial development in the national interest (Ibid.).

'Development' since the 1990s has also a new dimension, i.e., the consciousness of Delhi, Mumbai and other metropolises being 'world cities' with world-class infrastructure—good roads, flyovers, smooth traffic, malls and multiplex entertainment places. This imagination can equally overwhelm 'environment' questions. Thus, in December 2006, the Supreme Court refused to issue a stay order on construction at the Vasant Kunj Mall site in Delhi. This is, despite an affidavit from the Ministry of Forests and Environment that the topography of the site is similar to that of a ridge, requiring that environmental impact of construction should have been assessed beforehand. The order held the Delhi Development Authority culpable for having auctioned the site without requisite clearances, but held also that *since the corporate entities involved in the construction were not aware of this fact, they should not be penalised*. Construction was on in full swing at the time when conservationists filed a review petition. Even if there was incontrovertible evidence that there was irreversible ecological damage, it would have been too late to reverse the decision. (Express News Service 2006).

On the other hand, lack of awareness of the illegality of an action has never worked to the advantage of thousands of slum-dwellers evicted by Court order over the last decade, as we noted earlier in the Supreme Court judgement on the PIL of 2000, likening the 'encroacher' to a 'pickpocket'. In one such judgement in 2000,[8] the Supreme Court, denying that the government had any responsibility to find the estimated 300,000 people alternative accommodation, declared, 'Rewarding an encroacher on public land with a free alternate site is like giving a reward to a pickpocket'.

Similarly, while *suo motu* recognition was taken of the pollution of the Yamuna by slum clusters, as we saw earlier, the courts see no danger to the Yamuna or possible 'anarchy' arising from certain other encroachments on public land. Built right on the aquifer of the Yamuna River, the huge complex of the Akshardham temple got environmental clearance from the BJP-led National Democratic Alliance (NDA) in Central government at the time, in the teeth of opposition from environmentalist groups. Similarly, the Delhi Master Plan was modified in 2004 to accommodate an information technology park lying just south of the slums demolished in 2000, which had been already under construction for a year—in other words, a de facto regularisation of an illegal encroachment (Bhan 2006). Both these encroachments, in the eyes of the Supreme Court, were in the interests of the tourist-friendly global city.

The Godavarman order of 2002[9] is revealing for the set of preferences it outlines in the Environment/People/Development grid.

Initially the order makes a strong statement on the constitutional duty to protect and improve the environment, tracing this back to ancient Hindu sources (*Manusmriti* and *Arthashastra*) that enjoin punishments for harming nature. Nevertheless, it holds that 'no development is possible without some adverse effect on ecology and environment'. How to balance the two interests? 'Sustainable development' is then defined as 'essentially a policy and strategy for continued economic and social development without detriment to the environment and natural resources on the quality of which continued activity and further development depend'. In other words, continued development is impossible without the continued supply of natural resources and so strategies should be evolved to maintain these resources—environment is thus seen instrumentally as an input into development.

As for People versus Development:

> Where the commercial venture or enterprise would bring in results which are far more useful for the people, difficulty of a small number of people has to be bypassed. The comparative hardships have to be balanced and the convenience and benefit to a larger section of the people has to get primacy over comparatively lesser hardship.

That is, smaller groups of concrete people actually affected by development projects must sacrifice their lives and livelihood for the larger abstract entity of 'the people' who will benefit from 'development'.

The decision that emerges after this supposedly pro-environment analysis, however, is revealing. Having noted that the area in question was declared to be a reserved area in 1960 and again 1987, the decision of 2002 goes on *to permit mining till the end of 2005* 'by which time the weathered secondary ore available in the already broken area should be exhausted'. It seems hardly worth asking in whose interests it is that the secondary ore should be exhausted.

The Vedanta Alumina issue is another illustration of the formula—Environment over People, Development over Environment—and is worth a detailed look. There has been a powerful movement of resistance to bauxite mining by Vedanta in the Niyamgiri Hills, by environmentalists as well as the local indigenous tribes-people. It was the Ministry of

Environment and Forests during the United Progressive Alliance (UPA) government that had granted the company environmental clearance in September 2004, despite the fact that the Niyamgiri Hills are pristine forest lands and a Schedule V area as defined by the Indian Constitution, which prohibits transfer of tribal lands to non-tribals (Kohli 2006). In 2007, the Norwegian government's pension fund, convinced by the case put up by environmentalists, sold all its shares in Vedanta and blacklisted the company for environmental and human rights violations in India. Only then, and on the basis of the Norwegian government's report, did the Supreme Court stop Vedanta from carrying on mining in the Niyamgiri Hills.

However, simultaneously, it bailed out the company by holding that a subsidiary that did not bear the Vedanta tag could take over the mining project. Following the Supreme Court's order, Sterlite Industries, a subsidiary of Vedanta, filed an application before the Supreme Court's Central Empowered Committee (CEC) to set up a joint venture company with a public sector unit, Orissa Mining Corporation (OMC). The CEC, however, came up later with an alternative proposal, projected as a radical measure for 'inclusive growth'—that a non-profit company should be set up to carry out mining, in which the Orissa government would have 51 per cent shares, and Vedanta and OMC together would split the remaining shares. The reduction of Sterlite to a minority shareholder is projected as a measure that will address the 'environmental cost of developmental activity in an eco-fragile area ... Where such development is necessary in larger public interest, the balance of sustainability lies in balancing the environmental cost with public good and not private profit.' The profits earned by the new company are to be used for the welfare of local people, thus ensuring that disaffection among them would be minimised if not eliminated, says the CEC proposal (Mitta 2008).

In short, the 'environmental cost' for something called development will simply have to be paid, and the local people will be pacified with 'developmental measures' with which the poor in India are drearily familiar. That the currency this cost is being paid in is drastically limited, and fast running out, is not under consideration at all.

The point here is that despite apparently opposing arguments—whether exercising judicial restraint or undertaking judicial activism, whether meekly upholding government policy or taking the government to task—these judgements have a clear logic and are remarkably consistent in terms of their outcome. That outcome, as we have seen, takes the form: Environment trumps People, Development trumps Environment. This is why I argue that to continue to assess the judicial developments of the 1990s in terms that are internal to institutions (judiciary's role vis-à-vis legislature/executive) is not very useful. It is also a peculiarly liberal hangover to assume that the judiciary is a neutral institution that could render radically different effects if it followed one strategy rather than the other.

JUDICIARY, THE STATE AND THE POLITICAL ORDER

At this point we need to think through what we mean by 'the state'. What is the location and role of the judiciary within the state, and what is its relationship to 'government' (legislature/executive)? As we saw in several judgements, the pattern is that when the judiciary takes an adversarial position vis-à-vis the legislature/executive, it treats both corrupt practices in the latter as well as the constraints on it due to the pressure of democratic functioning as departures from principles. Thus, both corruption and something called 'populism' are equally decried, while the Court presents itself as a body above politics, objectively weighing evidence and taking the most rational decision.[10] However, when the judiciary upholds legislature/executive decisions, modestly exercising restraint, the government is represented by the Court as having weighed all possible options and taken a decision that the Court is not competent to evaluate.

Clearly, the judiciary and the government do not form a monolithic whole, nor do they work in tandem. Equally importantly, it is not always the same judges who take a particular kind of decision, and often we find such judgements from lower courts as well. How is it that particular outcomes seem to be assured once issues are taken to court? What are the processes that enable this to happen?

In order to address this question, we must first consider the assumption that the 'state' and 'society' are distinct spheres, which is the founding myth of the modern political order. Through this myth, the state and its institutions are seen as governing society, which stands apart from it. A striking illustration of this perspective is that of Marc Galanter, who, in an effort to build into the law a conception of identity as fluid and constituted by interaction and negotiation with other components of society, suggests that the law should adopt an 'empirical' rather than a 'formal' approach. The empirical approach does not attempt to resolve the blurring and overlap between categories; rather, it accepts multiple affiliations and addresses itself to the particular legislation involved, trying to determine which affiliation is relevant in that particular context. It is clear that Galanter assumes the courts and legislature to be independent of this shifting grid of affiliations, standing above society as a unified and self-transparent agency, interpreting the multiplicity of identities *outside* it (Galanter 1984: 357).

If, however, we recognise the boundary between state and society to be indistinct, the 'state' is no longer one coherent actor, but is shot through by extra-institutional loci of power. Similarly, law, as one of the institutions of the state, may seem to exist as an 'abstract, formal framework, superimposed above social practice' but in fact 'the mundane details of the legal process' are all 'particular social practices' (Mitchell 1991: 94).

It is productive here to invoke Partha Chatterjee's (1997) well-known conceptualisation of 'civil society' and 'political society'. Chatterjee (2001) thinks of civil society in Hegelian/Marxist terms as 'an actually existing arena of institutions and practices inhabited by a relatively small section' of people, marked by the 'characteristic institutions of modern associational life originating in western societies'(1997) and based on equality, freedom of entry and exit, contract, deliberative procedures of decision-making, recognised rights, and so on. Civil society is thus the sphere of modernity.

In terms of the formal structure of the state as given by the Constitution, all of society is civil society. But in actual fact, 'most of the inhabitants of India are only tenuously, and even then ambiguously and contextually, rights-bearing citizens in the sense imagined by the constitution'. However, they are not excluded from the domain of politics, rather, as 'populations' they have to be both looked after and controlled by various governmental agencies. This is the zone of 'political society', distinct from both state and civil society, the domain of democracy (Chatterjee 2001).

The 'hiatus' between civil and political society thus defined is 'the mark of non-western modernity', in which 'modernization' is an always incomplete project, to be carried out by an enlightened elite 'engaged in a pedagogical mission in relation to the rest of society' (Chatterjee 1997: 31).

Tweaking this formulation in which civil society and political society are realms set apart from the state, I wonder if it may not be more productive to see the state as inter-penetrating the two. In this sense, the judiciary in India since the 1990s is an exemplary instance of civil society in Chatterjee's sense, in action—shaped by the normative ideals of Western modernity and adopting a 'pedagogical mission of enlightenment' towards the vast mass of the population. So rather than noting 'the complicity' of the judiciary with 'the neo-liberal project', perhaps we need to recognise that the judiciary and the law *are* the neo-liberal project?

There is another way in which I would realign Chatterjee's formulation, formative as it is for my understanding of the contemporary moment in India. As we have seen in this essay, an important development of the 1990s that Chatterjee does not take on board is the fact that political society has ceased to be the target of development for civil society; it is viewed, rather, by civil society as the obstacle to development. Although Chatterjee (2003) does recognise the 'cleaning up' of Indian cities of the poor, by citizens' rights groups and an activist judiciary, he still claims that mobilisations in political society make demands for governmental welfare and that agencies of the state and NGOs deal with these people not as citizens, but as population groups deserving welfare. This was true enough till the 1980s, but needs to be rethought. Demands from these sections are no longer in the form of demanding 'welfare', and nor do government agencies assume that they 'deserve welfare'.

THE WILL TO RULE

After Foucault, we are compelled to see the state as 'but a temporary expression of a ubiquitous will to govern... There is no overarching source of authority...only a will to govern that runs through the polity at large and which produces multiple loci of power' (Bartelson 2001: 179). And, of course, in Foucault's understanding, modern forms of power do not simply oppress, they produce and regulate identity. An important technique by which this is achieved is, precisely, law. From this perspective, while 'rights of the poor and disadvantaged sections' may sometimes be protected by law, the function of the law is certainly not to do this.

To return then to the question of how particular outcomes seem to be certain once an issue is taken to court, Nikolas Rose poses the question this way:

> How is it possible for the calculations, strategies and programmes formulated within such centers [of government] to link themselves to activities in places and to activities far distant in space and time, to events in thousands of operating theatres, conferences, bedrooms, classrooms, prison cells, work-places and homes? (Rose 1999: 48)

His answer is 'translation'—Rose uses the term 'translation' to describe the relations between micro-practices of *government* ('where authorities of all types exercise their powers over the conduct of others') and what we may call *Government* (legislature/executive/judiciary) (Ibid.: 48).

It is through translation processes of various sorts that 'linkages are assembled' between government and the micro-practices of government (Rose 1999: 48). 'Rule "at a distance" becomes possible when each can translate the values of others into its own terms, such that they provide norms and standards for their own ambitions, judgments and conduct' (Ibid.: 50).

Further, Rose suggests that certain ideas serve to ground, at certain times, 'the abstract problematics of rule' (Ibid.). In the early twentieth century, he says, the notion of 'national efficiency' performed this function; in the 1980s in Britain it was the notion of 'enterprise'.

I suggest that a critical idea that performs this function in the late twentieth to early twenty-first century, globally, is Environment. We must read the Judicial Nineties and after in India in this context. In an era of corporate capitalist expansion, discourses of Environment serve the green judiciary to translate into local contexts, the global will to rule.

In this context, Thomas Lemke has pointed out that the discourse of 'sustainable development' is central to 'the government of new domains of regulation and intervention':

> One important aspect of the 'new world order' is the re-conceptualisation of external nature in terms of an 'ecosystem'. Nature, which once meant an independent space clearly demarcated from the social with an independent power to act, and regulated by autonomous laws, is increasingly becoming the 'environment' of the capitalist system... In an age of 'sustainable development', previously untapped areas are being opened in the interests of capitalization and chances for commercial exploitation. Nature and life itself are being drawn into the economic discourse of efficient resource management (2002: 55).

Or as Arturo Escobar puts it:

> the key to the survival of the rainforest is seen as lying in the genes of the species, the usefulness of which could be released for profit through genetic engineering and biotechnology in the production of commercially valuable products, such as pharmaceuticals. Capital thus develops a conservationist tendency, significantly different from its usual reckless, destructive form (1996: 47, cited by Lemke 2002: 56).

The key idea here is 'regulation'—the environment is to be regulated in the interests of long-term extraction. Within this perspective, even renewable sources of energy are envisaged as ensuring endless consumption; there is no sense that assumptions about consumption, urbanisation, and so on, will have to be drastically rethought. A characteristic statement illustrating this perspective is Barack Obama's Inaugural Address, in which he declared poetically, 'We will harness the sun and the winds and the soil'—to what end? 'To fuel our cars and run our factories.'[11]

The evolving principles of international environment law must be seen in this light.

RECALCITRANCE

The will to rule is, of course, not the end of the story. Here I return to Chatterjee's political society, and find that Chatterjee's formulation permits us to think of political society only as the passive target of government policy, or as petitioners of government. However, the poor, whether in Nandigram or on the streets of Seelampur in Delhi protesting the sealing of their small commercial establishments (Menon and Nigam 2006), are militantly claiming spaces and livelihoods as their own, not as largesse from the state. We need to see political society as recalcitrant, to use Foucault's term (1982), as resistant to the thrust of governmentality, not necessarily always in a politically aware sense, but simply in its quotidian forms of existence.

In other words, all too often 'the will to rule' *fails to translate.* For Foucault himself this recognition is crucial; indeed, what brings power relations to light is precisely resistance to them. Resistance acts as a 'chemical catalyst', revealing power relations, helping us locate their position and finding the methods used (Foucault 1982: 780).

'At the very heart of the power relationship, and constantly provoking it, are the recalcitrance of the will and the intransigence of freedom.' This is no essentialised human will to freedom, rather, it is an 'agonism—a relationship which is at the same time reciprocal incitation and struggle; less of a face-to-face confrontation that paralyses both sides than a permanent provocation' (Ibid.: 222).

It is worth remembering, for instance, that the spectacularly successful campaign against special economic zones in Goa was not built around carefully drafted PILs or a thoughtful judiciary, but through militant political mobilisation that cut across traditional battle lines from Left to Right (Mumtaz and Sardar 2008).

People fail to become recognisable subjects, they escape normalisation. It is this recalcitrance that law keeps coming up against. But there is another subject that discourses of governmentality do not recognise—nature. Eco-feminism has consistently drawn our attention to 'the relative autonomy of the environment',[12] and even Marxism, with all its nineteenth-century hubris, has struggled with a debate on ecology that recognised 'natural limits' to growth (Benton 1989).

The final recalcitrance will be that of nature itself.

NOTES

1. *Narmada Bachao Andolan v. Union of India and Ors* (2000) 10 SCC 664 (emphasis added).
2. *BALCO Employees Union v. Union of India* (2002) 2 SCC 343.
3. Ramnaq International Case (1999) 1 SCC 492.
4. *Prasanni Devi v. MCD* CW 2817/1999.
5. Judgement on PIL of Almitra Patel (2000) 2 SCC 679. Cited in Delhi Janwadi Adhikar Manch (2000: 21).

6. W.P. (Civil) No. 202 of 1995.
7. (1995) 6 SCC 483.
8. Almitra Patel (2000) 2 SCC 679.
9. (2002) 10 SCC 606.
10. A revealing analysis of judicial activism, terming 'judicial over-reach' to be a myth, puts it this way:

    > It is true that ideally, the social, economic and political aspects of justice should be left primarily to the law-makers.... But unfortunately...the legislative process in India, which is primarily a rule of majority rather than reason, fails to satisfy the ends of justice...it is in such situations that at times the courts have to step in to uphold the majesty of law... It will not be inappropriate to say that the so-called judicial activism, in most cases, is a result of 'inactivism' of the other wings of the state (Sharma 2008: 18).

    The author happens to be employed in the Tata group's legal department.
11. Transcript of Barack Obama's Inaugural Address, available at http://www.nytimes.com/2009/01/20/us/politics/20text-obama.html (accessed on 20 June 2009).
12. Professor Lata Mani uses this term in her intervention at the 'Judicial Nineties' Conference, School of Law, Christ College, Bangalore,10 May 2007.

REFERENCES

Bartelson, Jens. 2001. *The Critique of the State*. Cambridge: Cambridge University Press.

Baxi, Upendra. 1999. 'The Structural Adjustment of Judicial Activism'. In *Supreme Court on Public Interest Litigation Vol I*, ed. Jagga Kapur, A-A145-A – A-145-X. LIPS Publication.

Benton, Ted. 1989. 'Marxism and Natural Limits: An Ecological Critique and Reconstruction'. *New Left Review*, I (178): 51–86.

Bhan, Gautam. 2006. 'Whose Delhi Is It Anyway?' *Tehelka*, 17 October. Available at www.tehelka.com/story_main20.asp?filename=ne100706whose_Delhi.asp. Accessed on 6 August 2013.

Bhushan, Prashant. 2004. 'Supreme Court and PIL. Changing Perspectives under Liberalization'. *Economic and Political Weekly*, 39 (18): 1770–74. 1 May.

Chatterjee, Partha. 1997. 'Beyond the Nation? Or Within?' *Economic and Political Weekly*, 32 (1–2): 30–34.

———. 2001. 'Democracy and the Violence of the State: A Political Negotiation of Death'. *Inter-Asia Cultural Studies*, 2 (1): 7–21.

———. 2003. 'Are Indian Cities Becoming Bourgeois at Last?' In *Body.City: Siting Contemporary Culture in India*, eds Indira Chandrasekhar and Peter Seel, 170–85. New Delhi: Tulika.

Delhi Janwadi Adhikar Manch. 2000. *How Many Errors Does Time have Patience For? Industrial Closures and Slum Demolitions in Delhi*. Delhi.

Dhavse, Rasika. 2004. 'Updates on Our Forests'. *India Together*, July. Available at www.indiatogether.org/2004/jul/env-fcupdate.htm (accessed on 17 October 2012).

Down to Earth. 2003. 'Deep in the Woods'. 15 January.

Economic and Political Weekly. 2000. 'Editorial: Missed Opportunity'. *Economic and Political Weekly*, 35 (43–44): 3783–84. 28 October.

Express News Service. 2006. 'Work on Full Swing at VK Malls, No Clarity on Penalties'. *Indian Express*, 26 December.

Foucault, Michel. 1982. 'The Subject and Power', *Critical Inquiry*, 8 (4).

Galanter, Marc. 1984. *Competing Equalities: Law and the Backward Classes in India*. New Delhi: Oxford University Press.

Iyer, Ramaswamy R. 2006. 'Some Constitutional Dilemmas'. *Economic and Political Weekly*, 41 (21): 2064–71. 27 May.

John, Mathew. 2001. 'Interpreting Narmada Judgement'. *Economic and Political Weekly*, 36 (32): 3030–34. 11 August.

Kohli, Kanchi. 2006. 'Mine, What Mine? Ah Yes, the Mine'. *India Together*, December. Available at http://www.indiatogether.org/2006/dec/env-whatmine.htm (accessed on 19 June 2009).

Leena, D. 2006. 'Law vs. Justice'. Available at http://www.judicialreforms.org/files/Discussion%20paper%20for%20lawyers%20meeting.pdf (accessed on 19 June 2009).

Lemke, Thomas. 2002. 'Foucault, Governmentality and Critique'. *Rethinking Marxism: A Journal of Economics, Culture & Society*, 14 (3): 49–64.

Menon, Nivedita, and Aditya Nigam. 2006. 'Lambs at the Law's Guillotine'. *Tehelka*, 7 October. http://archive.tehelka.com/story_main20.asp?filename=op100706Lambs_at.asp. Accessed on 6 August 2013.

———. 2007. *Power and Contestation. India since 1989*. London: Zed Books; Hyderabad: Orient Longman.

Mitchell, Timothy. 1991. 'The Limits of the State: Beyond Statist Approaches and Their Critics'. *American Political Science Review*, 85 (1): 77–96.

Mitta, Manoj. 2008. 'Vedanta: Yet Another Twist'. *Times of India*, 29 April.

Mumtaz, Rifat, and Madhumanti Sardar. 2008. 'Goa. How the Battle was Won'. kafila.org. Available at http://kafila.org/2008/02/23/goa-how-the-battle-was-won/. Accessed on 6 August 2013.

Rajamani, Lavanya. 2007. 'Public Interest Environmental Litigation in India: Exploring Issues of Access, Participation, Equity, Effectiveness and Sustainability'. *Journal of Environmental Law*, 19 (3): 293–321.

Ramanathan, Usha. 2002. 'Of Judicial Power'. *Frontline*, 16–29 March. www.frontline.in/fl1906/19060300.htm. Accessed on 6 August 2013.

Rose, Nikolas. 1999. *Powers of Freedom: Reframing Political Thought*. Cambridge: Cambridge University Press.

Sathe, S. P. 2000. 'Supreme Court and NBA'. *Economic and Political Weekly*, 35 (46): 3990–94. 11 November.

Sharma, Sidharth. 2008. 'Myth of Judicial Overreach'. *Economic and Political Weekly*, 43 (10): 15–18. 8 March.

Upadhyay, Videh. 2000. 'Changing Judicial Power. Courts on Infrastructure Projects and Environment'. *Economic and Political Weekly*, 28 October.

4

Fundamental Rights and Public Interest Litigation in India

*Overreaching or Underachieving?**

VARUN GAURI†

The global (and perhaps national) reputation of Indian courts, as judicial innovators and as defenders of the interests of the disadvantaged and downtrodden rests largely on public interest litigation (PIL), a new set of procedures for expanding access to justice that were developed some thirty years ago. Although assessments of PIL in India range from the laudatory to the cynical, recent scholarship has developed a widely held narrative that runs as follows.[1] PIL or 'social action litigation', as some call it, originated in the late 1970s when the judiciary, aiming to recapture popular support after its complicity in Indira Gandhi's declaration of emergency rule, encouraged litigation concerning the interests of the poor and marginalised. To do so, they loosened rules and traditions related to standing, case filing, the adversarial process and judicial remedies. The Supreme Court pronounced a number of landmark social justice judgements in the 1980s and early 1990s, including key

* Acknowledgement: Reprinted with permission from *Indian Journal of Law and Economics*.

† The author would like to thank Afroza Chowdhury, Kabir Duggal, Kaushik Krishnan and Yamini Jaishankar for excellent research assistance. This essay has also benefited from very helpful comments from Daniel Brinks, Vikram Raghavan, Arun Thiruvengadam and the participants in a session of the Law and Social Sciences in South Asia Conference in New Delhi in 2009. The views presented in this essay are those of the author alone and do not necessarily represent the views of the World Bank or its executive directors.

rulings on the rights of prisoners, bonded labourers, pavement-dwellers and children.[2] The frequency of PIL cases in the Supreme Court and the high courts increased as claimants and their lawyers learned how to take advantage of the more liberal procedures associated with PIL.[3] By the middle to late 1990s, the range of issues the courts were addressing had expanded to include complex environmental concerns, such as urban pollution and solid waste disposal, as well as explicitly political issues, such as official corruption and elections. More recently, PIL has also addressed social issues, such as the decriminalisation of homosexuality in India (Mitta and Singh 2009). At the same time, some claimants and their lawyers learned to 'dress up' private disputes as PIL. Human rights activists began to grow disenchanted with courts' failure to enforce sweeping directives. Many have questioned the appropriateness of judicial intervention in the legislative and executive spheres, as well as the constitutionality of the courts' efforts to implement many of their expansive orders.[4]

Drawing on that narrative, concerns regarding the value and impact of PIL now take a number of forms. These will be described in more detail later, but in general terms, they can be categorised into two groups—questions related to the separation of powers, and a set of queries regarding judicial attitudes. The first group of concerns asks whether courts should be involved in environmental, social and economic matters at all. Are not the legislative and executive branches better equipped to address these matters? Does not 'judicial activism', precisely because the courts do not and cannot enforce many of their broad directives in these areas, erode the legitimacy of the courts? Are not PIL cases draining substantial resources from an already overburdened legal system in which ordinary civil cases can languish in courts for many years? Since many PIL cases are patently frivolous and many others never enforced, is not PIL a device for the judiciary to expand its own powers and autonomy under the mantle of a popular social justice agenda? A separate set of questions involves the beneficiaries of PIL: Do PIL cases continue to benefit the poor and disadvantaged, or have not lifestyle issues and middle class concerns become predominant in PIL cases? Are not judges manifestly less disposed to the interests of the poor and marginalised than they were two decades ago, during the 'heroic' years when PIL originated?

These queries regarding PIL are fundamentally normative claims, and are based on principled understandings of the role of judges and courts in India's democracy. At the same time, the validity of some of them rests on facts, albeit complex ones. For instance, the challenge related to separation of powers raises questions about judicial capacity—critics charge that courts cannot monitor and supervise complex 'polycentric disputes' (Fuller and Winston 1978: 359) whereas others respond that they can, or at least as well as parliaments can (Thiruvengadam 2009). The relative effectiveness of judicial supervision, if observed accurately and at scale, could help resolve this disagreement, at least for a subset of cases and in certain contexts. Similarly, whether or not PIL cases still address the concerns of the poor, and whether decisions are as supportive of their interests as in the past, are empirical questions. To date, the debate over PIL has largely been abstract (with some exceptions, to be described later). It has helped generate a set of normatively significant questions, but at this stage of the research cycle, empirical work may be more pressing. This essay contributes to that task by assessing PIL with empirical data.

The next section of this essay analyses the argument that PIL constitutes a case of judicial overreach. The contention that PIL weakens policy formulation and implementation in the legislative and executive branches is typically 'dressed up' as a separation of powers concern, but a more apt framework involves an assessment of the impact of PIL on sectoral governance, which is fundamentally an empirical matter, not a doctrinal one. The following section describes the charge that PIL favours middle class interests rather than the concerns of the poor and marginalised. The section then presents estimates, based on original data taken from Supreme Court records and online legal database, to assess that claim.

PUBLIC INTEREST LITIGATION: IS THE JUDICIARY OVERREACHING?

An old fashioned view of legal rights holds that most social and economic matters do not involve genuine rights because they require positive actions, not merely restraint, and have no single, identifiable duty-holder. Positive obligations, moreover, entail significant expenditures that are the purview of the other branches of government. Courts, therefore, should steer clear of the social, economic and environmental concerns at the heart of PIL. More contemporary views (Holmes and Sunstein 1999; Shue 1996) hold that 'for their fulfillment, all rights require restraint, protection, and aid from the entity from whom rights are claimed, and that a reasonably effective and well-funded state is a *sine qua non* for all rights' (Gauri 2004: 467).

Most of the criticisms of PIL in the Indian courts have not taken this somewhat old-fashioned form, perhaps because in a country where the scale of needs is so large it is hard to say that social and economic priorities are less commanding than civil and political ones. They have, argued rather, that the social and economic domain should largely be the prerogative of the other branches of government, which are better equipped to analyse, formulate and implement complex policies, and that much of PIL is inappropriate judicial 'activism' or 'adventurism'. For instance, in an assessment of the activities of the Supreme Court in the *M. C. Mehta v. Union of India (Delhi Vehicular Pollution)* and *Almitra Patel v. Union of India (Municipal Solid Waste Management)* cases,[5] Rajamani admonishes that 'policy, environmental and social, must emerge from a socio political process and must be considered in a legitimate forum not a judicial one' (2007: 319). Citing cases in which courts formulated explicit guidelines, such as cases related to vehicular pollution, the management of the Central Bureau of Investigation (CBI), adoption by foreign nationals, custodial torture and sexual harassment, Desai and Muralidhar note that 'while in some cases, the Court has expressed its reluctance to step into the legislative field, in others it has laid down detailed guidelines and explicitly formulated policy' (2000: 14). In their 2003 article, Rosencranz and Jackson welcome the environmental and health impact of the Supreme Court's 2001 decision[6] requiring the Delhi government to convert its commercial vehicles to a fleet running on compressed natural gas (CNG), but then plead for leadership on the part of the regulatory and legislative authorities: 'Some of the roadblocks to CNG implementation could have been avoided, or at least minimized, had the conversion been originally mandated through the normal legislative process' (Rosencranz and Jackson 2003: 252). Thiruvengadam documents a spate of similarly motivated criticism of PIL as an incursion into lawmaking from sitting and former judges of India's Supreme Court and high courts, including comments from

Justice Hidyatullah in 1984, Justice Srikrishna in 2005 and, perhaps most intemperately, Justice Katju in 2008 (Sharma 2008), who said PIL 'has developed into an uncontrollable Frankenstein' (Thiruvengadam 2009: 22).

One motivation for some of this criticism is a suspicion that the courts have used their post-Emergency popularity, to which PIL has significantly contributed, to expand their own powers and shield themselves from scrutiny and accountability. To some, it appears as though the courts may be spending time on frivolous and ineffectual PIL cases at the expense of the real administration of justice, and choose to do so because PIL burnishes their popularity.[7] Reported instances of frivolous PIL include prayers to rename India 'Hindustan',[8] rename the Arabian Sea 'Sindhu Sagar'[9] and replace the national anthem for one offered by the petitioner[10] (and partly sung before the chief justice) (Thiruvengadam 2007). At the same time, the systems of civil and criminal justice suffer enormous delays and arbitrary pre-trial detentions.

These concerns are echoed widely enough that there is now visible a clear backlash against this perceived usurpation of powers by the courts, including a Bill tabled in the Rajya Sabha in 1996 to regulate PIL (Jha, 'Problems Facing Public Interest Litigation in India'; Desai and Muralidhar 2000: 15), a 2007 statement by the prime minister warning against judicial overreach,[11] recent calls from the Bench to set parameters for PIL[12] and efforts to establish the National Judicial Council, a body to investigate complaints against judges. Some of these complaints involve corruption: there have been allegations that about 20 per cent of judges are corrupt (Dhavan 2002). Related complaints include the use of the law of privileges and contempt on the part of courts to shield themselves from criticism, resistance to efforts to require sitting judges to disclose their financial assets and the uncomfortably close relationship between some members of the judiciary and the Bar (Baxi 2006). Roy (2007) goes so far as to assert that judicial accountability is so low that 'we live in a sort of judicial dictatorship'.

A few comments about separation of powers are in order. First, policy formulation by the courts or its agents is, to some extent, inevitable. Judicial review of any sort requires ongoing commentary on laws and policies, including guidelines regarding their proper content. Because dispute resolution entails an elaboration and application of the normative structures of society as the necessary ground for the dispute-resolver's decision, judges inevitably involve themselves in rule making, which is a form of lawmaking whether in common law or civil law jurisdictions (Sweet 1999). Courts have not traditionally been significant actors in the area of social and economic policy; and resistance to PIL and the court directives it prompts in these areas may stem more from the novelty of the phenomenon than from anything like a real 'judicial dictatorship'. Reluctance on the part of the Indian judiciary to be held accountable for performance and probity is certainly problematic—from the point of view of democratic theory, it limits the power of the people to review public action. The expansion of judicial power in the area of social and economic concerns, on the other hand, catalyses legislative and executive activity more often than it paralyses it. That is because, as an empirical matter the world over, PIL typically spurs judicial dialogue with the other branches: rarely do courts issue all-or-nothing demands, backed with common law contempt power or its civil law counterparts,[13] in a way that requires the state to restructure its policy framework. 'Courts' decisions do not so much stop or hijack the policy debate as inject the language of rights into it and add another forum for debate' (Brinks and Gauri 2008: 304). As Fredman puts it, PIL allows the judicial forum to become, potentially, a space for democratic deliberation among equal citizens, rather than a place of interest group bargaining, which prevails in the legislature (Fredman 2008: 149).

In addition, an important use of PIL is to make public and scrutinise hidden or obfuscating information, including cost of potential social programmes, which the state and corporate entities on occasion have reasons to exaggerate or hide. In India, PIL during droughts in Rajasthan and Orissa in 2001 disclosed the extent of unreleased government grain stocks,[14] and subsequent PIL disclosed that state governments could in fact afford to widen several statutory food and nutrition programmes, including the midday meals scheme in schools, despite official protests to the contrary.[15] In the Delhi vehicular pollution debate, the Delhi health minister claimed that air pollution did not increase the risks of heart or lung disease; the Delhi government said that the timely installation of CNG stations would be impossible; the Ministry of Petroleum and Natural Gas argued that CNG bus conversion would not be sustainable in the long run; producers of commercial vehicles stated that the conversion to CNG was not economically cost-effective; and others argued that CNG is explosive. The Court, largely by empowering certain technical committees, played a significant role in helping to ascertain accurate information on these issues. It was, moreover, not an instance of judicial fiat but rather a judicial–executive branch collaboration: 'Government experts essentially became advisors to the Court as it drove policy implementation forward' (Bell et al. 2004: 35).

The argument that PIL constitutes judicial overreach, resulting in poor or inefficient decision making, is not really a separation of powers claim. The balance of power among government organs, as Madison conceived it, was not primarily about a strict separation of powers but 'the partial interpenetration of relatively autonomous and balanced powers' (O'Donnell 2003: 41). In other words, the separation of powers was not conceived as a design for the promotion of efficient decision making by preventing undue encroachment from one institution upon the prerogatives of another, but rather a check on the ability of any group or faction to dominate government from its enclave in a specific organisation. The doctrine of separation of powers seeks to accomplish this precisely by opening certain governmental tasks to competing competences and concurrent powers of review. Despite occasionally hyperbolic claims on the part of critics, Indian judges and their professional social classes are not using the courts as a staging ground to threaten the Indian state. There have been specific rulings, such as *Keshavananda Bharati*[16] or *Advocates-on-Record,*[17] or the ruling on the Jharkhand legislative procedures,[18] in which courts assumed powers not delineated in the Constitution. Even in those cases, it is arguable that in so doing the Court restored a constitutional balance because the executive and legislature had themselves been engaging in extra-constitutional activities.

These criticisms regarding separation of powers are better cast as concerns related to the impact of judicial intervention on sectoral governance. Does judicial involvement through PIL improve state performance in a given sector? Is forest policy, for example, more equitable, efficient and effective as a result of court involvement? That is an empirical question, but most treatments of the issue do not take the empirical challenge seriously. Rosencranz and Lélé believe that the Supreme Court's intervention following the *Godavarman v. Union of*

India[19] 'hurts the process of governance', but adduce little evidence about the capacity and authority of central and state executive agencies prior to and after the Court's assumption of powers (Rosencranz and Lélé 2008: 13). Writing in 2003 on the *Delhi Vehicular Pollution* case, Rosencranz and Jackson speculated that strengthening the pollution control boards (PCBs), rather than Supreme Court action, 'would seem to provide the most effective long-term solutions [to air pollution in India]' and worried that 'the Court's action seems likely to impede capacity building in the pollution control agencies, and thereby to compromise the development of sustained environmental management in India' (Rosencranz and Jackson 2003: 240, 249). This is fundamentally an empirical claim, and one can examine whether PCBs are weaker now than they were before the Court proceedings in the *Delhi Vehicular Pollution* case. A cursory review suggests that it is not obvious that they are weaker—the budget of the Central Pollution Control Board has nearly tripled since the year of the Court's order in 2002—and a number of efforts are underway to strengthen them and fill staffing vacancies in Central and state PCBs.[20] Another problem with criticisms like these is that they compare an ideal or hypothetical legislative intervention to a real judicial one when it is often the real-world failings of the other branches that prompted litigation in the first place. Thiruvengadam describes the deliberative failings of India's Parliament, noting that of the total thirty-six Bills passed in 2008, 'sixteen were passed in less than twenty minutes, most without any debate whatsoever' (2009: 32).

Why do analysts tend to describe issues of sectoral governance with the language of the separation of powers? The motivation stems in part from a belief, sometimes inarticulate, that governance should look similar the world over. In this case, courts, in order to be courts properly understood, must limit their tasks to interpreting laws, rather than writing or enforcing them. But it is a mistake to speak of 'courts' as such. The task of judicial institutions depends on the way they interact with the other institutions of their society. It is less useful to assess judicial activity against a preconceived institutional design than to evaluate, using 'normative benchmarks', the (positive or negative) contribution of courts to the key tasks of governance in any specific sector (Trebilcock and Daniels 2008). In the same way that careful studies of the institutional foundations of economic growth in East

Asia have challenged the rule of law orthodoxy, showing that successful market-sustaining institutions need not take the specific form that courts, corporate boards and bureaucratic agencies have taken in, say, the US or the UK (Ginsburg 2003), studies of PIL should recognise that courts may play a variety of roles in different settings. There is less institutional convergence in the world than believed, and it is important 'not to confuse institutional *function* and institutional *form*' (Rodrik 2003: 26, emphasis in original).

What, then, are the normative benchmarks that should be used to assess the contribution, or lack thereof, of courts towards sectoral governance? Those depend on the sector, of course—they would look different in health than in forestry. But, generalising, one can identify three key elements of governance for the broad category of tasks in government service delivery: the capacity and authority of the organisations charged with delivery or oversight, the availability of information and transparency regarding service delivery, and state accountability for performance. An empirically-minded assessment of PIL in India, then, would take the form of a series of case studies based on those normative benchmarks. The case studies would focus on these questions: Did the capacity and authority of institutions tasked with addressing the social problems increase or decline as a result of PIL? Was accurate information on sectoral concerns more widely available before or after judicial intervention? Were mechanisms of accountability, including legal and hierarchical oversight, markets and the power of actors to pursue their own interests, and social assessments of the motives of public officials, functioning more effectively before or after judicial intervention?

DOES PUBLIC INTEREST LITIGATION BENEFIT MARGINALISED INDIVIDUALS AND GROUPS?

The purpose of PIL in India, like most social causes, was likely over-determined; but most commentators agree that it was partly an effort on the part of the courts to speak to the poverty-ridden, socially excluded and powerless majority of citizens in India who continue to suffer.[21] Several commentators suspect, however, that this objective of PIL has not been realised, or indeed has been lost (Desai and Muralidhar 2000:

12–17). These criticisms take two forms. The first focuses on *beneficiary inequality*: the concern that the middle classes have more organisational and financial resources than the poor, which facilitate easier access to courts, and result in more benefits from PIL for them than for the poor. In some countries,[22] the Bar develops a *pro bono* practice that, to some extent, mitigates this inequality of access, but this has not emerged in a significant way in India. Compounding this problem, non-governmental organisations (NGOs) and social movements in India are wary of courts, and largely do not utilise litigation strategies to achieve their objectives (Krishnan 2003; Shankar and Mehta 2008: 153).

The second is *policy area inequality*: this is the concern that judges, because of their social class and ideological dispositions, are more alert to the concerns of the middle classes and the wealthy. This is evident, critics argue, in the demonstrable urban and middle-class bias of their rulings. Baxi believes that the interests of global economic elites now colour the thinking of the Indian judiciary, resulting in rulings that benefit those global elites, such as decisions in the cases involving World Trade Organization (WTO) accession, Union Carbide's liability for toxic emissions in Bhopal and the construction of the Narmada dam (Baxi 1980). Similarly, Rajagopal believes that the Indian courts have adopted the statist and development mindsets associated with the Indian state itself, and that the universal privileging of civil and political rights over socio-economic rights has affected the thinking of the Indian judiciary (Rajagopal 2007: 168–77). In a related vein, Ramanathan (2002) writes that 'increasingly, the constituency on whose behalf the enhancement of judicial power has been strengthened began to emerge as the casualty of the exercise of that power'.

These claims tend to be based on a set of exemplary cases, rather than a systematic review of PIL case law and implementation. It is also important to realise that judges, and the courts that they constitute, are creatures of their environment, and that patterns of judicial recruitment and appointment will almost always ensure that courts reflect the dominant political trends of their countries (Dahl 1957). Some argue that the Indian courts are an exception to this rule, having obtained as much, if not more, autonomy regarding judicial appointments than any other courts in the world. But that constitutional autonomy is constrained by the Indian civil service traditions under which courts operate, as well as the social dependence of judges on the Bar and on political and economic elites. 'Leaders of the Indian Bar,' writes Baxi, 'whether elected or otherwise, have always wielded historically disproportionate influence over the Justices' (2006: 10). In addition to the embedding of judges in their social and political milieu, strategic factors also limit judicial autonomy: courts in every country depend on the other branches of government for their political survival, so they will, by and large, take care that their decisions garner sufficient support from key political actors (Epstein and Knight 1998). In short, because ideological orientations in the larger Indian political economy have drifted rightward over the past two decades or so, it is to be expected that the courts will have followed. Assessments of the extent to which PIL supports the poor, then, need to develop an implicit benchmark of what can be expected of courts in the specific contexts in which they operate.[23]

To fill in some of the information needed for a more complete assessment of PIL in India, four different samples of PIL and fundamental rights cases at the Supreme Court level were examined: (i) cases that, according to the Supreme Court Registrar's office, the Court has itself classified as PIL from 1988 to 2007 (some 2,800 'cases' overall); (ii) all Supreme Court cases in the Manupatra database[24] that involved fundamental rights and that addressed concerns regarding women and children rights, whether or not explicitly admitted as PILs (86 cases); (iii) all Supreme Court cases in the Manupatra database that involved fundamental rights and were related to issues regarding Scheduled Castes/Scheduled Tribes/Other Backward Classes (SC/ST/OBCs), whether or not explicitly admitted as PILs (180 cases); (iv) all Supreme Court cases in the Manupatra database that the Supreme Court explicitly called a PIL (44 cases).

For the set of cases involving women and children's rights, these search terms, among others, were used: 'women' and 'children' and 'abuse'; 'violence' and 'women' and 'neglected children'; 'juvenile justice' and 'Article 21'; 'trafficking' and 'women' and 'Article 21'; 'labour' 'children' and 'Article 14'; 'custodial violence' and 'children'; 'education' and 'fundamental right' and 'Article 14'; 'gender and fundamental right'; 'prison rights and children'; 'rape' and 'Article 21'; 'emancipation' and 'women and children'. The SC/ST/OBC search used the terms 'scheduled caste' or 'scheduled tribe' or 'other backward classes' in conjunction with cases that addressed fundamental rights and constitutional concerns. Note that the data from the Supreme Court were a listing of orders related to PIL cases, and not necessarily a list of cases *per se*. But an examination of the names of the cases revealed that of the 2,800 separate orders, instances of duplicate or once repeating nearly identical plaintiff and defendant names occurred fourteen times, triplicates once, and quadruplicates once. Still, because of uncertainty regarding the basis for the listings, this essay refers to this list as constituting 'cases' rather than cases *per se*. The Manupatra database captures about 80–90 per cent of Supreme Court cases for which judgements are reported (Shankar and Mehta 2008: 152). While this results in something less than complete compendium of court decisions and orders in the selected topic areas, there is no evidence that the database censors certain categories of cases in a systematic fashion. There is no evidence, in other words, of significant sample bias.

Figure 4.1 shows the number of PIL 'cases' instituted per year, whether brought to the court for admission ('admission matters' in the Court's terms) or argued on the merits ('regular matters'), from 1997 to 2007, based on data from the Supreme Court itself. The figure shows

FIGURE 4.1: PIL Cases in the Indian Supreme Court

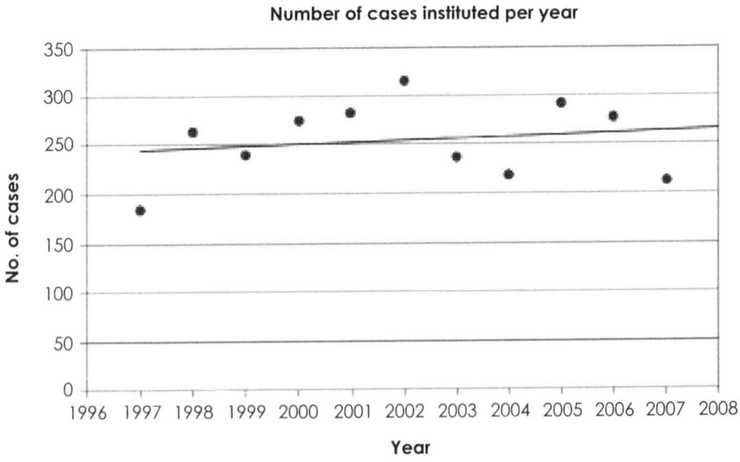

Source: Author's calculations.

that there has been a slight upward trend in PIL matters over the last ten years. It also shows that there are some 260 'cases' instituted per year, on average. This compares to about 60,000 'cases' per year overall, based on data publicly available in the Supreme Court's 'Court News' publication. So, on average, some 0.4 per cent of 'cases' before the Court involve PILs. This suggests that PIL does not drain significant court resources from the administration of day-to-day justice, contrary to the claims of some critics; but it also suggests that the outsized reputation of the Supreme Court's PIL work belies its modest scale. And, contrary to popular conceptions, the large majority of the 260 or so PIL 'cases' instituted in the Supreme Court each year are brought through formal channels; of the tens of thousands of letters and handwritten petitions that the Supreme Court receives from ordinary people each year, only a handful are converted into cases.[25]

The Court instituted a classification system for PILs in 1988. This might be used to determine whether the concerns cited in PILs have changed over the years, and if the 'cases' that appear before the Court have shifted to the concerns of the middle classes. Table 4.1 shows the breakdown by 'case' type and year. Unfortunately, the large majority of 'cases' fall in the category of 'other', so the classification scheme is not useful for tracking changes in PIL composition over time. Noteworthy, however, is the increase in 'cases' related to election commissions, and the relatively low share of 'cases' involving bonded labour and criminal justice, two of the concerns crucial in the early justifications for PIL.

Have increasing numbers of cases involved middle-class concerns? It is difficult to say for PILs more generally because an identifiable record of PIL cases is not available. To address this question, the essay used the set of fundamental rights cases described earlier. Fundamental rights cases, at least those related to women and children's rights and SC/ST/OBC concerns, may in fact underestimate the orientation of PILs to the middle classes because they exclude issues like urban quality of life that have been the concern of recent prominent litigation.

Figure 4.2 shows the number of cases in categories related to women's and children's rights or to SC/ST/OBC issues, or which the Supreme Court explicitly called a PIL, as reported in Manupatra, in which the claimant was likely to have been, on the basis of a review of the written opinion, a member of the 'advantaged classes'. For purposes of the coding,

TABLE 4.1: Fundamental Rights Cases in the Indian Supreme Court, % of Cases Submitted by Subject Matter

Subject	*1997*	*1998*	*1999*	*2000*	*2001*	*2002*	*2003*	*2004*	*2005*	*2006*	*2007*
Child Labour Matters Including Neglected Children		0.4						0.49		0.73	
Air Pollution Matters, i.e., Industrial, Vehicular, Power Stations, etc.	2.58	2.8	2.58	2.34	5.32	8.3	5.78	2.44	2.89	2.19	2.88
Water Pollution: Industrial, Domestic, Sewage, Rivers and Sea	1.94	6.4	2.58	4.3	2.84	0.72	2.22	1.46	18.18	2.19	1.44
Noise Pollution: Industry and Vehicular	0.65	1.2	0.43		0.35	1.81	1.33		0.83	1.46	
Ecological Imbalance: Protection and Conservation of Forests throughout the Country, Protection of Wildlife, Ban on Felling of Trees and Falling of Underground Water Level	8.39	3.2	3.43	2.73	3.19		4.44	5.85	7.85	16.06	12.98
Bonded Labour Matters	2.58	0.4	1.29			4.33					0.48
Matters relating to Custody Harassment, Jails, Complaint of Harassment, Custodial Death, Speedy Trial, Premature Release, Inaction by Police, etc.	3.87	2	1.72	1.56	0.35		0.44			0.36	0.96

(Table 4.1 contd.)

(Table 4.1 contd.)

Subject	*1997*	*1998*	*1999*	*2000*	*2001*	*2002*	*2003*	*2004*	*2005*	*2006*	*2007*
Matters Relating to Harassment of SC/ST/OBC and Women	0.65	0.4			1.42	0.36	0.89	0.49		0.36	0.48
Matters relating to Unauthorised Constructions including Encroachments, Sealing, Demolitions, Urban Planning	3.23	3.6	1.72	5.47	2.84		1.33	0.98	2.07	2.92	1.44
Matters relating to Election Commissions	1.29	1.6	1.72	0.39	1.42	3.25	0.44	7.8	3.72	3.28	5.77
Scam Matters	1.94		0.43	0.39		0.36		0.98	0.83	0.36	0.48
Others	72.9	78	84.12	82.81	82.27	80.87	83.11	79.51	63.64	70.07	72.6
Natural and Man-made Disasters Including Riots											0.48

Note: Numbers are in percentages.
Source: Author's calculations.

FIGURE 4.2: Fundamental Rights Cases

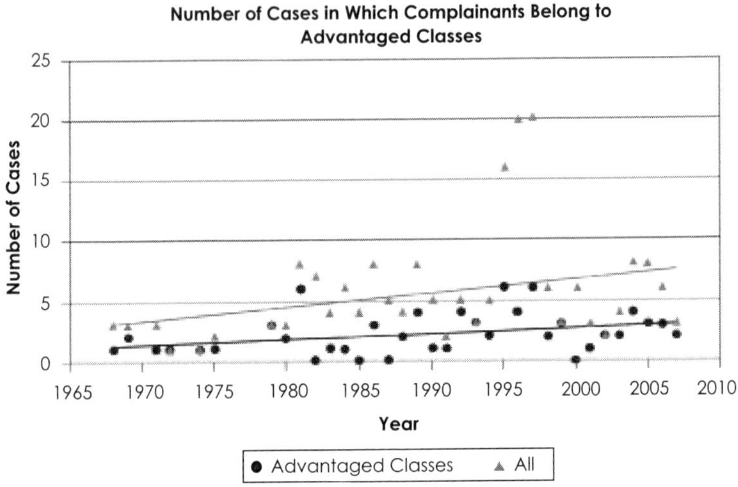

Source: Author's calculations.

a member of the advantaged classes included a professional (doctors, teachers, members of the armed services, etc.), a landowner or business person, or someone otherwise in the global middle class (including formal sector workers and civil service employees not designated as workers or labourers). Those not in the advantaged classes included those belonging to a SC or ST or a member of the OBCs (unless otherwise designated a member of an advantaged class), peasants, labourers and those detained in the criminal justice system. Where groups or publicly minded individuals made claims in courts, and where there was no obvious plaintiff, the coders attempted to identify the general social class of the individuals whose interests were being advocated or defended. In forty-eight of the 310 cases in the sample, the social class of the claimant(s) could not be discerned from the written opinion; or, and this was the more frequent problem, the social class was diffuse. Examples of this included cases concerning environmental protection of rivers and forest, challenges to the constitutionality of judicial action and challenges to the statutory definition of rape. For these cases, the calculations and figures later considered the observation to have a missing value for social class. For every case, an effort was made to identify the individual or class of individuals on whose behalf the case was instituted—in some instances, the lawyer or some other publicly minded individual is listed as the plaintiff/complainant in official records, but the claimant coded was the person or class of persons whose interests the case was seeking to advance (e.g., child bonded labourers).

Figure 4.2 plots the number of cases involving fundamental rights in the categories described earlier, and the number of cases in which the claimant was a member of the advantaged classes. Simple ordinary least squares estimates are used to identify trend lines, which are inserted in the figure. The trend lines show that the number of claimants from advantaged classes has increased at almost the same rate as the overall number of fundamental rights cases in these categories. This suggests that class bias concerns that stem from the organisational advantages of the advantaged class are not as pronounced as some have feared.

Another way to examine this problem of inequality in organisational resources is to look at the share of fundamental rights cases in which the rights violation originated in the BIMARU states (Bihar, Madhya Pradesh, Rajasthan and Uttar Pradesh).[26] Figure 4.3 plots the share of cases originating in the BIMARU states. (In 14 per cent of the cases, the location of the rights violation was national or otherwise impossible to pinpoint.) Figure 4.3 shows that although the number of cases of rights

FIGURE 4.3: Share of Fundamental Rights Cases from BIMARU States

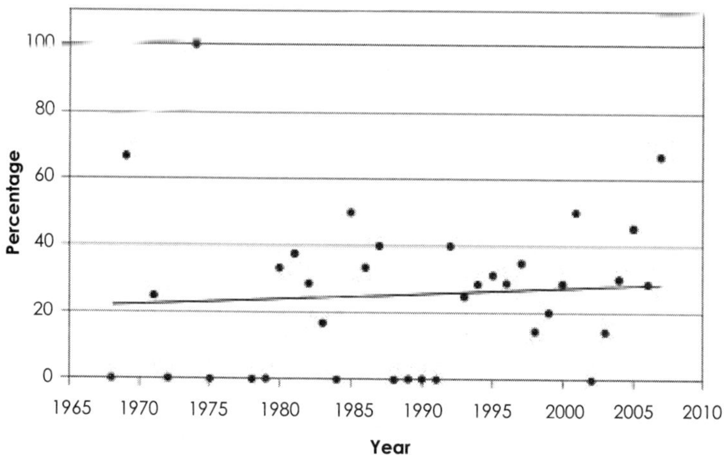

Source: Author's calculations.

violations originating in the BIMARU states has been increasing, it remains below the share of the national population residing in those states (some 40 per cent). This suggests that inequalities related to middle class legal mobilisation, though real according to this measure, are declining.

Finally, the data allow a third way to examine the issue of middle class legal mobilisation advantage—one can identify for each year the share of cases initiated by or involving an NGO or cooperative group. Cases that involve an NGO or cooperative are more likely to involve the concerns of the poor than the middle class, and are also more likely to result in generalised benefit than cases brought on behalf of individual private claimants by private lawyers (Gauri and Brinks 2008: 22–23). Overall, 15 per cent of cases were filed by cooperatives, groups or NGOs, while 80 per cent were filed by individual litigants (4 per cent of cases were unclear). Figure 4.4 shows that the annual number of cases filed by a cooperative/group and reported in Manupatra has been more or less flat since the 1970s, with a median number of about one per year, and has not grown as fast as cases involving fundamental rights filed by individuals. This suggests that although the absolute number of fundamental rights claims brought on behalf of disadvantaged classes has been increasing,

FIGURE 4.4: Fundamental Rights Cases

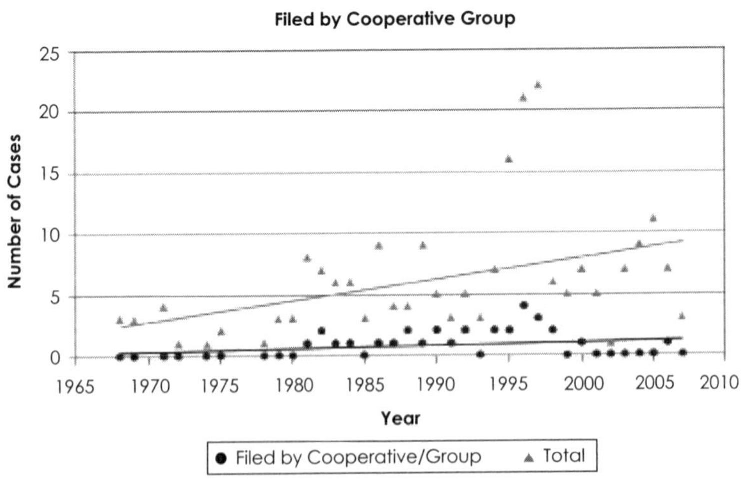

Source: Author's calculations.

as shown in Figure 4.2, this increase is not due to greater mobilisation by NGOs/civil service organisations; rather, it appears to have been the result of increased mobilisation by private individuals.

To examine policy area inequality, which is related to the content of judicial rulings on the cases that reach them, the study examined win–loss rates, both in general and for subsets of claims from advantaged classes, disadvantaged classes, members of SC/ST/OBC, and the middle and upper castes. Figures 4.5 and 4.6 show that claimants in cases involving women's and children's rights were more likely to win than claimants in cases involving SC/ST/OBC matters. Overall, the win rate for claimants in fundamental rights cases involving women's and children's rights was 84 per cent, compared to 51 per cent for cases involving SC/ST/OBC, and 72 per cent for the explicit PIL cases. In addition, the trend line for the win rate of claimants in SC/ST/OBC cases was sloped downwards. That suggests that judges may now be less favourably disposed to SC/ST/OBC claims than they were in the past.

But it is hard to tell whether this indicative trend is a function of the change in the composition of the claimants or a change in judicial attitudes; in other words, it is possible that judges are as favourably disposed to SC/ST/OBC concerns as they were in the past, and that win

FIGURE 4.5: Cases Involving Women and Children's Rights

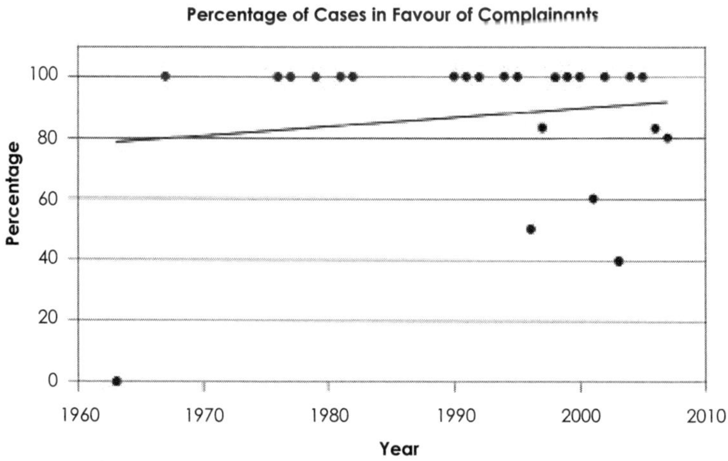

Source: Author's calculations.

FIGURE 4.6: Cases Involving SC/ST/OBC

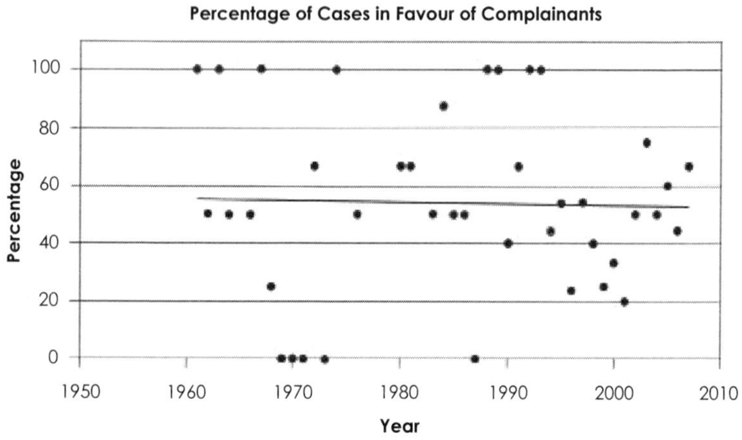

Source: Author's calculations.

rates in SC/ST/OBC cases have declined only because most claimants in these cases are now members of the advantaged classes. So the cases were further disaggregated on the basis of the social class of the claimant. Overall, 67 per cent of claimants in SC/ST/OBC cases were themselves members of SC/ST/OBC; but this falls to 60 per cent for cases admitted after 2000, indicating a recent increase in claims related to SC/ST/OBC by members of the middle and upper castes. For women's and children's rights cases, overall 72 per cent of claimants were members of the advantaged classes.

Figure 4.7 graphs the win rates in all fundamental rights cases for claimants who were and were not members of advantaged classes. It shows that the average annual win rate for claimants from advantaged classes was below the win rate of claimants who were not from advantaged classes until the late 1980s. Now claimants from advantaged classes have higher win rates than claimants not from advantaged classes. For example, advantaged class claimants had a 73 per cent probability of winning a fundamental rights claim for cases in which an order or decision was rendered from years 2000 to 2008, whereas the win rate for claimants not from advantaged classes for the same years was 47 per cent. For the 1990s, rates were 68 per cent and 47 per cent, respectively. But in the years prior to 1990, claimants not from advantaged classes

FIGURE 4.7: Fundamental Rights Cases

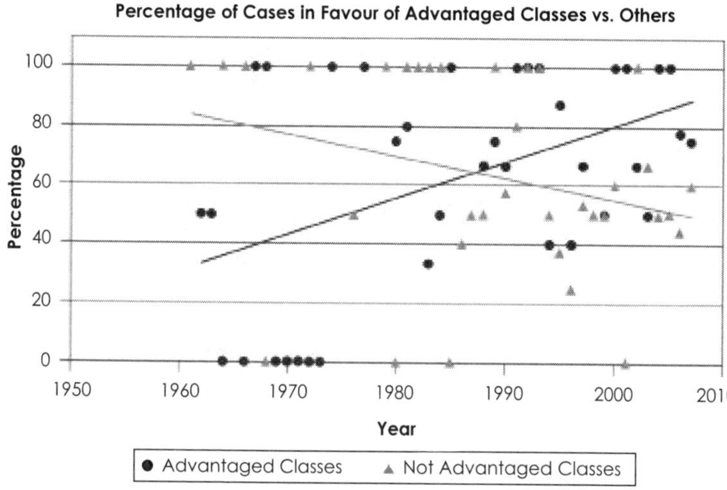

Source: Author's calculations.

enjoyed higher success rates than those from advantaged classes. The differences for the 1990s and 2000s are significantly different from each other, based on a simple chi-square test and a simple probit estimation (see Tables 4.2a and 4.2b).[27] Similarly, when one divides the claimants into those that are identified as members of SC/ST/OBC and those that are not, the same pattern emerges: Figure 4.8 shows that claimants who are not SC/ST/OBC now have a higher win rate than those who are. Even in the subset of cases involving SC/ST/OBC concerns, claimants who were not from SC/ST/OBC began to have higher average annual win rates than those who were, starting around 1990 (see Figure 4.9).[28]

TABLE 4.2a: Win Rates in Selected Fundamental Rights Cases before the Indian Supreme Court, Claimants from Advantaged and Disadvantaged Social Classes

Social Class	*1961–89*	*1990–99**	*2000–08**
Advantaged	57.9%	68.1%	73.3%
Disadvantaged	71.4%	47.1%	47.2%

Note: * probability of $\chi^2 < 0.05$.
Source: Author's calculations.

TABLE 4.2b: Probit Estimation of Win Rates for Advantaged Classes in Fundamental Rights Cases before the Indian Supreme Court, by Era

	1961–89	*1990–99*	*2000–08*
Advantaged class	–0.37	0.54*	0.69*
	(0.29)	(0.25)	(0.32)
Constant	0.57*	–0.07	–0.07
	(0.21)	(0.15)	(0.21)
Observations	80	114	66
Pseudo R^2	0.02	0.03	0.05

Note: Standard errors in parentheses; * significant at $p < 0.05$.
Source: Author's calculations.

FIGURE 4.8: Fundamental Rights Cases

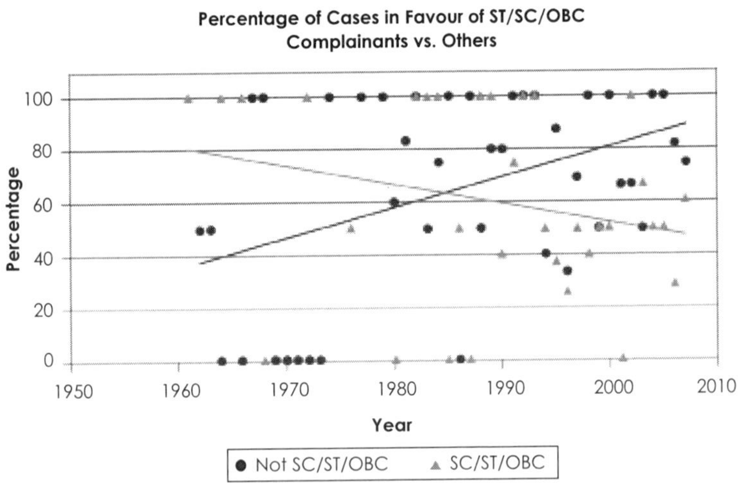

Source: Author's calculations.

These findings are consistent with the claim that judicial receptivity in the Supreme Court to fundamental rights claims made on behalf of poor and excluded individuals has declined in recent years. There are other explanations, however. The decline in the win rates for marginalised individuals could be attributed to the fact that cases brought on their behalf are weaker, on the merits, than they used to be, perhaps as a result of changes in statutes, decisions to litigate more challenging cases,

FIGURE 4.9: Cases Involving SC/ST/OBC

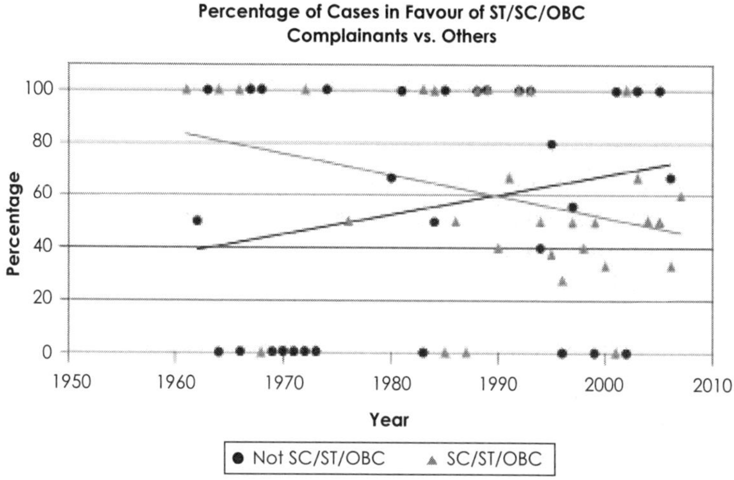

Source: Author's calculations.

or weaker legal representation. Each of these possibilities warrants careful scrutiny. Still, the data demonstrate not only a decline in the win rate for marginalised individuals but a simultaneous increase in the win rate for advantaged individuals. Though not impossible, it is unlikely that the quality of legal representation has simultaneously increased for the advantaged and decreased for the marginalised, and sufficiently to explain the significant reversal in win rates. Similarly, it is conceivable but not likely that advantaged clients started to select a less challenging set of cases at the same time that marginalised claimants did the reverse. The data here constitute a *prima facie* validation of the concern that judicial attitudes are less favourably inclined to the claims of the poor than they used to be, either as the exclusive result of new judicial interpretations or, more likely, in conjunction with changes in the political and legislative climate.

A number of criticisms of PIL have been voiced in recent years, including concerns related to separation of powers, judicial capacity and inequality. While critics have been persuasive when pointing to particular cases, the sheer number of cases, as well as the variation in tendencies over time and among court benches, have made reaching a general conclusion difficult. This essay has argued that complaints related to separation of powers concerns are better understood as criticisms of the impact of judicial interventions on sectoral governance, and that structured case studies of sectoral governance are necessary to assess those criticisms. On the issue of inequality, this essay contributes to an overall assessment by systematically examining the relative magnitude, case composition and geographical origins of, as well as legal representation and the claimant's social class in, PIL and fundamental rights cases that reached the Indian Supreme Court.

The analysis of PIL 'cases' shows that they do not appear to consume a significant share of the resources of the Supreme Court; they constitute less than 1 per cent of the overall case load. The subject matter of PIL cases and orders remains difficult to discern because over 70 per cent of them are classified as 'other', which is problematic from the point of view of judicial transparency. Concerns regarding inequality appear to be validated by some of the quantitative data on fundamental rights cases. On the one hand, the number of fundamental rights cases related to women's and children's rights and to the concerns of SC/ST/OBC, as well as cases explicitly called a 'PIL' in the Court's written opinions, appear to have increased; and the rate of increase has been similar for claimants belonging to both marginalised and advantaged population segments. The share of cases from BIMARU states also appears to be climbing. On the other hand, a very low share of the cases are brought by cooperative entities, such as NGOs, which is a useful predictor of the likelihood that benefits will generalise to the larger population. Most striking, win rates for fundamental rights claims are now significantly higher when the claimant is from an advantaged social group than when he/she is from a marginalised group. That constitutes a social reversal both from the original objective of public interest litigation and from the relative win rates in the 1980s.

NOTES

1. Elements of this broad narrative are supported in Baxi (1980); Rajeev Dhavan et al. (1985); Sathe (2002: 25–62); Cassels (1989: 496–97); Thiruvengadam (2009).

2. See, for example, *Sunil Batra v. Delhi Administration* (1978) AIR 1978 S.C. 1675 (prison conditions); *Upendra Baxi v. State of Uttar Pradesh* (1983) 2 S.C.C. 308 (prison conditions); *People's Union for Democratic Rights v. Union of India*, AIR 1982 S.C. 1473 (bonded labour); *Bandhua Mukti Morcha v. Union of India*, AIR 1984 S.C. 802 (bonded labour); *Olga Tellis v. Bombay Municipal Corporation*, AIR 1986 S.C. 180 (pavement-dwellers); *Sheela Barse v. Union of India*(1986) 3 SCC 596 (rights of children).
3. See, for example, Cassels (1989: 508) ('Perhaps of more immediate consequence, the relaxed test of standing and the expedited fashion in which cases can be brought in public interest matters put enormous strains on already extremely scarce judicial resources. Some high courts are reported to receive fifty to sixty public interest letters per day. In the fifteen months from 1 January 1987 to 31 March 1988, the Supreme Court received 23,772 letters.').
4. PIL has sparked concerns regarding judicial encroachment and the separation of powers that actually go back to the early days of the Indian Republic. Soon after independence, the Congress government enacted the First Amendment, creating the Ninth Schedule deemed beyond judicial review, out of concern that the judiciary would find planned land reforms unconstitutional, a belief soon to be substantiated in a set of cases in which the Supreme Court did just that. This back and forth over land reform, and over the Ninth Schedule, continued for decades. Famously, the Court held that Parliament did not have the power to amend the Constitution if such amendments abridged the fundamental rights guaranteed in the Constitution (*Golaknath v. State of Punjab*, AIR 1967 S.C. 1643) and/or altered the 'basic structure' of the Constitution itself (*Keshavananda Bharati v. State of Kerala*, AIR 1973 S.C. 1461), to which the Indira Gandhi government responded by departing from the seniority tradition in judicial appointments and attempting to dissolve the *Keshavananda* majority. On 'judicial sovereignty' in India, see Mehta (2007).
5. Writ Petition Number 13029 of 1985 and Writ Petition Number 888 of 1996, respectively. For a commentary on these cases, see Rajamani (2007: 296).
6. *M. C. Mehta v. Union of India*, S.C. Writ Petition (Civil) No. 13029/1985 (5 April 2002).
7. See, for example, Khosla (2008) ('The Supreme Court has failed to differentiate between frivolous petitions and appropriate representation').
8. *Petition To Rename India, Arabian Sea*, available at: http://heartx.sulekha.com/blog/post/2007/07/petition-to-rename-india-arabian-sea-3.htm (accessed on30 April 2010).
9. Ibid.
10. Ibid.
11. Shankar and Mehta (2008: 146). See also: *Indian Express* (2007).
12. *The Times of India*, 12 December 2007. See, for example, *Shri Sachidanand Pandey and Anrv. The State of West Bengal and Ors*, MANU/SC/0136/1987('Public interest litigation has now come to stay. But one is led to think that it poses a threat to courts and public alike. Such cases are now filed without any rhyme or

reason. It is, therefore, necessary to lay down clear guide-lines and to outline the correct parameters for entertainment of such petitions. If courts do not restrict the free flow of such cases in the name of Public Interest Litigations, the traditional litigation will suffer and the courts of law, instead of dispensing justice, will have to take upon themselves administrative and executive functions.').

13. These would include the *astreinte* in France; the *amparo* in Mexico and Venezuela; the *tutela* in Colombia; and the *mandado de segurança* in Brazil.
14. See Human Rights Features (2002).
15. Ibid.
16. *Keshavananda Bharati v. The State of Kerala and Others*, AIR 1973 S.C. 1461.
17. Satya Prakash, 'SC Rap for Advocates-on-record'. *Hindustan Times*. Available at http://www.hindustantimes.com/rssfeed/india/SC-rap-for-advocates-on-record/Article1-527171.aspx (accessed on30 April 2010).
18. See generally: Venkatesan (2005).
19. *T. N. Godavarman Thirumulpad v. Union of India (UOI) and Ors.*, (2008) 1MLJ 997 (SC).
20. The sanctioned budget was Rs 1,592.58 lakhs for 2001–02, and Rs 4,500 lakhs for 2007–08. These budgets are available at http://www.cpcb.nic.in/upload/AnnualReports/AnnualReport_6_annualreport2001-02.pdf (accessed on30 April 2010)and http://www.cpcb.nic.in/upload/AnnualReports/AnnualReport_34_final-report-06-07-A.pdf (accessed on 30 April 2010).
21. In a letter to the author dated 5 December 2008, former justice of the Supreme Court and member of the National Human Rights Commission, Hon'ble Justice Mrs Sujata Manohar opined: 'Public Interest Litigation was conceived as a means of providing to the underprivileged and downtrodden an access to the judicial system for redressal of wrongs.' She also states that, 'The raison de'tre [sic] behind public interest litigation is as valid to-day as it was when such an action was first permitted.... What is required is better regulation of Public Interest Litigation to make it more effective. It serves a vital public need and must be strengthened rather than discarded.'
22. See, for example: *The Bar Pro Bono Unit*, available at http://www.barprobono.org.uk/overview.html (accessed on30 April 2010) (for an instance of the bar pro bono efforts in the UK).
23. For an extended discussion of inequality in social and economic rights litigation, see Brinks and Gauri (2008: 334–42).
24. Manupatra is a popular online legal database.
25. Interviews with officers of the PIL section, Supreme Court, in New Delhi (13 January 2009).
26. The BIMARU states are states that continue to face severe poverty and socio-economic challenges in the country. See, for example, *The Times of India* (2005); Raghavan (2005).
27 The chi-square test is used to examine whether distributions of categorical variables differ from one another. The probit model is used to study the factors related to a binary outcome variable (in this case, winning or losing a case).

28. The social class of the claimant was not discernible in 1 per cent of the cases related to SC/ST/OBC, 34 per cent of cases related to women's and children's rights, and 45 per cent of explicit PIL cases.

REFERENCES

Baxi, Upendra. 1980. *The Indian Supreme Court and Politics*. Lucknow: Eastern Book Company.

———. 2006. 'Structural Adjustment of Judicial Activism'. Inaugural Lecture at the West Bengal National Academy of Juridical Sciences, 10 June.

Bell, Ruth G., Kuldeep Mathur, Urvashi Narain, and David Simpson. 2004. 'Clearing the Air: How Delhi Broke the Logjam on Air Quality Reforms'. *Environment* 46 (3). April.

Brinks, Daniel M., and Varun Gauri. 2008. 'A New Policy Landscape: Legalizing Social and Economic Rights in the Developing World'. In *Courting Social Justice: Judicial Enforcement of Social and Economic Rights in the Developing World*, eds Varun Gauri and Daniel M. Brinks, 303–52. New York: Cambridge University Press.

Cassels, J. 1989. 'Judicial Activism and Public Interest Litigation in India: Attempting the Impossible?' *American Journal of Comparative Law*, 37 (3): 495–519.

Dahl, Robert. 1957. 'Decision-Making in a Democracy: The Supreme Court as a National Policy-Maker'. *Journal of Public Law*, 6 (2): 279–95.

Desai, Ashok H., and S. Muralidhar. 2000. 'Public Interest Litigation: Potential and Problems'. In *Supreme but not Infallible: Essays in Honour of the Supreme Court of India*, eds B. N. Kirpal, Ashok H. Desai, Gopal Subramanian, Rajeev Dhavan and Raju Ramachandran., 159–92. New Delhi: Oxford University Press. Available at http://www.ielrc.org/content/a0003.pdf (accessed on 30 April 2010).

Dhavan, Rajeev. 2002. 'Judicial Corruption'. *The Hindu*, 22 February. Available at http://thehindujobs.com/thehindu/2002/02/22/stories/2002022200031000.htm (accessed on 30 April 2010).

Dhavan, Rajeev, R. Sudarshan, and Salman Khurshid. eds. 1985. *Judges and the Judicial Power: Essays in Honour of Justice V.R. Krishna Iyer*. London: Sweet & Maxwell.

Epstein, Lee, and Jack Knight. 1998. *The Choices Justices Make*. Washington, DC.: CQ Press.

Fredman, S. 2008. *Human Rights Transformed: Positive Rights and Positive Duties*. Oxford, UK: Oxford University Press.

Fuller, L. L., and K. I. Winston. 1978. 'The Forms and Limits of Adjudication'. *Harvard Law Review*, 92 (2): 353–409.

Gauri, Varun. 2004. 'Social Rights and Economics: Claims to Health Care and Education in Developing Countries'. *World Development*, 32 (3): 465–77.

Gauri, Varun, and Daniel M. Brinks. 2008. 'The Elements of Legalization, and the Social and Economic Rights Triangle'. In *Courting Social Justice: Judicial Enforcement of Social and Economic Rights in the Developing World*, eds Varun Gauri and Daniel M. Brinks, 1–37.

Ginsburg, Tom. 2003. *Judicial Review in New Democracies: Constitutional Courts in Asian Cases*. New York: Cambridge University Press.

Hidayatullah, Justice M. 'Highways and Bye-Lanes of Justice', (1984) 2 SCC J-1.

Holmes, Stephen, and Cass R. Sunstein. 1996. *The Cost of Rights: Why Liberty Depends on Taxes*. New York: W. W. Norton & Co.

Human Rights Features.2002. 'Right to Food: The Indian Experience'. Available at http://www.hrdc.net/sahrdc/hrfeatures/HRF58.htm (accessed on 30 April 2010).

Indian Express. 2007. 'Line Dividing Activism and Over-Reach is a Thin One: PM's Caution to Bench'. 9 April.

Jha, Geetanjali. 'Problems Facing Public Interest Litigation in India'. Available at http://www.legalservicesindia.com/articles/pil_ind.htm (accessed on 30 April 2010).

Khosla, Madhav. 2008. 'Bitter PIL'. *Indian Express*, 18 November.

Krishnan, Jayanth K. 2003. 'Social Policy Advocacy and the Role of the Courts in India'. *American Asian Review*, 21.

Mehta, P. B. 2007. 'The Rise of Judicial Sovereignty'. *Journal of Democracy*, 18 (2): 70–83. April.

Mitta, Manoj, and Smriti Singh. 2009. 'India Decriminalizes Gay Sex'. *The Times of India*, 3 July. Available at http://timesofindia.indiatimes.com/articleshow/4726608.cms (accessed on 30 April 2010).

O'Donnell, Guillermo. 2003. 'Horizontal Accountability: The Legal Institutionalization of Mistrust'. In *Democratic Accountability in Latin America*, eds Scott Mainwaring and Christopher Welna, 34–54. Oxford, UK: Oxford University Press.

Raghavan, B. S. 2005. 'BIMARU or bimari?' *The Hindu*, 12 August. Available at http://www.thehindubusinessline.com/2005/08/12/stories/2005081200521000.htm (accessed on 30 April 2010).

Rajagopal, Balakrishnan. 2007. 'Pro-Human Rights but Anti-Poor?: A Critical Evaluation of the Indian Supreme Court from a Social Movement Perspective'. *Human Rights Review*, 18 (3): 168–77.

Rajamani, Lavanya. 2007. 'Public Interest Environmental Litigation in India: Exploring Issues of Access, Participation, Equity, Effectiveness and Sustainability'. *Journal of Environmental Law*, 19 (3): 293–321.

Ramanathan, Usha. 2002. 'Of Judicial Power'. *Frontline* 19.Available at http://www.thehindu.com/fline/fl1906/19060300.htm (accessed on 4 June 2010).

Rodrik, Dani. 2003. 'Growth Strategies'. 26, National Bureau of Economics Research Working Paper No. 10050.

Rosencranz, Armin, and Michael Jackson. 2003. 'The Delhi Pollution Case: The Supreme Court of India and the Limits of Judicial Power'. *Columbia Journal of Environmental Law*, 28 (2): 223–54.

Rosencranz, A., and S. Lélé. 2008. 'Supreme Court and India's Forests'. *Economic and Political Weekly*, 43 (5): 11–14.

Roy, Arundhati. 'Scandal in the Palace'. Available at http://www.zmag.org/znet/viewArticle/14376 (accessed on 30 April 2010).

Sathe, S. P. 2002. *Judicial Activism in India: Transgressing Borders and Enforcing Limits*. New Delhi: Oxford University Press.

Shankar, Shylashri, and Pratap Bhanu Mehta. 2008. 'Courts and Socioeconomic Rights in India'. In *Courting Social Justice: Judicial Enforcement of Social and Economic Rights in the Developing World*, eds Varun Gauri and Daniel M. Brinks, 146–82. New York: Cambridge University Press.

Sharma, Tannu. 2008. 'Court Monitoring Committees Illegal .. Stop PIL Blackmail: Justice Katju Slams His Own'. *Indian Express*. Available at http://www.indianexpress.com/news/court-monitoring-committees-illegal...stop-pil-blackmail-justice-katju-slams-his-own/295916/0 (accessed on 30 April 2010).

Shue, Henry. 1996. *Basic Rights: Subsistence, Affluence, and U.S. Foreign Policy*. 2nd edition. Princeton, New Jersey: Princeton University Press.

Srikrishna, Justice B. N. 'Skinning a Cat', (2005) 8 SCC (J) 3.Available at http://www.ebc-india.com/lawyer/articles/2005_8_3.htm(accessed on 30 April 2010).

Sweet, Alec S. 1999. 'Judicialization and the Construction of Governance'. *Comparative Political Studies*, 32 (2): 147–84.

The Times of India. 2005. '"Bimaru" States Hampers India's Growth'. 7 September. Available at http://timesofindia.indiatimes.com/articleshow/1223697.cms (accessed on 30 April 2010).

Thiruvengadam, Arun K. 2007. 'Recent PIL Cases Decided by the Supreme Court'. Available at http://lawandotherthings.blogspot.com/2007/07/recent-pil-cases-decided-by-supreme.html. (accessed on 22 July 2013).

———. 2009. 'Evaluating Contemporary Criticisms of "Public Interest Litigation": A Progressive Conception of the Role of a Judge'. Paper presented at the 2009 inaugural LASSNET Conference, New Delhi.

Trebilcock, Michael J., and Ronald J. Daniels. 2008. *Rule of Law Reform and Development: Charting the Fragile Path of Progress.* Northampton: Edward Elger.

Venkatesan, J. 2005. 'Supreme Court's Indelible Record'. *The Hindu*. Available at http://www.hindu.com/2005/12/30/stories/2005123003391600.htm (accessed on 30 April 2010).

5

Social Justice and the Supreme Court

SUDHIR KRISHNASWAMY and MADHAV KHOSLA

> The Indian Supreme Court has achieved world-wide acclaim in fashioning new rights under Part III of the Constitution and also using Directive Principles as interpretive devices for giving a contemporaneous meaning to Part III ... The ultimate justification for the creation of new rights and renewed emphasis on implementation of statutory rights is that they have to be made justifiable, simply because of their primacy in living a life with dignity and the matching recognition thereof with the values that our Constitution inheres.
>
> – Justice S. B. Sinha, Supreme Court of India[1]

The judicial enforcement of socio-economic rights is gaining support around the world. Scholars now suggest that courts have the democratic legitimacy to enforce such rights,[2] and the institutional capacity to adjudicate polycentric issues.[3] Academic writing in support of socio-economic rights enforcement often draws on the Indian experience to show that the Supreme Court has 'adapted its processes so that the voices of the poor and disadvantaged can be heard' (Fredman 2008: 124). In India, however, recent debates have called into question the Supreme Court's commitment to socio-economic rights enforcement. It has been observed in recent times that the judiciary has increasingly narrowed the field on issues of socio-economic rights and distributive justice. It is argued that the judiciary has taken a conservative turn and the judicial output of the Court in such cases is seen in terms of a 'rise and fall'. The Supreme Court is portrayed as having developed a sound approach to public interest litigation (PIL) and socio-economic rights adjudication in 1970s and 1980s, while post the 1990s the Court is no longer 'taking suffering seriously' (Baxi 1985: 289). Comments by some judges like Justice M. Katju on PIL and judicial activism strengthen this narrative.[4] In the first part of this essay, we resist this narrative of a rise and fall in the judicial enforcement of socio-economic rights as it is neither empirically tested nor doctrinally sustainable. We examine recent accounts suggesting a regression in socio-economic rights enforcement and show why these accounts fail to establish the general proposition. Moreover, the metaphor of a 'rise and fall' obscures serious issues in the enforcement of socio-economic rights. Hence, in the remaining section we turn to critical issues in the judicial enforcement of these rights which we believe deserve greater academic, activist and judicial engagement.

MEASURING THE ENFORCEMENT OF SOCIO-ECONOMIC RIGHTS

In a recent account of socio-economic rights enforcement, Shylashri Shankar conducts an empirical analysis of the enforcement of such rights by the Indian Supreme Court (Shankar 2009). She concludes that:

> [j]udgments after 1988 were 17 per cent less likely to favour health/education rights than those issued before 1988 ... Judgments after 1993 were 16 per cent less likely to favour an outcome beneficial to a citizen's right to health or education ... Similarly, judges appointed before 1993 were significantly more likely to favour such outcomes (Ibid.: 177).

Shankar explains these statistical conclusions by offering contingent historical and political reasons. For example, she posits that the Supreme Court was keen to restore its reputation as an institution that upheld rights and safeguarded freedom after the Emergency in 1975, thereby focusing on the achievement of social justice. She observes that 'after the Emergency, judges were keen to use social rights to enhance the institutional prestige of the courts, but a decade later the courts did not need to do so and reverted to seeing affordability of the state as a key criteria for delivering social rights judgments' (Ibid.).

In this essay, we are not concerned with Shankar's explanations as much as with the methodology that leads to her conclusions. Shankar adopts a quantitative approach to show that the success rate in socio-economic rights cases has declined over the years. Unquestionably, if true, this is an important trend in judicial behaviour in the Indian Supreme Court. However, the study has several limitations. First, we should note at the outset that the claim is overbroad as the sample of cases is restricted to reported cases which are a subset of cases decided by the Supreme Court. Second, and more significantly, the study does not enquire into the reasons for decision. Consequently, the higher rejection rate may well be a result of the admission of a higher number of cases which are poorly drafted or pleaded. It could also be a result of new claims (however meritorious) that have arisen under certain rights. In order to show that there has been a conservative turn in the Supreme Court's approach to socio-economic rights we must have evidence to suggest that the 1990s Supreme Court chose not to enforce a right which, under similar facts and circumstances, the 1980s Supreme Court would have. In other words, the data does not reveal that the Court has treated similar cases differently. Third, as Shankar acknowledges, her research is limited to the fields of health and education, and thus may not be sufficient for an overall conclusion on the Court's behavioural patterns (Ibid.: 174).

Prashant Bhushan, in his analysis of judicial behaviour towards socio-economic rights, adopts a different methodology (Bhushan 2009: 32). He anecdotally asserts that in a chosen sample of cases socio-economic rights have been unjustifiably denied. Bhushan relies heavily on the *Narmada*[5] decision to support his claim, as well as recent cases like *Tata Housing Development Company v. Goa Foundation*.[6] However, in order to show that there has been significant doctrinal regression in the enforcement of socio-economic rights, it is inadequate to rest the argument on a few cases where protection to rights may have been denied. To show that the 'Judicial Nineties' have been a lean period for socio-economic rights one must demonstrate that the Supreme Court has either reversed its recognition of rights or refused to grant remedies for rights which were hitherto enforced. Did *Narmada* and *Tata Housing* alter the recognition of socio-economic rights available under the Constitution or recast the conditions under which rights are likely to be enforced? Were any earlier cases overruled in these judgements? Bhushan may well be right that the Court erred in its decisions in both these cases but he does not establish that there has been a doctrinal shift that changes the nature of the rights or the capacity of the Court to protect them.

In this section we have examined some recent writing that suggests the Supreme Court has reneged on its earlier promise to enforce socio-economic rights. We argue that the existing literature in the field does not establish this claim with analytical rigour or empirical robustness. In order to establish such a general claim about the enforcement of particular socio-economic rights, we must examine the entire body of cases in a particular area—right to food or the right to shelter—and show that an analysis of the judicial output of the court that pays attention to the strength of the bench and the ratio of the cases leads us to conclude that we have indeed lost several cherished and previously protected rights. A stronger version of such a claim (Gloppen 2009) may seek to establish whether the Supreme Court's capacity or willingness to craft suitable remedies for socio-economic rights violations has resulted in a social transformation measured through empirically verifiable social and economic indicators.[7]

The development of socio-economic rights in the last six decades of the Indian Constitution has been uneven. In any given period of the Court's history some rights have been recognised and developed, others have remained moribund and under-enforced, while in the case of some rights there have been minor regressions. We believe that the 'Judicial Nineties' are no exception.[8] For instance, in the right to food case,[9] the Court went further than it had previously by utilising the remedy of continuing mandamus to direct the implementation of its orders within strict time frames.[10] Similarly in the 1990s the Supreme Court followed the *Olga Tellis*[11] judgement in several cases, highlighting, in contrast to *Narmada*, that there was no regression in the right to housing.[12]

If the argument in this section is correct, then we may usefully engage with more enduring themes and conceptual problems with public interest litigation and the enforcement of socio-economic rights, and which persist across the last four decades of socio-economic rights adjudication in India.

STANDING, PROCESS AND JUDICIAL REVIEW

The case of *Peoples' Union for Democratic Rights v. Union of India* (*PUDR v. UOI*)[13] is a celebrated case for proposing an 'Indian model' of public law adjudication with new rules on standing, new process requirements and new remedies. This claim was supported by some academic literature at the time. This view that *PUDR* pioneered a form of public law adjudication that was unique in the common law world is surprising considering that Fuller, Chayes and Fiss had already discussed these very issues and the evolving nature of public law adjudication in the 1970s.[14] The recent controversies in India regarding PILs and judicial activism may be attributed in some measure to the lack of academic attention to serious questions relating to this form of adjudication in India. It is useful to analyse these problems shorn of the rhetorical flourishes in which they are often presented. Hence, discussions on PIL may be understood primarily as a problem related to the rules of standing and the overblown concern with 'judicial activism' is a proxy for a necessary debate about judicial process and remedies in writ litigation.[15] As many cases which seek to enforce socio-economic rights are initiated as PIL, this section reviews the present issues in the standing rules in constitutional rights cases.

In cases where more than one litigant approaches the court on behalf of another, the standing rule may need to be modified suitably. Peter Cane, in his analysis of representative standing, distinguishes between three types of representative standing: 'associational standing', 'public interest standing' and 'surrogate standing'.[16] There may be a case of associational standing which relates to groups formed by several individuals who are all individually affected by the state action and hence decide to collectively litigate. This is akin to class action in writ proceedings, which is a form of standing recognised in civil proceedings and finds mention in Order 2, Rule 2 of the Code of Civil Procedure 1908. 'Public interest standing' may be said to exist where the group or person before the court is not directly affected by the state action and can show no constitutional injury, but claims to have a special concern in a matter of public interest. In such cases, the court must develop an account of when a person may be said to act in the 'public interest'. 'Surrogate standing' is where one person (the nominal applicant) represents the interests of another (the real applicant).

Unfortunately, courts in India have failed to develop principles of ascertaining how appropriate representation will be determined. In several cases the Supreme Court has highlighted the problem of frivolous PIL petitions.[17] However, in attempting to resolve the issue, the Court has blurred the distinction between frivolous litigation and appropriate representation.[18] The failure to address the issue of appropriate representation has provided little clarity on how courts weigh factors such as the specialised knowledge that petitioners may have, and the relationship that he/she shares with the persons whom he/she is seeking to represent. For example, in the *Narmada* case, the Supreme Court initially refused to regard the Narmada Bachao Andolan (NBA) as an authentic representative of the interest of those who were ousted by the dam.[19] Yet, a closer study reveals that NBA may well satisfy the criterion for both associational standing as well as public interest standing. However, in other cases such as *Sarbananda Sonowal v. Union of India*,[20] a member of legislative assembly (MLA) who failed to win the election was allowed to raise the issue of the application of the Foreigners Act, 1946 to the state of Assam as a matter of 'public interest'. The failure of the Court to recognise different types of standing rules and the criteria which it must apply in each of these cases has resulted in the haphazard development of PIL.

Courts must also provide guidance on how petitions will be characterised in complex situations where there may be multiple petitioners. For instance, in *Yashpal v. State of Chhattisgarh*,[21] a PIL petition was filed under Article 32 of the Indian Constitution challenging the constitutionality of a state legislation establishing private universities. The first petitioner, Professor Yashpal, was a former chairman of the University Grants Commission of India, and was thus held to have satisfied the requirement of acting bona fide in the public interest. The second petitioner, a resident of the state concerned, however, had suffered an economic loss after being defrauded by a private university and approached the Court because he was, ostensibly, 'concerned with the quality of education in his State'.[22] Strangely, the Court did not reflect on the personal motivations of the first and second petitioner, and the petition was treated as a valid PIL petition.[23] However, had the Court dealt with these petitioners' motivations, it remains unclear how it would have responded. Indian courts must determine the approach to be adopted in situations where some petitioners satisfy the standing requirements but others do not.

In addition to the doctrinal developments that are needed to determine appropriate representation in representative litigation, there is a need for greater engagement with the impact of socio-economic rights adjudication and representative litigation on the judicial process. While there has been a great deal of stress on the institutional capacity and democratic legitimacy of courts to adjudicate socio-economic rights, there has been little emphasis on how this may impact the judicial process. Carol Harlow, in an analysis of PIL, observes how groups entering the judicial process convert courts into another forum for politics and affect the 'independence, objectivity and finality' of the process (Harlow 2002: 65). While some authors have suggested that certain safeguards must be built into the system,[24] there needs to be further discussion on what these safeguards are and on whether evolved principles for determining appropriate representation can respond to some of these concerns.

A third issue that requires attention is the form of judicial review in socio-economic rights cases. Through studying the South African approach of a non-individualised remedy in socio-economic rights cases,[25] Mark Tushnet has recently put forth the possibility of weak-form judicial review in socio-economic rights cases. According to Tushnet, a weak-form judicial review model responds to both legitimacy and capacity concerns regarding socio-economic rights adjudication by 'providing an institutional mechanism for the *provisional* identification and enforcement of social and economic rights' and can 'reconcile democratic self-governance with constitutionalism' (Tushnet 2007: xi. Emphasis in the original). Other scholars have also suggested different ways in which rights and remedies may be structured to provide for the legitimate and effective enforcement of socio-economic rights.[26] Evidence from the waste management[27] and Delhi pollution[28] cases reveals the ineffectiveness of certain remedial models and suggests that the subject of effective remedies requires greater examination in the Indian context.[29] It is also worth exploring the degree to which Tushnet's typology may be applicable in India, and if the Indian experience can be better understood through disaggregating the nature of the right enforced and the type of remedy provided. One of us has attempted to undertake this enterprise in a recent essay, and we hope that it will stimulate debate in this area (Khosla 2010).

The discourse emphasising the Supreme Court's regression on issues of social justice is inadequate in several ways. Apart from the fact that a close reading of cases reveals the Court has done less in earlier decades than many suppose (Khosla 2011), it is important to investigate how the adjudication of social rights in India is informed by the relationship between Directive Principles and Fundamental Rights under the Constitution, and what the Court's interpretation of Articles 21 and 37[30] reveals about its understanding of this relationship (Khosla 2012: 119–36). We have therefore turned to certain issues which we believe merit greater attention. The first of these deals with standing, and suggests some possible ways in which PIL may be reformed. A closely related issue is the impact that PIL and socio-economic rights adjudication may have on the judicial process. Finally, we have suggested that the Indian discourse may be informed by the debates emerging from the South African Constitutional Court's adjudication of socio-economic rights. We need to investigate the form of judicial review currently undertaken by Indian courts in socio-economic rights, and consider whether greater sensitivity to the relationship between rights and remedies can enhance our understanding of the Indian experience. While we must no doubt engage with the politics of the Supreme Court and its adjudication, we need to simultaneously develop rigorous analyses of the Court's doctrine and judicial process to refine any assessment of the Supreme Court's impact on the achievement of social justice.

NOTES

1. *State of UP v. Jeet S. Bisht*, (2007) 6 SCC 586, pp. 615, 617.
2. See, for example, Fabre (2000). A seminal article on the legitimacy of justiciable socio-economic rights is Michelman (1973). See also Michelman (1969, 2003, 2008). For a recent discussion on Michelman's work, see Liu (2008).
3. See, for example, King (2008) (for a discussion on how taxation law is also polycentric). The argument that courts should not adjudicate polycentric issues has its origins in Fuller (1978). For the classic response to Fuller, see Fiss (1979: 39–44).
4. See Sharma (2008); *Divisional Manager, Aravali Golf Club v. Chander Hass*, 2007 (14) SCALE 1.
5. *Narmada Bachao Andolan v. Union of India*, (2000) 10 SCC 664.
6. (2003) 7 SCALE 54.
7. For such a study in the American context, see Rosenberg (2008). We do not endorse Rosenberg's conclusions, and it is not clear whether his model of assessing

the remedial impacts of decisions is accurate. For an important criticism of Rosenberg's methodology that emphasises the multi-causal nature of events, see Ackerman (2007: 1762–763). Nonetheless, Rosenberg does present a far more rigorous study than those witnessed in the Indian context.

8. For a detailed account of the Indian Supreme Court's approach towards socio-economic rights during the 1990s, see Kothari (2007: 191–92). ('The experience of the last decade has shown that the Indian Supreme Court has refashioned its institutional role to readily enforce social rights and even impose positive obligations on the state.')
9. *Peoples Union for Civil Liberties (PUCL) v. Union of India & Others* WP (Civil) No 196/2001.
10. Kothari (2007: note 15, pp. 176–82).
11. *Olga Tellis v. Bombay Municipal Corporation (BMC),* (1985) 3 SCC 545.
12. See *Shantistar Builders v. Narayan K. Totame,* (1990) 1 SCC 520; *Chameli Singh v. State of UP,* (1996) 2 SCC 549; *Ahmedabad Municipal Corporation v. Nawab Khan Gulab Khan,* (1997) 11 SCC 121.
13. AIR 1982 SC 1473.
14. See Chayes (1976); Fuller (1978); Fiss (1979).
15. For a critique of the 'judicial activism' discourse in India, see Khosla (2009).
16. See Cane (1995).
17. See, for example, *Ashok Kumar Pandey v. State of W.B.,* (2004) 3 SCC 349; *Dr. B. Singh v. Union of India,* (2004) 3 SCC 363; *N. K. Prasada v. Government of India* (2004) 6 SCC 299; *Dattaraj Nathuji Thaware v. State of Maharashtra* (2005) 1 SCC 590; *Gurpal Singh v. State of Punjab* (2005) 5 SCC 136.
18. See Khosla (2008).
19. See Fredman (2008: note 4, pp. 140–41).
20. (2007) 1 SCC 174.
21. (2005) 5 SCC 420.
22. *Yashpal v. State of Chhattisgarh,* note 38, p. 429.
23. See Dam (2006: 112). ('Clearly, the petition while acting in so-called "public interest" was motivated by pecuniary interests.... The inability of the Supreme Court to see through the motivations of the second petitioner is perplexing at best and crafty at worst.')
24. See Desai and Muralidhar (2000: 159).
25. See *Government of the Republic of South Africa v. Grootboom,* 2000 (11) BCLR 1169; *Minister of Health v. Treatment Action Campaign,* 2002 (10) BCLR 1033.
26. See Dixon (2007). See also Klein (2008).
27. Writ Petition Number 888 of 1996.
28. Writ Petition Number 13029 of 1985.
29. For a study of how these cases have not resulted in governance-related reform, see Rajamani (2007).
30. See Krishnaswamy (2010).

REFERENCES

Ackerman, Bruce. 2007. 'The Living Constitution'. *Harvard Law Review*, 120 (7): 1737–1812.

Baxi, Upendra. 1985. 'Taking Suffering Seriously: Social Action Litigation in the Supreme Court of India'. In *Judges and the Judicial Power: Essays in Honour of Justice V. R. Krishna Iyer*, eds Rajeev Dhavan, R. Sudarshan and Salman Khurshid, 289–315. Bombay: N. M. Tripathi.

Bhushan, Prashant. 2009. 'Misplaced Priorities and Class Bias of the Judiciary'. *Economic and Political Weekly*, 44 (13): 32–37.

Cane, Peter. 1995. 'Standing Up for the Public'. *Public Law*, 276–87.

Chayes, Abram. 1976. 'The Role of the Judge in Public Law Litigation'. *Harvard Law Review*, 89 (7):1281–1316.

Dam, Shubhankar. 2006. 'Unburdening the Constitution: What has the Indian Constitution got to do with Private Universities, Modernity and Nation-States?' *Singapore Journal of Legal Studies*, 48 (1): 108–47.

Desai, Ashok H., and S. Muralidhar. 2000. 'Public Interest Litigation: Potential and Problems'. In *Supreme but not Infallible: Essays in Honour of the Supreme Court of India*, eds B. N. Kirpal, Ashok H. Desai, Rajeev Dhawan and Raju Ramachandran, 159–92. New Delhi: Oxford University Press.

Dixon, Rosalind. 2007. 'Creating Dialogue about Socioeconomic Rights: Strong-Form versus Weak-Form Judicial Review Revisited'. *International Journal of Constitutional Law*, 5 (2): 391–418.

Fabre, Cecile. 2000. *Social Rights under the Constitution: Government and the Decent Life*. Oxford: Oxford University Press.

Fiss, Owen M. 1979. 'The Supreme Court, 1978 Term—Forword: The Forms of Justice'. *Harvard Law Review*, 93(1): 1–58.

Fredman, Sandra. 2008. *Human Rights Transformed: Positive Rights and Positive Duties*. New York: Oxford University Press.

Fuller, Lon L. 1978. 'The Forms and Limits of Adjudication'. *Harvard Law Review*, 92: 353–409.

Gloppen, Siri. 2009. 'Legal Enforcement of Social Rights: Enabling Conditions and Impact Assessment'. *Erasmus Law Review*, 2 (4): 465–80.

Harlow, Carol. 2002. 'Public Law and Popular Justice'. *Modern Law Review*, 65 (1): 1–18.

Khosla, Madhav. 2008. 'Bitter PIL'. *Indian Express*, 18 November. Available at http://www.indianexpress.com/news/bitter-pil/386940/ (accessed on 10 June 2009).

———. 2009. 'Addressing Judicial Activism in the Indian Supreme Court: Towards an Evolved Discourse'. *Hastings International and Comparative Law Review*, 32 (1): 55–100.

———. 2010. 'Making Social Rights Conditional: Lessons from India'. 8 *International Journal of Constitutional Law (I-CON)*, 8: 739–65.

———. 2012. *The Indian Constitution*. New Delhi: Oxford University Press.

King, Jeff A. 2008. 'The Pervasiveness of Polycentricity'. *Public Law*, 101–24.

Klein, Alana. 2008. 'Judging as Nudging: New Governance Approaches for the Enforcement of Constitutional Social and Economic Rights'. *Columbia Human Rights Law Review*, 39 (2): 351–422.

Kothari, Jayna. 2007. 'Social Rights Litigation in India: Developments of the Last Decade'. In *Exploring Social Rights: Between Theory and* Practice, eds Daphne Barak-Erez and Aeyal Gross, 171–92. Oxford: Hart Publishing.

Krishnaswamy, S. 2010. 'Horizontal Application of Fundamental Rights and State Action in India'. In *Human Rights, Justice and Constitutional Empowerment*, eds Raj Kumar, C. Rajkumar and K. Chokalingam, 47–95. Oxford University Press.

Liu, Goodwin. 2008. 'Rethinking Constitutional Welfare Rights'. *Stanford Law Review*, 61 (2): 203–70.

Michelman, Frank I. 1969. 'The Supreme Court, 1968 Term—Foreword: On Protecting the Poor Through the Fourteenth Amendment'. *Harvard Law Review*, 83: 7–59.

———. 1973. 'In Pursuit of Constitutional Welfare Rights: One View of Rawls' Theory of Justice'. *University of Pennsylvania Law Review*, 121: 962–1019.

———. 2003. 'The Constitution, Social Rights, and Liberal Political Justification'. *International Journal of Constitutional Law*, 1 (1):13–34.

———. 2008. 'Socioeconomic Rights in Constitutional Law: Explaining America Away'. *International Journal of Constitutional Law*, 6 (3) 663–86.

Rajamani, Lavanya. 2007. 'Public Interest Environmental Litigation in India: Exploring Issues of Access, Participation, Equity, Effectiveness and Sustainability'. *Journal of Environmental Law*, 19 (3): 293–321.

Rosenberg, Gerald N. 2008. *The Hollow Hope: Can Courts Bring about Social Change?* 2nd edition. Chicago: University of Chicago Press.

Shankar, Shylashri. 2009. *Scaling Justice: India's Supreme Court, Anti-Terror Laws, and Social Rights*. New Delhi: Oxford University Press.

Sharma, Tannu. 2008. 'Court Monitoring Committees Illegal… Stop PIL Blackmail: Justice Katju Slams His Own'. *Indian Express*, 12 April. Available at http://www.indianexpress.com/story/295916.html (accessed on 9 May 2008).

Tushnet, Mark. 2007. *Weak Courts, Strong Rights: Judicial Review and Social Welfare Rights in Comparative Constitutional Law*. Princeton: Princeton University Press.

6

Swallowing a Bitter PIL?

Reflections on Progressive Strategies for Public Interest Litigation in India

ARUN K. THIRUVENGADAM*

The introduction to this volume suggests that there has been a shift in the nature and role of the Judiciary in India between the 1980s and the 1990s. Following this, this essay focuses on the following two questions: (i) What exactly is the nature of the shift that has taken place within the judiciary (specifically, the Supreme Court of India) on issues of social rights and distributive justice? (ii) Should this shift lead progressives to abandon the site of legal intervention?

In formulating responses to these two questions, this essay in turn advances two arguments. The first argument seeks to assess the shift in the approach of the Supreme Court to issues of human rights and public interest litigation (PIL) between the 1980s and the 1990s. The second argument urges progressives to increase—rather than abandon—engagement with the law and the courts. In advancing both these arguments, my effort will be to engage with the other contributors to this volume, as well as existing scholarly work on these issues.

* I thank the editors, Siddharth Narrain and Mayur Suresh, for their comments on a previous draft which helped me sharpen and explain my central argument. I also thank Mayura Baweja and Madhav Khosla for their constructive comments and suggestions for change. This is a revised version of the original paper presented at the conference on Judicial Nineties held in Bangalore in 2008. It draws from and builds upon an expanded analysis in Thiruvengadam (2013).

THE CHANGING CHARACTER OF PIL: THE DEBATE OVER ASSESSING THIS CLAIM

In many of the contributions to this volume, a consistent theme has been the transformation of PIL from the time of its inception in the late 1970s to the causes it embraced in the 1990s. Aditya Nigam refers to the original phase of PIL as being concerned with reaching out 'to the ordinary person, cutting out the cumbersome formalities that made it so unapproachable' and as being focussed upon the concerns of 'the "people"... the poor and the disadvantaged' (see Nigam's essay in this volume). In Nigam's view, PIL in the 1990s began reflecting the wider ideologies of 'neo-liberalism' and 'corporate-capitalism' and emerged as 'the champion of the new order'. Nivedita Menon's chapter confirms this assessment by undertaking a survey of cases decided by the Supreme Court in the 1990s which, according to her, 'have a clear logic and are remarkably consistent in terms of their outcome [which inevitably is]...: Environment trumps People, Development trumps Environment' (see Menon's essay in this volume). Going a step further than Nigam, Menon asserts that rather than being complicit with the neo-liberal project, 'the judiciary and the law *are* the neo-liberal project'.

This seeming consensus among progressives on a shift in the Supreme Court's stance is questioned by Sudhir Krishnaswamy and Madhav Khosla in their co-authored chapter. Focusing specifically on socio-economic rights, Krishnaswamy and Khosla argue that the 1990s are not an exception to the trend across the history of the Supreme Court, where '[i]n any given period... some rights have been recognised and developed, others have remained moribund and under-enforced, while in the case of some rights there have been minor regressions'. They seek to emphasise this point by focusing on recent Supreme Court decisions that have sought to implement the rights to food and housing, which are classic socio-economic rights and were not seriously implemented even in the original phase of PIL. Krishnaswamy and Khosla thus express scepticism about claims asserting that the Supreme Court has taken a 'conservative turn'. While expressing doubts about a particular statistical survey, Krishnaswamy and Khosla advance what is a credible way of testing such claims: they emphasise that this would require 'evidence to suggest that the 1990s Supreme Court chose not to enforce a right which, under similar facts and circumstances, the 1980s Supreme Court would have'. The arguments advanced by Krishnaswamy and Khosla remind us that the empirical basis for the consensus among progressives may not be as sound as is generally assumed.

Even as I acknowledge the importance of the points raised by Krishnaswamy and Khosla, my own view is that those asserting the existence of a 'conservative turn' can rely on various forms of evidence to back their claims. My first argument, therefore, seeks to bolster the claim of a 'conservative turn' by describing the terrain while relying upon scholarly assessments and actual court decisions. In setting out this argument, I will use the points raised by Krishnaswamy and Khosla as a foil for my own view.

In its early stages, the Court's focus in PIL cases was on very specific causes, almost all of which affected constituencies that were particularly disempowered. Very often the Court cited the fact that most such constituencies would not have ready access to justice, to justify its admittedly adventurous steps to improve their situation. Thus, for instance, a number of these early cases (especially those involving Justice V. R. Krishna Iyer, who had a particular interest in ameliorating prison conditions having undergone incarceration himself) focussed on the rights of prisoners. Clearly, prisoners were a category of citizens who were severely handicapped in being able to pursue the rights that were due to them. The Supreme Court held, for instance, that those charged with criminal offences had positive rights to legal aid[1] and speedy trial.[2] On the negative side, prisoners were held to have constitutional rights against the following: solitary confinement;[3] bar fetters;[4] handcuffing;[5] delayed execution;[6] custodial violence;[7] and against public hanging.[8] Other groups whose causes were addressed in early PIL cases were the following: migrant labourers;[9] pavement-dwellers;[10] children;[11] and mentally ill persons.[12] All of these groups fit the general category of cases that were the focus of the early phase of PIL cases, as each of these groups faced special difficulties in being able to espouse its grievances through the regular channels of democratic politics and access to justice.

Things began to change in the 1990s. To illustrate briefly what these changes entailed, I rely on a comprehensive survey of PIL cases that were decided in the 1997–98 period. In the conclusion of the survey,

S. Muralidhar presciently observed: 'The cases that were taken up for detailed consideration by the courts reflected a perceptible shift to issues concerning governance' (Muralidhar 1997–98: 525). This was the period during which the Supreme Court became proactive in its efforts towards: (i) cleaning up the political process by focusing on corruption at the highest levels of the political set-up in the *Hawala* case[13] and the *Fodder scam* case;[14] (ii) solving the chaotic traffic and pollution in Delhi;[15] (iii) cleaning up the Taj and its surrounding area;[16] (iv) regulating the disposal of hazardous waste;[17] (v) regulating the manufacture and sale of pesticides;[18] (vi) addressing the issues of sexual harassment[19] and female foeticide;[20] and (vii) regulating the collection and distribution of blood by blood banks.[21]

Owing to constraints of space, I will rely primarily upon the scholarly work of Usha Ramanathan which documents the changing nature of PIL in the mid-1990s. Ramanathan describes the original constituency of PIL as being that portion of the Indian population which was 'caught in the throes of severe disenfranchisement, dispossession and rightlessness' and includes within this category 'the bonded labourer, the incarcerated undertrial, the labouring child, migrant labour, and women in custodial institutions' (Ramanathan 2002: 1). In her telling, PIL cases across the 1980s and into the 1990s began to focus on a vast range of issues, most of which centred on concerns affecting the middle classes in India, as opposed to the marginalised sections. Ramanathan states that in this new phase, which emerged more clearly in the 1990s, the Supreme Court had to balance competing interests, and it gradually began to turn away from protecting the interests of the original constituencies of PIL. Ramanathan describes these competing interests in vivid terms:

> The right of over 30 per cent of the residents of Delhi to their shelter in the slum settlements was pitted against the need to 'clean up' the city. The right to a relatively unpolluted environment by means of the relocation of industries was pitted against the right of the working classes to their livelihood. The right to life, livelihood and protection from immiseration and exploitation of communities displaced along the Narmada was pitted against the right to water that the dam was expected to reach to the people in parts of Gujarat; it was also pitted against the enormous amounts of money that had already been expended on the

> dam. Even the right of the victims of the Bhopal gas disaster to receive compensation was pitted against the bureaucratic imperative of winding up the processing of claims (Ibid.).

Ramanathan therefore argues that 'the constituency on whose behalf the enhancement of judicial power' had been justified in the first phase of PIL, 'began to emerge as the casualty of that exercise of power' in the new phases of PIL that appeared in the 1990s (Ramanathan 1996, 2005). More recently, Rakesh Shukla has reached a similar conclusion after examining a body of case law relating to civil liberties, slum clearance and labour rights, all of which directly affect the conditions of the poor in India: 'From the beginnings of PIL as pro-poor and trying to effectuate the rights of the exploited, it is increasingly taking *a diametrically opposite direction*' (Shukla 2006: 3757).

The analysis offered by Ramanathan and Shukla (among others) meets the test suggested by Krishnaswamy and Khosla. The former does in fact argue that the Supreme Court in the 1990s and in the current decade is refusing to enforce rights which the Court of the 1980s would have. Krishnaswamy and Khosla have argued that one would need more rigorous evidence of such a 'conservative turn'. One measure of this would have to be a quantitative analysis. In support of their arguments, the critics of PIL cite several significant decisions to make good their claim, which can be classified under three categories. One category of cases includes the following three cases: *Narmada Bachao Andolan v. Union of India* (2000),[22] *N. D. Dayal v. Union of India* (2003)[23] and *Tata Housing Development Company v. Goa Foundation* (2003)[24]—all of which involved the displacement of thousands of people as a result of large dam and housing projects that were ultimately endorsed by the Supreme Court. A second set of cases which have been consistently attacked for their neglect of the concerns of migrant workers is the series of orders passed in the long-running *M. C. Mehta v. Union of India* (1986) case[25] that oversaw the relocation of thousands of polluting industries outside of the limits of the city of Delhi. The third category of cases which attracts the ire of the critics is cases such as *Almitra Patel v. Union of India* (2000),[26] where the Supreme Court ordered the demolition of slums and unauthorised structures set up by migrant workers and the poor. Even if these cases are few in number, one has to recall that the impact of each of these cases was typically felt on a large section of the population, and in that sense, each case had a potentially huge impact.

Krishnaswamy and Khosla critique a statistical survey undertaken by Shylashri Shankar (2009) where she asserts that the success rate in socio-economic rights cases (specifically in the health and education sectors) had declined from the 1980s to the 1990s. The fact that Shankar's study was primarily focussed upon cases relating to health and education and would not be 'sufficient for an overall conclusion on the Court's behavioural patterns' (Krishnaswamy and Khosla's essay in this volume) seems like a reasonable objection. In addition, Krishnaswamy and Khosla note that Shankar's study relied upon reported cases, which form a small subset of the actual cases decided by the Supreme Court. This too is a valid critique. Charles Epp, in conducting a similar quantitative study of the Supreme Court's record on rights cases, has called this the difference between the Court's 'public agenda' (consisting of decisions on major issues that are published in law reports) and its 'routine agenda' (consisting of tens of thousands of routine decisions, forming the bulk of the caseload of the Court, which remain unpublished and are known only to the lawyers and the parties to the case) (Epp 1998: 90).

A more comprehensive study that is relevant for our purposes is that conducted by Varun Gauri, who has attempted to empirically test the claims of the critics of PIL in a systematic way (Gauri 2009). Anticipating some of the criticisms advanced by Krishnaswamy and Khosla, Gauri's study covers a wider spectrum. Like Epp, Gauri appears to have worked in tandem with the Supreme Court Registry, as is indicated by the description of his dataset:

> i) cases that, according to the Supreme Court registrar's office, the Court has itself classified as PIL from 1988–2007 (some 2800 'cases' overall); (ii) all Supreme Court cases in the Manupatra database that involved Fundamental Rights and that addressed concerns regarding women and children rights, whether or not explicitly admitted as PILs (86 cases); (iii) all Supreme Court cases in the Manupatra database that involved Fundamental Rights and were related to issues regarding SC/ST/OBCs, whether or not explicitly admitted as PILs (180 cases); (iv) all Supreme Court cases in the Manupatra database that the Supreme Court explicitly called a PIL (44 cases) (Ibid.: 2009: 9).

Gauri concludes that his findings are 'consistent with the claim that judicial receptivity in the Supreme Court to Fundamental Rights claims made on behalf of the poor and excluded individuals has declined in recent years'. His data shows 'not only a decline in the win rate for marginalised individuals but a simultaneous increase in the win rate for advantaged individuals'. Gauri concludes that his findings

> constitute a prima facie validation of the concern that judicial attitudes are less favorably inclined to the claims of the poor than they used to be, either as the exclusive result of new judicial interpretations or, more likely, in conjunction with changes in the political and legislative climate (Gauri 2009: 13).

As Gauri concedes, the ambiguous manner in which the Supreme Court Registry classifies PIL cases creates difficulties in making definitive determinations about trends in PIL cases. Also, the specific methodological choices made by Gauri in seeking to conduct his study may also be open to debate, especially the factors he uses to assess success rates of the categories that he terms as 'marginalised', 'disadvantaged' and 'advantaged'. It cannot be doubted, however, that Gauri's study is an important step towards making quantitative assessments of the PIL jurisprudence of the Supreme Court.

It would appear that a number of public interest organisations and non-governmental organisations (NGOs) have, for some time now, acted in a way which shows an appreciation of the conclusions reached by Gauri. This is what is suggested by Jayanth Krishnan who argues, based on an extensive survey of seventy-three prominent social advocacy groups, that the changed reality is leading to a situation where the most prominent social advocacy groups tend to avoid litigation as a deliberate strategy (Krishnan 2003: 9). Krishnan explains that groups like the People's Union for Democratic Reforms (PUDR) have become disenchanted with the slow pace and inconsistent progress of PILs, and prefer to focus on alternative strategies, such as grassroots political mobilisation (as suggested by Menon in her contribution to this volume). For several other groups (Krishnan specifically identifies the Centre for Law and the Environment, Conservazone, Lokayan, the National Federation of Women, Saheli and the National Alliance of Women), the costs and institutional focus required for mounting and sustaining long-drawn PIL campaigns have caused them to avoid using them altogether. Overall, Krishnan emphasises that social groups are beginning to shy away from using PILs in their strategies.

For these reasons, I support the view advanced by a number of progressive scholars that the Supreme Court has, in a process which began in the 1990s and has continued over the current decade, transformed the nature of PIL and in some cases turned away from concerns it embraced in its original phase. I take Krishnaswamy and Khosla's methodological objections on board, while reiterating their call for more comprehensive and empirically rigorous research to be undertaken to facilitate a firmer grasp on the actual practice of contemporary PIL.

THE WAY FORWARD

I now turn to the second question set out earlier: what should progressives do when faced with an increasingly bleak situation where judges of the Supreme Court have turned their back on at least some of the central progressive causes and concerns?

Nigam and Menon do not, in their contributions to this volume, offer direct prescriptions on the way forward. There are, however, hints about where they think the focus of progressives should lie. Both are extremely critical of the vast powers taken upon themselves by judges, and express deep concerns about the extent of this power. Nigam focuses on an extra-judicial speech delivered by Justice Ruma Pal to express his surprise at the self-perception of Supreme Court judges as the ultimate interpreters and arbiters of constitutional text and values (Nigam, this volume). Menon is equally critical of the power wielded by the Supreme Court in cases involving environmental issues, and concludes by noting that more recently, the poor are 'militantly claiming spaces and livelihoods as their own'. At another point in her conclusion, she observes that 'the spectacularly successful campaign' against Special Economic Zones in Goa relied not on 'carefully drafted PILs or a thoughtful judiciary' but on '*militant* political mobilisation' (Menon, this volume; emphasis added). Although this is only an interpretation of their silence on this issue, I suspect that both Nigam and Menon would counsel progressives to abandon the site of legal intervention and focus instead on '*militant* political mobilisation'.

Krishnan's (2003) study suggests that a number of social organisations and advocacy groups have already acted upon this advice. In my view, this is an alarming trend and needs to be reversed. What is the alternative? Some progressives have implicitly suggested that what is required is a return to the original phase of PIL. In essence, they could be seen as demanding that a new generation of judges in the mould of Justices Iyer, Bhagwati, Chinappa Reddy and Desai be appointed to redeem the potential of PIL for progressive causes. I believe that such a view is both unrealistic and problematic.

The contemporary situation, which is characterised by excessive and overweening judicial power, where judges adopt 'command-and-control' strategies in PIL cases, may well be a direct result of the exhortations offered by the generation of progressive scholars who sought to influence and shape the discourse of PIL in its founding era. Looking at some of the landmark scholarly literature from the 1980s, one finds an astonishingly instrumental vision advanced for the judiciary. I focus here on the writings of Upendra Baxi, whose role and influence in that founding era has been widely acknowledged. In an article that was widely cited and came to symbolise the dominant thinking among progressives at the time, Baxi exhorts judges to become 'activist'. For Baxi, an activist judge is

> a judge who is aware that she wields enormous executive and legislative power in her role as a judge and this power and discretion have to be used *militantly* for the promotion of constitutional values.[27]

I find this statement problematic on two counts. First, the presumption here appears to be that only 'activist' judges can provide deliverance from the many social ills that afflicted India by promoting constitutional values. Noticeably, no other social actor is relevant in this scenario: grassroots movements, social organisations, lawyers and even clients are completely missing from this picture. The only people who seem to be important for bringing about the necessary social change are 'activist' judges. Second, the task of interpreting and promoting constitutional values is also presumed to be straightforward, and entirely free from either complexity or problems. Baxi appears to suggest that the text of the Indian Constitution inexorably points to progressive ends, ignoring the reality that there can be several conflicting interpretations of what exactly the constitutional values are and, more importantly, how they are to be achieved. Justice Bhagwati, one of the pioneers of the PIL movement, offers very similar advice in a much cited article (Bhagwati 1985: 561).

In another article written around the same time, Baxi offers a more nuanced perspective, acknowledging that PIL was not without problems. Here, Baxi specifically notes that despite encouraging signs, the crucial phase of PIL between 1980 and 1982 had shown that use of PIL had continued apace with the judiciary making 'constitutional compromises' which 'create new sources of anxiety'.[28] Baxi also concedes that the movement in its early years could be viewed as 'relatively minor exercises in class-transcendence'. Yet, this nuance gets drowned out in the overall message of the article, which celebrates early successes in PIL cases and exhorts other judges on the Supreme Court to convert to the cause.

Many judges of the Supreme Court, having taken these messages to heart, began to flex their muscles particularly in the 1990s when the weakened political executive had no choice but to tolerate such judicial adventurism. Part of the problem was also the fact that the judges favoured by progressives (referred to more recently by Baxi as the Four Musketeers[29]) had retired and were replaced by other judges who did not always share the same judicial philosophy or values. Baxi once referred to the evolution of PIL in India as 'at best an "establishment revolution"' (Baxi 1987a: 49). The story of PIL in the 1990s seems to be consistent with the historical storyline of the weak records of other establishment-led revolutions.

When Aditya Nigam, writing in the twenty-first century, asks how Supreme Court judges came to believe that they wield untrammelled authority when deciding PIL cases, at least part of the answer can be tracked to progressive scholarship in the 1980s, which counselled judges to believe that they were all powerful and fully justified in incorporating their own understanding of the values of the Constitution into their decisions. So, when Justice Kirpal wrote in a judgement about encroachers being akin to pickpockets,[30] he was merely incorporating his own value judgements into the task of adjudication—and was thus directly acting on the questionable advice offered by progressive writings in the 1980s. The deification of activist judges by progressives seems, albeit with the benefit of hindsight, a mistake. (For a different critique of such advocacy of judicial activism, see Khosla [2009: 55, 60–71].)

Progressive scholars and judges do not seem, while offering this advice, to exhibit a genuine belief in the values of constitutionalism and the rule of law. In adopting such an instrumental view of the task of judging, they seem to be unconcerned with maintaining the institutional credibility and neutrality of judges, to enable them to speak authoritatively while deploying the language of constitutionalism and the rule of law. Much of the initial criticism by some judges of the Supreme Court was indeed directed at the potential harm such nakedly ideological actions would cause to the credibility of the Supreme Court.[31] Progressive scholars like Baxi were quick to dismiss these valid criticisms as being outdated and regressive, but in doing so, ignored the sensible pleas made to focus on a credible conception of the judicial role for handling PIL.

In charting strategies for the future, I believe progressives should avoid making the same mistake, and must instead advocate a role for judges where they can justifiably lend support to PILs without appearing to act in partisan or ideologically motivated ways. The first move in this regard is a negative one, where I seek to rely on what progressive judges should *not* do in PIL cases. In many PIL cases, judges seek to dominate the agenda of the proceedings, and adopt 'command-and control' (Sabel and Simon 2004: 1016, 1019) measures, where they mimic bureaucracies by laying down fixed and specific rules, which prescribe the inputs and operating procedures of the institutions they seek to regulate.

By way of illustration, I focus on two examples drawn from different eras of PIL cases. One can see symptoms of this tendency in the early 1980s PIL that sought to regulate inter-country adoption of children, where detailed orders were issued to the authorities to solve the problem.[32] Although the Court did seek to solicit participation from NGOs and government agencies dealing with the issue of inter-country adoption, its final order reads like a legislative enactment, complete with the setting of age limits and precise procedures for conducting specified tasks. It was unclear exactly how the Court obtained the background information to base its definitive conclusions upon. The inflexibility of the rule-like 'guidelines' laid down by the Court later led to problems of implementation and confusion, after the case was finally disposed off by the order. A more recent example of a PIL where the Court exercised an extraordinary degree of overweening control over the proceedings is the *Hawala case* (*Vineet Narain v. Union of India* [1998]).[33] To recall, the PIL was brought by two journalists and two lawyers, seeking investigation by the Central Bureau of Investigation (CBI) on details of illegal payments made by way of hawala transactions to several politicians for favours in the award of government contracts. Over a period of two years, the Court (especially after the case began to be heard by a bench headed by Justice J. S. Verma) adopted a posture that has been described by a sympathetic observer as 'dynamic, fearless and dominating'.[34] As Muralidhar describes it, the Court's actions achieved many things, including infusing investigatory authorities like the CBI with autonomy and insulating them from executive interference. Yet, in the process of doing so, the Court displaced the actual petitioners and appointed a senior advocate as *amicus curiae* to assist the Court. At the same time, intervention in the proceedings by everyone else was shut out, while some of the hearings were held *in camera*, by shutting out the public. Muralidhar, whose credentials as a PIL litigant and astute and insightful chronicler of its development are impeccable, is critical of these aspects of the case, which 'defeat ... the very purpose of the jurisdiction', 'deprive ... public-spirited petitioners of their right to espouse a public cause' and render the participation of other organs of the state redundant. These criticisms echo those made by others about the overweening attitude of court-appointed *amicus curiae*, committees and the judges themselves.

I argue that progressives should critique such modes of adjudication and urge judges to abandon the 'command-and-control' strategies that are currently on display. Judges should instead be encouraged to adopt a far more modest, *facilitative* role, where the focus is on the citizens who suffer, the social movements who organise their interests, and the lawyers who represent them. This will enable an avoidance of some of the problems of domineering judges, individual lawyer–dominated agendas and idiosyncratic judicial preferences that have plagued PIL in more recent times.

Elsewhere (Thiruvengadam 2009, 2013: 359–66), I have discussed what such a facilitative role would entail in its details. Due to constraints of space, I can only outline the broad details of that conception here. Judges in India gain legitimacy for their extravagant actions in PIL cases from the fact that they are seen as making up for the deficiencies of the elected branches. Indeed, in several PILs, the Court has consciously sought to act as a deliberative forum for policy-making, and has used the judicial process to solicit—even mandate—responses from all wings of government. In doing so, the Court has reached beyond the Central government to seek responses from state governments on issues that affect them; required all ministries potentially affected by its decisions to provide their considered inputs, etc. My assertion is that judges should continue to be sensitive to the need to focus upon filling the deliberative gap, rather than seeking to impose their own subjective choices upon the judicial process. They must remember that their primary role should be to *facilitate* the reaching of sound policy decisions in cases that come up before them.

This *facilitative* role can be enhanced by a focussed change in mindset which eschews the domineering methods noted in the two examples earlier. What is required, instead, is a much more decentralised form of intervention, where the emphasis is on enabling all possible stakeholders to contribute meaningful inputs. Such inputs should be used to design flexible rules that are capable of responding to changing—and sometimes unpredictable or hostile—circumstances on the ground. Throughout this process, the emphasis should be on making every stage of the judicial process transparent.[35]

Progressives also need to attend to other worrying features of contemporary PIL. We have already noted Krishnan's disturbing findings that public interest organisations and social organisations have begun to abandon the route of PIL. This trend makes sense if we take account of the contemporary PIL scene, which is dominated by individual lawyers who file PILs quite often with no direct connection to the clients or causes they seek to represent. This is followed by a 'top-down' process employed by the judges who subsequently hear the case and decide on its future development with inputs from 'experts', and 'court-appointed amici' who, once again, have very little direct contact with affected interests.

In his provocative study of PIL in India, Epp (1998: 108) concludes that the Indian case offers a paradox: despite having one of the most activist courts in the world, which is also the most supportive of egalitarian and procedural rights, India has been 'unable to develop a sustained and deep agenda' on rights. Epp argues that this is primarily because 'the Indian support structure for legal mobilization—the complex of financial, legal and organizational resources necessary for appellate litigation—remains weak and fragmented' (Ibid.: 108).

If PIL is to truly become a vehicle for addressing concerns of the marginalised in Indian society, its future will have to be crafted for it to be able to do so effectively and meaningfully. It is imperative that progressives focus on strengthening the network of social organisations that can build grounded and bottom-up litigation strategies, which seek to genuinely represent the concerns of the actual clients in PIL cases. Arguably, the recent Right to Food PIL represents one example of such a trend.[36] Another example—albeit drawn from comparative law—is the *Treatment Action Campaign* case[37] decided by the South African Constitutional Court where an AIDS NGO was able to use the courts to thwart the South African government's opposition to plans to distribute a free drug that would significantly reduce mother–child transmission of AIDS (Belani 2004: 24–31; Forbath et al. 2011).

These examples provide hope that once such a 'support structure' is in place, judges will feel obliged to adopt more modest roles by deferring to the greater credibility and representational capacity enjoyed by a strengthened support structure.

In this short essay, I have sought to highlight specific questions about the changing character of PIL through the 1980s to the 1990s, while acknowledging the need for more detailed and rigorous empirical studies of the issue. While agreeing with other contributors about several worrying aspects of contemporary PIL, I find myself disagreeing with the general cynicism exhibited towards a continued engagement with the law. I believe that PIL has achieved many successes, and what is required is not abandonment but renewed engagement with its foundational ideas. I have sought to show how progressives of the 1980s made mistakes in charting strategies for the future of PIL, and how these will need to be corrected and remedied as we conceive of its future in the current moment.

Like many others who have contributed to this volume, I too am fully conscious of the seductive power of the law, and how it has historically frustrated and belied progressive hopes. Yet, like the British historian E. P. Thompson, I believe that the law *matters* and is of deep consequence for progressive causes. I conclude with these words from his revealing study of the tradition of the rule of the law in eighteenth-century England:

> In a context of gross class inequities, the equity of the law must always be in part sham. Transplanted as it was to even more inequitable contexts, this law could become an instrument of imperialism. But even here the rules and rhetoric have imposed some inhibitions upon the imperial power. If the rhetoric was a mask, it was a mask which Gandhi and Nehru were to borrow, at the head of a million masked supporters.
>
> I am not starry-eyed about [the law].... I am insisting only upon the obvious point, *which some modern Marxists have overlooked*, that there is a difference between arbitrary power and the rule of law. We ought to expose the shams and inequities which may be concealed beneath this law. But the rule of law itself, the imposing of effective inhibitions upon power and the defence of the citizen from power's all-intrusive claims, seems to me to be an unqualified human good. To deny or belittle this good is, in this dangerous century when the resources and pretentions of power continue to enlarge, a desperate error of intellectual abstraction. More than this, it is a self-fulfilling error, which encourages us to give up the struggle against bad laws and class-bound procedures, and to disarm ourselves before power. It is to throw away a whole inheritance of struggle about law, and within the forms of law, whose continuity can never be fractured without bringing men and women into immediate danger (Thompson 1975: 266, emphasis added).

Much as we may have reason to be disappointed with the achievements of Indian constitutionalism, we must broaden our vision to see how we have fared comparatively. When one looks across South Asia, and the post-colonial nations in Asia and Africa more generally, one begins to appreciate the value of the struggles of Gandhi and Nehru to establish the foundations of constitutional government in India. If they held fast to a belief in the power of the rule of law while struggling against the dark forces of imperialism, surely we can do so when faced with the challenges of the contemporary?

To 'abandon the site of legal intervention', as has been suggested by some, would, in my view, be a mistake of monumental proportions and would also amount to 'throw[ing] away a whole inheritance of struggle about law'. What is required of progressive communities, instead, is a fulsome re-engagement with the enterprise of PIL with a view to correcting strategic errors of the past and reclaiming ownership over its future.

NOTES

1. *M. H. Hoskot v. State of Maharashtra*, MANU/SC/0119/1978.
2. *Hussainara Khatoon v. Home Secretary*, State of Bihar, MANU/SC/0084/1980.
3. *Sunil Batra v. Delhi Administration*, MANU/SC/0184/1978.
4. *Charles Sobhraj v. Supt. Central Jail*, MANU/SC/0070/1978.
5. *Prem Shankar Shukla v. Delhi Administration*, MANU/SC/0084/1980.
6. *T. V. Vatheeswaran v. State of T.N.*, MANU/SC/0383/1983.
7. *Sheela Barse v. State of Maharashtra*, MANU/SC/0382/1983.
8. *A.G. of India v. Lachma Devi*, MANU/SC/0059/1985.
9. *Bandhua Mukti Morcha v. Union of India*, AIR 1984 SC 802.
10. *Olga Tellis v. Bombay Municipality*, AIR 1985 SC 180.
11. *Lakshmikant Pandey v. Union of India*, AIR 1984 SC 469.
12. *Upendra Baxi v. State of Uttar Pradesh*, (1983) 2 SCC 308.
13. *Vineet Narain v. Union of India*, (1998) 1 SCC 226.
14. *Union of India v. Sushil Kumar Modi*, (1997) 4 SCC 770.
15. Suo Moto Proceedings in Re: Delhi Transport Department, (1998) 9 SCC 250.
16. *M. C. Mehta v. Union of India*, (1998) 9 SCC 381; (1998) 9 SCC 711; (1998) 8 SCC 711.
17. *Research Foundation for Science and Technology v. Union of India*, 1997 (5) SCALE 495.
18. *Dr. Ashok v. Union of India*, (1997) 5 SCC 10.
19. *Vishaka v. Union of India*, (1997) 6 SCC 241.
20. *Chetna v. Union of India*, (1998) 2 SCC 158.
21. *Common Cause v. Union of India*, (1998) 2 SCC 367.
22. 2000 10 SCC 664. Here the Supreme Court allowed the Sardar Sarovar project, which created one of the world's largest dams, to proceed even though a comprehensive environment appraisal had not been conducted. In addition, this affected thousands of tribals and other disempowered groups of people who were forcibly relocated without adequate rehabilitation efforts or compensation.
23. 2003 7 SCALE 54. Again, the Court approved of a large dam project by dispensing with the requirement of an environmental impact assessment programme, and by ignoring an expert committee report which pointed to serious environmental problems.
24. 2003 7 SCALE 589. In this case, the Supreme Court approved a housing project that was to come up on forest land. Its order, according to Bhushan, effectively deprived hundreds of poor fishermen of their livelihood.
25. AIR 1996 SC 2231; MANU/SC/1181/1996. The original case was initiated in 1985, but has had several off-shoots over the years. Several of the orders issued by

the Supreme Court over the last two decades have been helpfully catalogued and reproduced at http://www.elaw.org/resources/regional.asp?region=Asia. (Accessed on 6 August 2013). (See the cases listed as '*M. C. Mehta v. Union of India*'.)

26. (2000) 2 SCC 166; MANU/SC/2767/2000.
27. Baxi (1987a: 172, emphasis added). The same article appeared in the *Indian Bar Review* in 1984, and was probably written in the early 1980s.
28. Baxi (1987b: 32). This piece has appeared in print in several different versions, the earliest of which was in the *Delhi Law Review* in 1979.
29. Baxi (2007: 5). The reference is to Justices Krishna Iyer, Bhagwati, O. Chinappa Reddy and D. A. Desai.
30. *Almitra Patel v. Union of India*, MANU/SC/2767/2000 at para 14.
31. See, for instance, the criticisms voiced by Justices Tulzapurkar and Hidayatullah during the initial stage of the development of PIL, pointing to several troubling aspects of the phenomenon. Tulzapurkar (1983) and Hidayatullah (1984).
32. *Lakshmikant Pandey v. Union of India*, AIR 1984 SC 469.
33. (1998) 1 SCC 226.
34. S. Muralidhar, 'Public Interest Litigation', 33–34 *Annual Survey of Indian Law*.
35. My normative views are influenced by the experimentalist modes of intervention that have been reconstructed by Sabel and Simon after studying successful recent examples of public law litigation in the U.S. See Sabel and Simon (2004).
36. See http://www.righttofoodindia.org/links/updates/update14.html. Accessed on 6 August 2013.
37. *Minister of Health and Ors. v. Treatment Action Campaign*, (2002) 5 SA 721 (CC).

REFERENCES

Bhagwati, P. N. 1985. 'Judicial Activism and Public Interest Litigation'. *Columbia Journal of Transnational Law*, 23 (56): 561–76.

Baxi, Upendra. 1987a. 'On the Shame of Not being an Activist: Thoughts on Judicial Activism'. In *The Role of the Judiciary in Plural Societies*, eds Neelan Tiruchelvam and Radhika Coomaraswamy, 168–78. London: Frances Pinter.

———. 1987b. 'Taking Suffering Seriously'. In *The Role of the Judiciary in Plural Societies*, eds Neelan Tiruchelvam and Radhika Coomaraswamy, 32–60. London: Frances Pinter: London.

———. 2007. 'The Promise and Peril of Transcendental Jurisprudence'. In *Human Rights, Justice and Constitutional Empowerment*, eds C. Raj Kumar and K. Chockalingam, 3–5. New Delhi: Oxford University Press.

Belani, Aarthi. 2004. 'The South African Constitutional Court's Decision in TAC: A "Reasonable" Choice?' Center for Human Rights and Global Justice Working Paper.

Bhushan, Prashant. 2004. 'Supreme Court and PIL: Changing Perspectives under Liberalisation'. *Economic and Political Weekly*, 39 (18): 1770–74. 1 May.

———. 2009. ' Misplaced Priorities and Class Bias of the Judiciary'. *Economic and Political Weekly*, 44 (14): 32–37. 4 April.

Epp, Charles. 1998. *The Rights Revolution: Lawyers, Activists and Supreme Courts in Comparative Perspective*. Chicago: University of Chicago Press.

Forbath, William, with assistance from Zackie Achmat, Geoff Budlender, and Mark Heywood. 2011. 'South Africa's Treatment Action Campaign'. In *Stones of Hope: How African Activists Reclaim Human Rights to Challenge Global Poverty*, eds Lucie E. White and Jeremy Perelman, 1–90. Stanford: Stanford University Press.

Gauri, Varun. 2009. 'Public Interest Litigation in India: Overreaching or Underachieving?' World Bank Policy Research Working Paper No. 5109, November. Available at http://elibrary.worldbank.org/content/workingpaper/10.1596/1813-9450-5109 (accessed on 13 September 2012).

Hidayatullah, M. 1984. 'Highways and Bye-lanes of Justice'. 2 SCC 1-7.

Khosla, Madhav. 2009. 'Addressing Judicial Activism in the Indian Supreme Court: Towards an Evolved Debate'. *Hastings International and Comparative Law Review*, 32: 55–100.

Krishnan, Jayanth. 2003. 'Social Policy Advocacy and the Role of the Courts in India'. 21 *American Asian Review*, 91.

Muralidhar, S. 1997–98. 'Public Interest Litigation'. 33–34 *Annual Survey of Indian Law*. 525.

Ramanathan, Usha. 1996. 'Displacement and Law'. *Economic and Political Weekly*, 31 (24): 1486–91.

———. 2002. 'Of Judicial Power'. *Frontline*, 19 (6). Available at http://www.flonnet.com/fl1906/19060300.htm (accessed on 13 September 2012).

———. 2005. 'Demolition Drive'. *Economic and Political Weekly*, 40 (27): 2908–12.

Sabel, Charles F., and William H. Simon. 2004. 'Destablization Rights: How Public Law Litigation Succeeds'. *Harvard Law Review*, 117 (4): 1015–1101.

Shankar, Shylashri. 2009. *Scaling Justice: India's Supreme Court, Anti-terror Laws, and Social Rights*. New Delhi: Oxford University Press.

Shukla, Rakesh. 2006. 'Rights of the Poor: An Overview of Supreme Court'. *Economic and Political Weekly*, 41 (35): 3755–59.

Thiruvengadam, Arun. 2009. 'Evaluating Criticisms of Contemporary "Public Interest Litigation": A Progressive Conception of the Role of the Indian

Judge'. Draft presented at the LASSNET Conference. New Delhi: Jawaharlal Nehru University.

———. 2013. 'Revisiting "The Role of the Judiciary in Plural Societies (1987)": A Quarter-Century Retrospective on Public Interest Litigation in India and the Global South'. In *Comparative Constitutionalism in South Asia*, eds Sunil Khilnani, Vikram Raghavan and Arun K. Thiruvengadam, 341–69. New Delhi: Oxford University Press.

Thompson, E. P. 1975. *Of Whigs and Hunters: The Origins of the Black Act*. New York: Pantheon Books.

Tulzapurkar, V. D. 1983. 'Judiciary: Attacks and Survival'. *All India Reporter*: 9–18.

7

A Meandering Jurisprudence of the Court

The Evolving Case Law Related to Water

PHILIPPE CULLET

Courts have for many years engaged closely with a variety of water law issues. The spectrum ranges from discussion of the fundamental right to water to irrigation and issues of water pollution. The judiciary has played an important role in adjudicating disputes on the basis of existing legal principles and statutes as well as in developing water law and water-related legal principles.

Since the early 1990s, two significant changes have taken place in the water sector. These fall squarely in the context of the overall process of economic reforms, and direct links between reforms in the water sector and economic reforms can be identified. First, at the policy level, a series of 'water sector reforms' have been introduced to restructure in particular the governance of the water sector with particular emphasis on the management of water.[1] This includes, in particular, proposals to restrict the role that the government plays in managing water resources and institutional reorganisation from the local to the state level.[2] These reforms are in line with the broader economic reforms that have swept through the country since the early 1990s. Second, over the past decade, an attempt has been made to entrench water sector reforms through the introduction of a series of water law reforms (Cullet 2010: 38). Most of these new laws are based on the principles of water sector reforms and seek to ensure the viability of reforms beyond project-specific interventions. These reforms have quick-started a process that will likely lead to an overhaul of water law in coming years.

Over the past two decades, the response of the courts to the unfolding changes has not been linear. Indeed, the case law illustrates that courts have given completely different responses to the issues they were asked to address in different contexts and there is thus no single trend that can be identified. This essay seeks to highlight some of the salient trends of the case law since the early 1990s in the context of water-related cases through the analysis of a limited number of selected cases. The case law reviewed here is neither limited to issues that can be strictly defined as issues of water law nor including all relevant water-related issues since water can be a factor in numerous situations in an indirect manner.

WATER-RELATED DECISIONS IN THE CONTEXT OF WATER SECTOR REFORMS

Courts have taken many water-related decisions since the early 1990s. These decisions have concerned a number of issues ranging from fundamental rights and constitutional issues to private rights. The courts have achieved a number of widely different things through their decisions in the different cases under review. There is no overall trend that comes out of the decisions taken but, in fact, there emerge potential contradictions between different decisions taken in different contexts.

Basic Structure of Water Law

Courts have since 1990 concerned themselves in various cases with the basic structure of water law. Broad statements of the courts generally emphasise the key role of water for life on earth.[3] Courts have recognised the government's duty to 'keep the rivers in the country pure and clean so that the water there is drinkable and free of diseases'.[4] They have also used the basic life-supporting role of water as a basis for inter-state allocation of water, as in the case of the dispute between Delhi and Haryana over additional water supply for Delhi's increasing population.[5]

Fundamental Human Right to Water

Courts have repeatedly discussed water in relation to fundamental rights and have repeatedly asserted the existence of a human right to water. The right has in general been linked to Article 21 and the broader perspective on the right to life that has informed the case law for the past couple of decades.[6]

This right has been upheld at a theoretical level in a variety of decisions at the state and Union levels. Some key characteristics can be highlighted here. Over the past two decades, courts have done little more than confirm and restate the existence of a human right to water. In other words, they have not focussed on the scope and content of the right but rather used it as a building block for the specific decisions they were taking. In certain situations, courts have attempted to circumscribe the scope of the right, as reflected in *Venkatagiriyappa v. Karnataka Electricity Board*, indicating that the right to water does not cover water for irrigation and business purposes.[7] The Karnataka High Court did not consider, however, whether irrigation water for subsistence crops and for livelihood should be treated in the same way, thus refraining from engaging with the more difficult issues concerning the scope of the right.

The more recent case of *Shajimon Joseph v. State of Kerala* addressing the drinking water concerns of the city of Alappuzha makes a useful contribution to the definition of the scope of the right.[8] It specifically provides that the government 'is bound to provide drinking water to the public' and that this should be the foremost duty of the government.[9] Additionally, the judges ruled that the failure of the state to 'provide safe drinking water' to citizens amounted to a violation of Article 21 of the Constitution.[10]

In some cases, the human right to water has been linked first to Article 47 of the Constitution. In *Hamid Khan v. State of Madhya Pradesh*, the government was sued for not taking appropriate precautions to ensure that the drinking water supplied through handpumps in Mandla district was free from excessive fluoride.[11] It was ruled that under Article 47, the state has the responsibility to 'improve the health of public providing unpolluted drinking water'.[12] The judges first ruled on this 'primary responsibility' of the state and then went on to state that Article 21 *also* covers the issue. They concluded on the basis of Articles 47 and 21 that the state has a duty 'towards every citizen of India to provide pure drinking water'.[13]

The case law has also linked water, health and sanitation. In *Dr K. C. Malhotra v. State of Madhya Pradesh*, it was alleged that the Municipal

Corporation of Gwalior and the public health and public health engineering departments had failed in their duty to avoid the spread of an epidemic of cholera, resulting in the death of twelve children in 1991 and further deaths in 1992.[14] The judges ruled that all individuals, even from backward classes and weaker sections, benefit from the protection of Article 21. This put a duty on the government to ensure, for instance, that the *nallah* should be covered and regularly cleaned public conveniences should be provided.[15]

Courts have also engaged with the inter-state aspects of the realisation of water. In *D. M. Singhvi v. Union of India*, the High Court of Rajasthan debated issues related to water that Rajasthan is entitled to receive from the Ravi Beas water under a 1981 agreement.[16] The court determined that the issue was not an inter-state issue because it only concerned control over the supply of water allocated. In the present suit, the concern was to ensure that the state of Punjab was replaced by the Bhakhra Beas Management Board to ensure that Rajasthan gets its full share of water. The High Court ruled in favour of this change on the basis of an argument framed around the fundamental right to water. The court asserted that it was concern for the realisation of the fundamental right to water of farmers in Rajasthan that led it to intervene. It ruled that the dependence of the population in several famine-stricken districts on the water of the Indira Gandhi Nahar for their supply of drinking water for human and cattle was the motive for its intervention.[17] While this case did not directly discuss the responsibility of the state of Punjab towards citizens of another state of the Union, it makes an important link and highlights the need for solidarity between different states of the Union in terms of the realisation of the fundamental right to water.

The aforementioned cases confirm that courts have frequently upheld the human right to water and used it in different contexts. In most cases, the assertion of the human right to water has been made in a context which seeks to expand the realisation of the right to all citizens. There are, however, some cases which are more problematic. This is in particular the case of the 2000 judgement concerning the Sardar Sarovar dam which strongly asserted the right to water of the citizens who were the potential beneficiaries of the project without taking into account the implied negative impacts of this decision on the realisation of the right to water of the oustees.[18]

Ownership of Water

Beyond discussions on the human right to water, courts have engaged with basic principles of water law. In particular, the Supreme Court determined in 1997 that the principle of public trust applies in India to all surface waters.[19] In *M. C. Mehta v. Kamal Nath*, the dispute revolved around interference with the course of a river by property developers as they were seeking to force back the Beas River into a course which would not affect their property interests. The Court started from the premise that '[t]he area being ecologically fragile and full of scenic beauty should not have been permitted to be converted into private ownership and for commercial gains'.[20] It then expanded existing legal concepts and determined that water is covered by the public trust doctrine. The Supreme Court then concluded that where the public trust applies, such resources are meant for public use and cannot be converted into private ownership.[21] This recognition has been re-affirmed.[22] In different words, the High Court of Rajasthan has further stated that '[w]ater is the property of the people of India and is dedicated to their use'.[23]

The crucial recognition by the Supreme Court that water is a public trust has, however, had no impact in practice beyond the specific decisions where courts have used this principle. Indeed, neither have states amended legislation that recognises state ownership of water nor have any of the many legislative enactments concerning water adopted since 1997 taken any notice of this principle. Further, some cases have tended to restrict the application of the principle. In *Mrs Susetha v. State of Tamil Nadu*, the Supreme Court used an earlier statement it had made that the public trust 'does not exactly prohibit the alienation of the property held as a public trust'.[24] In the context of the case at hand where a shopping complex had been sanctioned at the spot of a disused temple tank, the Court found that since there was no shortage of water in the village and since the tank had been unused for a long time, it had to take a 'pragmatic view' of the doctrine of sustainable development and could thus condone the alienation of the property.[25] The only additional element the Court requested was to direct the state and gram panchayat to ensure that *other* tanks in and around the village were properly maintained. This decision seems to empty the principle of public trust from its inner substance since the Court did not base its decision on an assessment of the water needs of the area in long term but only balanced present-day use against availability. One of the basic points of the public trust doctrine is to take a long-term view of the resource conservation and use, something which is in fact also central to the doctrine of sustainable development used here as a basis for the decision.

Overall, in the context of basic issues such as the fundamental right to water and the development of broad principles such as the public trust, two general trends can be noticed. First, courts have not concerned themselves with the detail of the broad principles they have introduced in the legal framework and restricted their contribution to broad pronouncements. Second, neither the legislature nor the executive have taken much notice of courts' decisions. The result is that the legal framework today conceptually includes progressive developments like the formal recognition of the human right to water but little has been done to translate this into the actual instruments that make a difference to people's lives.

Courts have, in certain situations, taken decisions that have had somewhat more immediate large-scale practical consequences. This is, for instance, the case with groundwater where the Supreme Court ignored the lack of specific legislation in this area and, on the basis of existing environmental legislation, directed the Ministry of Environment and Forests to set up a Central Groundwater Authority with the main object of regulating indiscriminate boring and withdrawal of groundwater.[26] The Authority that was set up is mandated to notify 'over-exploited' and 'critical' areas and to regulate groundwater withdrawals in such areas.[27] It does not, however, have a broad mandate to regulate groundwater in general and is not credited with having had much impact in its decade of existence (Shah 2008: 116).

Traditional Water Law Issues

In the long run, courts have devoted most of their attention to water issues in the context of disputes related to real property rights and inter-state issues. Concerning property rights-related issues, frequent recourse to the courts is linked to the absence of a framework water legislation regulating access to and control over water and the reliance of the legal framework for the past many decades on common law principles that link in direct and indirect ways water and land rights. Inter-state issues have been the focus of attention in part because of the existence of a Union legislation that provided a framework for the consideration of disputes between states sharing a watercourse. Since the beginning of the reforms, courts have still considered 'traditional' water issues in a number of cases.

First, courts still discuss water in terms of the property rights of the state. This was not surprising in the case of *N. Sankappa Shetty v. State of Karnataka* that was decided before the 1997 decision making the public trust effective throughout the country.[28] What is more surprising is that in the 2004 *Tekaba v. Sakumeren* decision, where two clans of two villages of Nagaland brought a dispute over the sharing of a source of water governed by customary rules, the Supreme Court simply restated that the 'state is the sovereign dominant owner' of water.[29] This does not coincide with the decisions concerning the public trust and tends to indicate that even at the level of the case law, a clear trend in the development of water law principles can, in fact, not be identified.

Second, courts still concern themselves with property rights-related water claims in different types of cases. Since traditional common law rules link access to water and land rights, the disputes relate in most cases around property rights concerns rather than water concerns. There is, however, nothing fundamentally new to this trend since it is the very structure of riparian and other common law rights that triggers this. In *Orient Papers and Industries Limited v. Tashildar-cum-Irrigation Officer*, a riparian owner had been drawing water since 1939 for the manufacture of paper and for domestic use of employees working in the attached colony. Following the construction of the Hirakud dam, a dispute ensued because it was averred that the riparian owner had lost their pre-existing rights since they were now drawing water from the reservoir of the dam. The conflict was thus over whether the impoundment of the dam had affected the rights of the owner over the river. In substance, the Supreme Court analysed whether riparian rights can be trumped by rights of the state.[30] The Court found that the construction of a dam that creates a reservoir displaces the rights that landowners can claim over running water at common law. This tends to confirm that the state has wide-ranging power over water even where private rights are well established.

In the case of groundwater, where the link between land rights and access to water is even stronger than in the case of surface water, the ongoing litigation concerning a Coca Cola bottling plant in Kerala has brought to the fore the need for significant changes in the basic rules of water law. The first judge who looked at the issue proposed that common law principles were not relevant in the present scenario anymore and the public trust notion should apply to groundwater as well.[31] A subsequent decision of the high court reversed this and suggested that traditional rules that give landowners and occupiers largely unfettered access to groundwater should be upheld.[32] Any future decision of the Supreme Court may suggest extending the application of the public trust to groundwater, but even if this is the case, it is unlikely to do so without qualifications. In the context of this section, the Coca-Cola case illustrates the fact that water law rules introduced in the nineteenth century and that were possibly never appropriate for this country are in any case outdated and need the intervention of the legislature or the courts. In the case of Kerala, the legislature has made a first attempt at moving beyond common law rules with the adoption of groundwater legislation.[33] This is insufficient to address all the social and environmental shortcomings of existing rules because the new legislative framework is built around a technocratic rather than environmental or social perspective. Yet, recent years do not show a trend in favour of building new rules and principles reflecting the present needs of the country. In effect, the single judge's decision in the Coca-Cola case is more the exception that confirms the rule.

Third, courts have continued to address inter-state issues in a number of cases. This includes specific issues such as the sharing of water between Delhi and Haryana concerning the supply of drinking water to Delhi. In *Delhi Water Supply & Sewage Disposal Undertaking v. State of Haryana*, the Court analysed water use from an inter-sectoral perspective and came to the conclusion that the use of water for drinking purposes should prevail.[34] The Court also argued that 'it would be mocking the nature to force the people who live on the bank of a river to remain thirsty', a statement that takes a tint of dark irony when looked at together with the Yamuna Pushta cases analysed later.[35] The Supreme Court has also had occasion to intervene in the broader conflicts concerning the management of watercourses shared by different states even where a special tribunal was set up. This includes interventions in the case of the Cauvery dispute and major decisions in the case of the Sardar Sarovar dam referred to later.

Drinking Water

As indicated in numerous judgements, courts have not failed to give drinking water the priority it deserves in all cases where issues of inter-sectoral allocation of water have arisen. Drinking water has also been frequently mentioned in the context of discussions on the fundamental right to water since it constitutes the core content that all decisions give to the right implied under Article 21 of the Constitution. Yet, while decisions discussing the human right to water mention drinking water on many occasions, drinking water is the immediate focus only in some instances, as in the case of *F. K. Hussain v. Union of India*.[36]

In other cases, drinking water may be conceived within the general context of the fundamental right but addressed from a different perspective. This is, for instance, the case of *Comdr. Sureshwar D. Sinha v. Union of India* wherein the Court considered the issue of drinking water in terms of inter-state allocation of water but did not consider issues related to the use of the water in terms of access to this water by the most disadvantaged groups in Delhi.[37]

In *DLF Universal Ltd v. Prof. A. Lakshmi Sagar*, drinking water was considered from a health and environment perspective in the context of the construction of buildings next to a reservoir used for urban drinking water needs. The Court put a number of conditions for the acceptability of new buildings but did not specifically put drinking water and water quality before other concerns.[38]

In *Municipal Corporation Chandigarh v. Shantikunj Investment* the Court discussed, in the case of commercial properties, whether drinking water should be part of the amenities provided by the municipal corporation. It decided that there was no obligation on the part of the authorities to provide such amenities and that this did not preclude the full enjoyment of the leased properties. In deciding that the lack of amenities such as drinking water did not provide the private investors the right not to pay the amount due under the lease, the Supreme Court only attempted to balance this with a request to the high court to consider whether the lack of such amenities could provide the basis for 'proportionate relief' to the leaseholders.[39] It is likely that the Court would have taken a different view of the matter in the case of residential buildings but this decision seems to indicate that the provision of drinking water to any building, regardless of the use to which it is put, is not compulsory. This is problematic, in particular, in the context of all so-called unauthorised residential colonies.

Courts have also addressed drinking water from the point of view of economic interests involved in its provision. In *Lucknow Grih Swami Parishad v. State of Uttar Pradesh* the Court adjudicated a dispute over the levying of water charges by the Jal Sansthan.[40] In *M/s Noorulla Ghazanfarulla v. Municipal Board of Aligarh,* the Court adjudicated a dispute between a former private supplier of drinking water and the Municipal Board of Aligarh following the revocation of the licence to ensure better supply to the residents.[41] In this case, the Court was concerned with the economic consequences of the takeover and did not specifically consider the issues posed in terms of drinking water.

The question of water quality has also been addressed directly and indirectly in the context of bottled drinking water. In *Cauvery Mineral Waters Private Limited v. Bureau of Indian Standards,* it was found that water which can be used for human consumption as drink or food is not excluded from the definition of food under the Prevention of Food Adulteration Act, 1954.[42] Further, in *Bureau of Indian Standards v. Pepsico India Holdings Private Limited,* in the context of a dispute over the labelling of drinking water as 'pure', it was found that the Bureau of Indian Standards (BIS) has ample power in relation to the labelling of articles and that it can prohibit activities which mislead the public about the nature, origin, composition and properties of any good or article sought to be marketed under the BIS standard mark.[43]

Environment and Water

As indicated in several other chapters of this book, courts have devoted significant attention to environmental issues over the past couple of decades. Their interventions can be divided in two different strands. First, in a number of cases that have been shaping people's perception of the judicial system in India, the Supreme Court has taken a number of decisions often seen as very progressive. Second, in another series of cases, courts have taken decisions that can, at best, be qualified as regressive from a social and environmental point of view (Bhushan 2004). This section examines some of the decisions that have given the court a good name while the next section examines the more problematic decisions, many of which concern water.

In the context of the broad field of decisions seeking to expand the scope of environmental law and strengthen its content, courts have taken a number of decisions that concerned water. The following sample is only representative of decisions framed in an environmental context with water as one of the underlying issues but does not constitute a sample of all relevant environmental decisions.

Courts have often addressed the question of water pollution. The general context for these decisions is often the Water Act, 1974, a water law legislation that is often considered as part of environmental law. In *M. C. Mehta v. Union of India (Calcutta tanneries)*, the case revolved around water pollution caused by tanneries.[44] The Court discussed at length the shifting of the polluting units and the possibility of setting up effluent treatment plants. The importance of this decision is that it affirmed the relevance of the prevention and precautionary principles in the context of water. These central principles of environmental law were thus recognised as applicable to water and by extension as principles of water law in general. Courts have also considered issues of water pollution arising directly under the Water Act.[45]

In *Indian Council for Enviro-Legal Action v. Union of India*, the Court addressed the issue of the pollution of the drinking water sources of the inhabitants of the village of Bicchri in Rajasthan from the point of view of Article 21 of the Constitution. The severe pollution caused by industrial units led the Court to discuss remedial measures from the point of view of liability rules. In a significant move it indicated that the principles developed a decade earlier following the Bhopal tragedy were applicable to the damage caused to the soil and groundwater.[46] This also has indirect consequences on the extent of landowners' control over groundwater as this case clearly indicates that even under the common law rules that still prevail, interests beyond those of the landowners are at stake, at least in the worst cases.[47]

In *Andhra Pradesh Pollution Control Board II v. Prof. M. V. Nayudu (Retd)*, the Supreme Court ruled that the fundamental objective of the Water Act is to provide clean drinking water to people.[48] It decided that the state government was not in a position to grant to a given industry an exception to rules seeking to protect sources of drinking water from pollution. Not only did the Court determine that this was arbitrary and contrary to public interest, but it also ruled that it was a violation of the fundamental right to clean water.[49] Additionally, the Court made the link with the precautionary principle, thus confirming that there can be no distinction between water law, environmental law and human rights.

In the more recent *Tirupur Dyeing Factory Owners Association v. Noyyal River Ayacutdars Protection Association*, the Supreme Court restated the central position of the prevention and precautionary principles and of the guiding notion of sustainable development. The Court acknowledged the central role played by Tirupur in the export of fine garments and the contribution of about Rs 10,000 crores it makes to the nation in addition to providing livelihoods to large number of persons. At the same time, it found that on balance they should ensure no pollution to the river and that industrial units must 'carry out their industrial activities without polluting the water'.[50] Further, it noted that it was the responsibility of the polluting units to meet the expenses involved in tackling environmental damage.

Environment, Water and Fundamental Rights

The intrinsic relationship between water, the environment and human rights has ensured that courts have had to address the links between these different issues. In fact, since water and the environment are also fundamental rights in themselves, the link is always present, though not necessarily acknowledged or visible. In this context, several types of decisions can be highlighted.

First, in some cases, courts have attempted to deal separately with the different issues that arise. In *M. C. Mehta v. Union of India (Calcutta tanneries)* mentioned earlier, the Court addressed the issue mainly from an environmental perspective. Yet, a place is made at the end of the judgement for the consideration of the consequences for workers of the relocation of the tanneries.[51]

Second, courts have sometimes addressed conflicts between different actors. In *Kachchh Jal Sankat Nivaran Samiti v. State of Gujarat*, the high court considered the claims of the people of Kachchh to a higher allocation of the Narmada water allocated to Gujarat.[52] The Court disposed of the case by stating that there was no obligation on the state of Gujarat to revisit the water allocation proposed by the Narmada Water Disputes Tribunal in 1979 and that the petitioners had no enforceable right to demand such a revision.[53] The noteworthy aspect of this case is that the petitioners argued in effect for reviewing water allocation on the basis of water needs, environmental considerations and equity, Kutch being much drier than the rest of the state, less well endowed in water resources and economically poorer. While the government may in principle be in a better position to determine such issues, it is surprising to see the Court siding with the government on the basis that no further time should be wasted depriving the people of the benefits of the Sardar Sarovar Project (SSP).[54] This is even more surprising in a context where the expected benefits of SSP, a project that the government of Gujarat has been promoting for the past several decades, are yet to be delivered to people, even though most of the dam is built (Parasuraman et al. 2010). The Supreme Court refused to interfere with the decision of the high court in its 2011 order.[55]

Third, courts have addressed in several cases the immediate intersection between water, environment and human rights in the context of dam-induced displacement. One of the cases that have attracted most attention over the past couple of decades is that of the SSP. In the main judgement delivered by the Supreme Court on SSP in 2000, judges were forced to consider the different rights of different categories of people. The main judgement adopted a clear line.

On the one hand, Justice Kirpal saw SSP as a project that provided significant benefits to the country as a whole. He went as far as stating that 'large-scale river valley projects per se all over the country have made India more than self-sufficient in food'.[56] He thus approached the issue from the point of view of the benefits of SSP. One of the consequences was that one of the justifications he gave for the project was the realisation of the human right to water of project beneficiaries, a right he clearly acknowledged as part of fundamental rights.

On the other hand, Justice Kirpal determined that displacement did not 'per se result in the violation of [the oustees'] fundamental or other rights'.[57] In his view, the government was in fact making oustees a favour in displacing them. He stated that it was 'not fair that tribals and the people in undeveloped villages should continue in the same condition without ever enjoying the fruits of science and technology for better health and have a higher quality of life style'.[58] As a result, ousting people becomes a positive feature of the dam that will provide the basis for their 'assimilation in the mainstream of the society [and this] will lead to betterment and progress'.[59]

One of the important aspects of Justice Kirpal's judgement is that he turned on their head various principles that are otherwise well settled to justify the catastrophic displacement of an acknowledged 40,827 families (as per the 2000 judgement). Thus, in effect the judgement excludes oustees from the protection of the fundamental right to water and determines without factual basis that their fundamental rights will be better realised after displacement. This is all the more ironical in the case of the fundamental right to water since the people who have been and are being displaced all lived close to the Narmada River that fulfilled in direct and indirect ways most of their fundamental living needs, as well as livelihood needs.

The environmental dimension of the project was also a major issue in the context of the 2000 judgement. Indeed, whether the required environmental clearance was in fact granted in 1987 or not, the main issue is that since 1994 a legal framework made it binding to undertake a full environmental impact assessment that was valid for only five years.[60] On any of these counts, SSP should have been subjected to a full impact assessment procedure. Justice Kirpal, however, chose a different line of argument and not only condoned the insufficient assessment undertaken but also justified the dam on other grounds by, for instance, arguing that in an era where global warming matters, a dam that displaces more people than a thermal power plant is preferable because the 'pollution caused by the thermal plant and the adverse effect on the neighbourhood could be far greater than the inconvenience caused in shifting and rehabilitating the oustees of a reservoir'.[61]

The 2000 judgement has been followed by a string of other judicial interventions in the case of SSP. While the judgement given in 2005 by the Court showed that the plight of the oustees had eventually been heard with a kinder ear by the judges, a string of orders coming up in the following year was again on the whole unfavourable to the grievances of the oustees who were at this stage not even asking for the project to be stopped but only for the promised rehabilitation package to be effectively implemented (Cullet 2007: 1). Yet, the actual clearance for the last remaining stretch of the dam was not provided immediately and it was only in early 2010 that a 'conditional' clearance was granted by the environment sub-group of the Narmada Control Authority while further litigation goes on (Parsai 2010).

Fourth, courts have in the past decade taken an increasingly keen interest in matters of urban planning. In Delhi, in particular, courts have been proactive in using environmental arguments to justify displacement. Beyond cases concerning industry relocation that are not water-specific, one of the cases that attracts attention in the context of this chapter is the displacement of people in the area known as Yamuna Pushta. The decisions taken here must be seen in the context the Delhi-Haryana case mentioned earlier where the Court argued that people living near the bank of the river should not remain thirsty.

Yamuna Pushta was a settlement near the river. In the broader process of so-called beautification and preparation for the Commonwealth Games 2010, the whole settlement was destroyed. This was challenged in the high court. In *Wazirpur Bartan Nirmata Sangh v. Union of India*, the court made a number of significant findings. First, it asserted that the pollution that affects the Yamuna is caused not only by the dumping of industrial or medical waste but also caused by the fact that the river's embankment has been 'unauthorizedly and illegally encroached by construction'.[62] Second, in a city where a large part of the sewage flows into the same Yamuna River untreated, the court lambasted the residents of Yamuna Pushta for constructing houses with no drainage facility.[63]

The court then used the holy status of the Yamuna in religious terms to label its present pollution as 'shocking'.[64] This led the court to put a duty on all residents of Delhi to cooperate in addressing this problem but at the same time to single out the special duty of people living along the banks of the river. As a result, the court could say that the removal of houses on the embankment would 'help not (*sic*) few but all the citizens of Delhi as river Yamuna is the lifeline, for the Capital'.[65] In an earlier order, the court had been even more precise in determining who had what kinds of rights. On the one hand, it found that the residents of Yamuna Pushta had no legal right to stay in the bed of the Yamuna. It also termed the destruction of their houses and consequent displacement an 'inconvenience'.[66] On the other hand, it argued in effect that the other residents of Delhi had a right to demand this sacrifice from their co-residents because the construction of houses on the river bed would 'convert Yamuna into a huge sewage drain causing irreparable damage to the vast majority of the citizens of Delhi'.[67]

One of the key points to emerge from this judgement is the court's statement that '[t]he right of people of Delhi to have clean potable water from river Yamuna and health and friendly environment from its bed and embankment is a constitutional right'.[68] This confirms Justice Kirpal's rationale in the 2000 Sardar Sarovar judgement that justified the project in terms of the fundamental rights of the people of India while deciding that oustees were being made a favour by the state. In other words, in Delhi it is only certain kinds of people that benefit from the constitutional or fundamental rights that the court recognises.

EVOLVING CASE LAW AND WATER SECTOR/LAW REFORMS

The survey of some of the decisions taken by courts during the period that has seen the introduction of major economic reforms and more specifically major reforms in the water sector as well as significant changes in water law shows that there is no single trend that emerges.

First, water law remains relatively undefined in the sense that water law is made of various layers including constitutional principles, Union and state acts, common law principles and customary principles. Additionally, what constitutes water law itself is subject to debate because water, like the environment, pervades many other areas of the law. This is possibly more acute in the context of water where the only Union legislation adopted since the 1970s is the Water (Prevention and Control of Pollution) Act, 1974, which has been considered as much as an environmental legislation as part of water law. The response of courts to what is in effect a legal maze is understandably not straightforward. Additionally, water law has been quickly evolving over the past fifteen years in the context of water sector reforms. This explains in part why certain decisions focus on certain principles or provisions while others do something different. Yet, this is problematic because it is, for instance, in part the lack of a clear understanding of the scope of the fundamental human right to water that leads some judges to take decisions that in effect prioritise the realisation of the right for certain categories of people at the expense of others who are usually among the poorer and more disenfranchised sections of society.

Second, the case law is not consistent with regard to the principles that are applied. Thus, whereas the principle of public trust has been clearly accepted as applicable throughout the country, this has not stopped the same Supreme Court affirming that the state is the sovereign dominant owner of water. With regard to the human right to water, a similar phenomenon surfaces. On the one hand, the right has been repeatedly asserted in a variety of contexts. On the other hand, in cases like dam-related or urban displacement, the fundamental right is used in such a way that its realisation for some comes at the cost of the realisation of human rights for other people. The argument according to which oustees are only 'inconvenienced' and that certain things need to be done for the broader social or environmental welfare is suspicious in a fundamental rights context because it undermines the very essence of a human rights perspective that emphasises the primacy of the situation of the poorest and most disenfranchised.

Third, the case law of the period that has seen significant economic and water sector reforms does not reflect the tremendous policy and law changes that have occurred over the past fifteen years. To some extent, this reflects the fact that decisions taken by the courts often concern issues that arose long before they reach the higher judiciary. This is also due to the fact that water sector reforms were in the first place introduced mostly through projects that did not necessarily imply changes in the existing legal framework. Further, this reflects the lack of attention that civil society has given to the adoption of all the new water laws that have come up over the past decade or so. Indeed, water law reforms have been characterised by their lack of visibility. As a result, while water has been one of the areas where major reforms largely based on the broader principles of overall economic reforms have been adopted, this has not yet reached the stage where courts adjudicate cases related to water law reforms. The present case law points to two different directions that courts may take when faced with water law reform-related cases. On the one hand, they may use these cases to give more content to some of the broad principles they have introduced or recognised in the legal framework such as the public trust and the human right to water. On the other hand, they may follow the kinds of arguments used in displacement-related cases by emphasising the new economic rationale that recent water laws give to most issues in the water sector and confirm, for instance, that water being an economic good, urban-dwellers are worthier of accessing it than the people displaced by a dam that contributes to the drinking water supply of cities.

Fourth, the case law reviewed shows that certain issues are recurrent while other issues do not surface. This is in part due to the types of cases that are brought to courts but the point is still to be noted. Some of the issues that attract significant judicial attention include property rights-related issues, broad issues such as constitutional principles, adjudication related to major development projects such as dams and urban planning. Some of the issues that do not feature prominently in the case law include drinking water needs in rural areas, irrigation needs of small farmers and the problems associated with urban/rural inequalities inbuilt in the drinking water policy framework.

Water has been, is and will be one of the most fundamental issues that the judiciary has to address in terms of its importance to people's daily lives and the environment in general. The progression of the case law shows that courts have over the past couple of decades attempted to address some of the shortcomings of water law with respect to the lack of a framework legislation that sets out the basic principle governing water. Courts have also attempted to react to the fact that a lot of water law on the statute books as well as other general principles of water law are in a number of cases antiquated and not adapted to current realities.

At the same time, courts have looked at water with traditional eyes when it comes to certain issues such as major economic development projects or urban planning and development. Rather than emphasising the basic nature of water as key to human survival, agriculture and civilisation, courts have looked at water from the perspective of its contribution to aggregate economic development and thereby emphasised the position of the already privileged people in society. While this has not taken place directly in the context of ongoing water law reforms, these decisions fall within the broader paradigm of the economic reforms and the new economic ethos that has developed over the past two decades. On this basis, it is not impossible that the case law will evolve towards further radicalisation when judges start adjudicating disputes related to new legal frameworks. Given the emphasis on the notion that water is an economic good in ongoing water sector reforms and water law reforms, it is likely that the case law may increasingly foster the approach proposed in all the policy documents adopted over the past decade.

NOTES

1. For example, World Bank, Water Resources Sector Strategy: Strategic Directions for World Bank Engagement (2004).
2. For example, World Bank, India—Water Resources Management Sector Review: Report on the Irrigation Sector (Report No. 18416 IN, 1998), Chapter 3. Accessed on 27 July 2013.
3. *D. M. Singhvi v. Union of India* AIR 2005 Raj 280 (High Court of Rajasthan [Jaipur Bench], 2005), available at ielrc.org/content/e0513.pdf. Accessed on 27 July 2013.
4. *Mahendra Prasad Sonkar and Surya Prakash Singh v. State of Uttar Pradesh through Secretary Urban-Development* (High Court of Allahabad, 2004), available at ielrc.org/content/e0414.pdf. Accessed on 27 July 2013.
5. *Delhi Water Supply and Sewage Disposal Undertaking v. State of Haryana* AIR 1996 SC 2992 (Supreme Court, 1996), available at ielrc.org/content/e9603.pdf. Accessed on 27 July 2013.
6. *Subhash Kumar v. State of Bihar* AIR 1991 SC 420 (Supreme Court, 1991), available at ielrc.org/content/e9108.pdf. Accessed on 27 July 2013.
7. *Venkatagiriyappa v. Karnataka Electricity Board, Bangalore* 1999 (4) KarLJ 482 (High Court of Karnataka, 1998), available at ielrc.org/content/e9813.pdf. Accessed on 27 July 2013.
8. *Shajimon Joseph v. State of Kerala*, 2007 (1)KLT368 (High Court of Kerala, 2006), available at ielrc.org/content/e0631.pdf. Accessed on 27 July 2013.
9. Ibid.: para 5. Similarly, in *Lucknow Grih Swami Parishad v. State of Uttar Pradesh* 2000(3)AWC2139 (High Court of Allahabad [Lucknow Bench], 2000) (available at ielrc.org/content/e0013.pdf, accessed on 27 July 2013), para 4, the Court ruled that 'it is the bounden duty of the State to assure the supply of sufficient amount of qualitative drinking water to its people'.
10. *Shajimon Joseph v. State of Kerala*, para 5.
11. *Hamid Khan v. State of Madhya Pradesh* AIR 1997 MP 191 (Madhya Pradesh High Court, 1996), available at ielrc.org/content/e9613.pdf. Accessed on 27 July 2013.
12. Ibid.: para 6.
13. Ibid.
14. *Dr K. C. Malhotra v. State of Madhya Pradesh* AIR 1994 MP 48 (Madhya Pradesh High Court, 1993), available at ielrc.org/content/e9310.pdf. Accessed on 27 July 2013.

15. Ibid.: para 14.
16. *DM Singhvi v. Union of India.*
17. Ibid.: para 15.
18. *Narmada Bachao Andolan v. Union of India* AIR 2000 SC 3751 (Supreme Court, 2000), available at ielrc.org/content/c0001.pdf. Accessed on 27 July 2013. See further the section 'Environment, Water and Fundamental Rights'.
19. *M. C. Mehta v. Kamal Nath* (1997) 1 SCC 388 (Supreme Court, 1996), available at ielrc.org/content/e9615.pdf. Accessed on 27 July 2013.
20. Ibid.: para 22.
21. Ibid.: para 34.
22. *Intellectuals Forum, Tirupathi v. State of Andhra Pradesh* AIR 2006 SC 1350 (Supreme Court, 2006), available at ielrc.org/content/e0606.pdf. Accessed on 27 July 2013.
23. *DM Singhvi v. Union of India*, para 15.
24. *Intellectuals Forum, Tirupathi v. State of Andhra Pradesh*, para 60.
25. *Mrs Susetha v. State of Tamil Nadu* AIR 2006 SC 2893 (Supreme Court of India, 2006), para 9, available at ielrc.org/content/e0608.pdf. Accessed on 27 July 2013.
26. *M. C. Mehta v. Union of India* (groundwater case) (1997) 11 SCC 312 (Supreme Court, 1996).
27. Ministry of Environment and Forests, Gazette Notifications SO38 and SO1024 of 14 January 1997 and 6 November 2000.
28. *N. Sankappa Shetty v. State of Karnataka* 1992 (3) Kar LJ 474 (High Court of Karnataka, 1992), available at ielrc.org/content/e9212.pdf. Accessed on 27 July 2013.
29. *Tekaba v. Sakumeren* AIR 2004 SC 3674 (Supreme Court, 2004), available at ielrc.org/content/e0408.pdf. Accessed on 27 July 2013.
30. *Orient Papers and Industries Limited v. Tashildar-cum-Irrigation Officer* AIR 1998 SC 3330 (Supreme Court, 1998), available at ielrc.org/content/e9807.pdf. Accessed on 27 July 2013.
31. *Perumatty Grama Panchayat v. State of Kerala* 2004 (1) KLT 731 (High Court of Kerala, 2003), available at ielrc.org/content/e0415.pdf. Accessed on 27 July 2013.
32. *Hindustan Coca-Cola Beverages v. Perumatty Grama Panchayat* 2005 (2) KLT 554 (High Court of Kerala, 2005), available at ielrc.org/content/e0515.pdf. Accessed on 27 July 2013.
33. Kerala Ground Water (Control and Regulation) Act, 2002, available at ielrc.org/content/e0208.pdf. Accessed on 27 July 2013.
34. *Delhi Water Supply and Sewage Disposal Undertaking v. State of Haryana* AIR 1996 SC 2992 (Supreme Court, 1996), available at ielrc.org/content/e9603.pdf. Accessed on 27 July 2013.
35. Ibid. and see the section II.6.
36. *F. K. Hussain v. Union of India* AIR 1990 Ker 321 (High Court of Kerala, 1990), available at ielrc.org/content/e9002.pdf.

37. *Comdr Sureshwar D. Sinha v. Union of India* (2000)8 SCC 368 (Supreme Court, 2000), available at ielrc.org/content/e0006.pdf.
38. *DLF Universal Ltd v. Prof. A. Lakshmi Sagar*, AIR 1998 SC 3369 (Supreme Court, 1998), available at ielrc.org/content/e9805.pdf.
39. *Municipal Corporation Chandigarh v Shantikunj Investment* AIR 2006 SC 1270 (Supreme Court, 2006) available at ielrc.org/content/e0613.pdf.
40. *Lucknow Grih Swami Parishad v. State of Uttar Pradesh* 2000(3) AWC 2139 (High Court of Allahabad [Lucknow Bench], 2000), available at ielrc.org/content/e0013.pdf.
41. *M/s Noorulla Ghazanfarulla v. Municipal Board of Aligarh*, AIR 1995 SC 1058 (Supreme Court of India, 1995), available at ielrc.org/content/e9504.pdf.
42. *Cauvery Mineral Waters Private Limited v. Bureau of Indian Standards* 2003 (1) KarLJ265 (Karnataka High Court, 2002), available at ielrc.org/content/e0224.pdf.
43. *Bureau of Indian Standards v. Pepsico India Holdings Private Limited* 2008 INDLAW DEL 1591 (Delhi High Court, 2008), para 23.
44. *M. C. Mehta v. Union of India* 1996 (9) SCALE 397 (Supreme Court, 1996), available at ielrc.org/content/e9710.pdf. Accessed on 27 July 2013.
45. *State of Madhya Pradesh v. Kedia Leather & Liquor Ltd* AIR 2003 SC 3236 (Supreme Court, 2003), available at ielrc.org/content/e0311.pdf; and *Akhil Bharat Gosewa Sangh v. State of Andhra Pradesh* 2006 (3) SCALE 617 (Supreme Court, 2006), available at ielrc.org/content/e0615.pdf.
46. *Indian Council for Enviro-Legal Action v. Union of India* AIR 1996 SC 1446 (Supreme Court, 1996), available at ielrc.org/content/e9605.pdf. Accessed on 27 July 2013.
47. For the current understanding of groundwater rules in less extreme cases, see *Hindustan Coca-Cola Beverages v. Perumatty Grama Panchayat* 2005 (2) KLT 554 (High Court of Kerala, 2005), available at ielrc.org/content/e0515.pdf. Accessed on 27 July 2013.
48. *Andhra Pradesh Pollution Control Board II v. Prof. M. V. Nayudu (Retd)* 2000 (3) SCALE 354 (Supreme Court, 2000), available at ielrc.org/content/e0010.pdf. Accessed on 27 July 2013.
49. Ibid.: para 43.
50. *Tirupur Dyeing Factory Owners Association v. Noyyal River Ayacutdars Protection Association* (Supreme Court, 2009), para 27, available at ielrc.org/content/e0904.pdf. Accessed on 27 July 2013.
51. *M. C. Mehta v. Union of India* 1996 (9) SCALE 397 (Supreme Court, 1996), available at ielrc.org/content/e9710.pdf. Accessed on 27 July 2013.
52. *Kachchh Jal Sankat Nivaran Samiti v. State of Gujarat* (High Court of Gujarat at Ahmedabad, 2005), available at ielrc.org/content/c0509.pdf. Accessed on 27 July 2013.
53. Ibid.: para 33.
54. Ibid.: para 25.

55. *Kachchh Jal Sankat Nivaran Samiti v. State of Gujarat* 2011 (8) SCALE 26 (Supreme Court, 2011), available at ielrc.org/content/c1104.pdf. Accessed on 27 July 2013.
56. *Narmada Bachao Andolan v. Union of India* AIR 2000 SC 3751 (Supreme Court, 2000), available at ielrc.org/content/c0001.pdf, para 265. Accessed on 27 July 2013.
57. Ibid.: para 91.
58. Ibid.: para 267.
59. Ibid.: para 91.
60. Environmental Impact Assessment Notification, 1994.
61. *Narmada Bachao Andolan v. Union of India* AIR 2000 SC 3751 (Supreme Court, 2000), available at ielrc.org/content/c0001.pdf, para 278. Accessed on 27 July 2013.
62. *Wazirpur Bartan Nirmata Sangh v. Union of India* (High Court of Delhi, 29 September 2006), para 9.
63. Ibid.: para 9.
64. Ibid.: para 10.
65. Ibid.: para 10.
66. *Wazirpur Bartan Nirmata Sangh v. Union of India* (High Court of Delhi, 20 July 2006).
67. *Wazirpur Bartan Nirmata Sangh v. Union of India* (High Court of Delhi, 1 June 2006).
68. Ibid.

REFERENCES

Bhushan, Prashant. 2004. 'Supreme Court and PIL'. *Economic and Political Weekly*, 39 (18): 1770–74.

Cullet, Philippe. 2007. 'The Sardar Sarovar Dam Project: An Overview'. In *Sardar Sarovar Dam Project: Selected Documents*, ed. P. Cullet, 1–4. Aldershot: Ashgate.

———. 2010. 'Water Law—Evolving Regulatory Framework'. In *Water Governance in Motion: Towards Socially and Environmentally Sustainable Water Laws*, eds P. Cullet, A. Gowlland-Gualtieri, R. Madhav, and U. Ramanathan, 26–52. New Delhi: Cambridge University Press.

Parasuraman, S., H. Upadhyaya and G. Balasubramanian. 2010. 'Sardar Sarovar Project: The War of Attrition'. *Economic and Political Weekly*, 45 (5): 39–48.

Parsai, Gargi. 2010. 'Conditional Clearance for Crest Gates at Narmada Dam'. *The Hindu*, 8 May. Available at http://www.thehindu.com/todays-paper/tp-national/tp-newdelhi/conditional-clearance-for-crest-gates-at-narmada-dam/article763121.ece. Accessed on 27 July 2013.

Shah, T. 2008. 'Groundwater Management and Ownership: Rejoinder'. *Economic and Political Weekly*, 48 (17): 116–19.

World Bank. 1998. *India—Water Resources Management Sector Review: Report on The Irrigation Sector*. World Development Sources. WDS 1998-3. Washington, DC. http://documents.worldbank.org/curated/en/1998/09/442139/india-water-resources-management-sector-review-report-irrigation-sector. Accessed on 27 July 2013.

———. 2004. 'Water Resources Sector Strategy: Strategic Directions for World Bank Engagement'. Washington. DC.: World Bank.

8

The Judicial Nineties

Of Politics, Power and Dissent

UJJWAL KUMAR SINGH

The 1990s have often been seen as marking a significant turn in the way in which public and political institutions have responded to and simultaneously embodied the changes that informed the decade and endured thereafter.[1] Following the course of its neo-liberal policies, the state in the 1990s withdrew steadily from certain social and economic sectors, relinquishing them to private and global capital. This selective withdrawal was accompanied, however, with the state's hyper-visibility with the expansion of 'governmentality' and 'law and order' functions. Enframed by the logic of masculinist protection,[2] the state reincarnated itself as the security state, with an unprecedented reinforcement of its coercive apparatus through the enactment of new extraordinary laws and vigorous application of existing ones against a range of people's struggles.[3] The politics of negation, passive obedience and willing submission that the security state is embedded in, was ironically unfolding in a period of a deepening of the social base of electoral democracy in India, and popular movements around issues concerning livelihood, land, access to natural resources, struggle for regional autonomy and self-determination.

In the light of the aforementioned, in this essay one would examine the manner in which the Supreme Court has emerged as 'an institution of the 1990s'. As an institution located simultaneously in the domain of the state entrusted with certain 'refereeing' and 'restraining' functions (Kapur and Mehta 2005: 10), and in the realm of social action devolving from its constitutional role as the custodian and guarantor of people's rights (Baxi 2002), the judiciary manifests a precarious ambivalence. Even as it has discharged its constitutional mandate as the guardian of the fundamental rights of citizens, the Supreme Court has shown inconsistency in the way it has looked at personal liberties and civil rights, and the socio-economic and cultural rights of groups, collectivities and communities, especially those that are articulated by radical movements and people's struggles and reside in the residual domain of people's natural rights, rather than in the realm of enumerated/legal rights.

In this essay, one would show how in the 1990s the judiciary took a 'conservative turn', often becoming a surrogate state itself. This conservative turn, one would argue, was characteristic of the functioning of public institutions, which despite differentiated interests show a degree of interlocking, convergence and ideological homogeneity. Yet, even under the most homogeneous of ideological constellations, public institutions often compete with each other, setting limits to other institutions (Kapur and Mehta 2005: 9). Moreover, while public institutions in their structure and functioning represent some degree of state power, they also embody the conflict that lies at the heart of modern politics, between the universal ideals of individual freedoms and equal rights, and the demands for differential treatment of particular groups on grounds of vulnerability, backwardness or historical injustice (Chatterjee 2004). This opposition, argues Chatterjee, characterises the transition that has occurred in modern politics, from a conception of democratic politics grounded in the idea of popular sovereignty to one which is shaped by governmentality. At a more fundamental level, even when the relative powers of the judiciary and the political and representative organs of the state, in particular the legislature, have been a matter of contest, wielding a fair share of state-power, the courts have veered towards a preservation and conservation role.

It may be possible to see the 'state-power' aspect of the Supreme Court as having followed and strengthened in the post-Emergency phase, through an accumulation of social action litigation and judicial activism whereby it also got deeply embroiled in governing and making policy interventions. It may be possible also to propose at this point that the judiciary's active involvement in governance coincided with changes in the electoral-political process. The disintegration of the 'Congress system' and the reconfiguration of the party system into a 'competitive multi-party system' accompanied by the 'second democratic upsurge',[4] opened up spaces for marginal political parties and intensified electoral contests. It is no less significant that this period was also marked by a progressive decrease in trust in the political process and representative institutions, and a commensurate increase in the credibility of non-elected public institutions such as the Election Commission and the Supreme Court. Located outside 'criminalised' politics, these institutions could garner a fair degree of trust among people, and step into the public domain as bodies that could be called upon to monitor and regulate the multitudinous churnings in politics.

These two processes—the active role of the Supreme Court in the processes of governance and policy-making, and its emergence as a visible and trusted organ of the state—unfolded in the late 1980s and in the 1990s in the phenomenon of 'judicialisation of politics', whereby the judiciary became a surrogate for political engagements between the state and the 'people' and also participated in the legitimation practices of the neo-liberal security state. This is evident in the manner in which the Supreme Court upheld the constitutional validity of extraordinary laws (Armed Forces Special Powers Act [AFSPA], Terrorist and Disruptive Activities (Prevention) Act [TADA] and Prevention of Terrorism Act [POTA]) and accepted a 'hands-off' approach in economic policy matters. Moreover, in its surrogacy and legitimation functions the judiciary subscribed to the reason of state, demurred from expanding the domain of people's rights and legitimated curbs on personal liberties of citizens by taking recourse to a procedural argument hinged on legislative competence. On the other hand, as a referee institution it widened the scope of political rights (in particular the right to political participation and the freedom of speech and expression) in the electoral domain, and determined the relative powers of political and statutory institutions. Ironically, the rights which were affirmed by the Supreme Court as crucial for the effective functioning of electoral democracy were not considered critical for citizens when the court set them aside while affirming extraordinary (anti-terror) laws. Significantly, while curbing civil liberties and democratic rights under the regime of extraordinary laws, the court espoused the position that rights are granted by the state and can therefore also be withdrawn by the state.

To explore the aforementioned, this essay identifies two sets of judgements—those delivered in the *Union of India v. Association for Democratic Reforms and Another*, affirming the citizen's 'right to know', and another set of judgements upholding TADA (*Kartar Singh v. State of Punjab 1994*) and AFSPA (*Naga People's Movement of Human Right v. Union of India 1997*) and those delivered in various TADA cases. The decision of the Supreme Court in the first set of judgements was premised on the claim by the judges that judicial interpretation should consistently aim at the expansion of fundamental rights. A different figuration of rights is seen in the second set of judgements in which the Supreme Court accepted the definition of exceptional circumstances in which the personal liberties of citizens may be curtailed and expression of political dissent thwarted.

ELECTORAL/POLITICAL PARTICIPATION: THE CITIZEN-VOTER AND THE 'RIGHT TO KNOW'

The Supreme Court judgement affirming 'the right to know' of the citizen-voter came in the context of an appeal by the Central government against a Delhi High Court judgement of 2 November 2000, directing the Election Commission to seek information on the background, assets and capability of candidates contesting elections. The judgement came in response to a petition filed by the Association for Democratic Reforms (ADR) asking for directions from the court for the implementation of the recommendations made in the 170th report of the Law Commission. Armed with the mandate to suggest measures for making the electoral process fair, transparent and equitable, the Law Commission reviewed the Representation of the People Act, 1951, and recommended that a candidate contesting elections must furnish details of criminal cases against him/her and assets owned by him/her and dependent family members. Upholding ADR's petition the high court stressed that in order to make the right choice, the voter needed to know whether the candidate was worthy of his/her vote. It directed the Election Commission to 'secure' such information for the voters.

The Central government joined by the Indian National Congress appealed the Supreme Court against the high court's judgement contending that instead of the Election Commission, the Court should have addressed Parliament for the implementation of the Law Commission's recommendations. The petitioners argued that while disqualifications based on offences and corrupt practices and procedures for filing nomination papers were already present in the Representation of the People Act, 'non-disclosure' of information was *not* a disqualification under the Act and the Election Commission's directions to elicit such information should not, therefore, have been issued. Making 'disclosure' of facts binding on candidates, the Supreme Court, like the high court, asserted that the courts were ultimately addressing the fundamental rights of the people and the principles of democratic participation. Declaring that democracy could not survive 'without free and fair elections, without free and fairly informed voters', that votes cast by 'uninformed voters' would be 'meaningless', the judges enunciated the right of voters *to know*. Construing the 'casting of votes' as a form of 'speech and expression', they averred that 'the voter speaks out ... by casting the vote'. In order for the act of voting to be meaningful and fulfilling for both the voter and for the political community of which the citizen-voter was a part, they argued for enabling conditions, which would compel the 'little man'...'to think'...'before making his choice of electing law-breakers as lawmakers'.

Significantly, while articulating the citizen's right to know, the Supreme Court also widened the scope of the Election Commission's constitutional powers to superintend and conduct elections. The judges expanded the scope of Article 324, not merely vesting residuary powers in the Election Commission, but also envisaging it as a 'reservoir of powers', 'where law [was] silent' (*Mohinder Singh Gill v. The Chief Election Commissioner*, New Delhi 1978: SC 405), giving scope for the exercise of residuary power in an infinite variety of situations.[5]

In a 'rare show of consensus' the political parties rejected the Election Commission's directive which made it mandatory for candidates contesting the Parliament and state assembly elections to furnish 'disclosures'. Claiming the privilege of representing the 'political domain' and its authority to legislate on matters concerning it, Parliament sough to 'neutralise' the Supreme Court order and the Election Commission directives by promulgating the Representation of the People (Amendment) Ordinance on 24 August 2002, replaced later by the Representation of the People (Third) Amendment Act. Under the amended Act, a candidate contesting election was not required to disclose his/her assets and liabilities, the criminal charges against him/her and his/her educational qualification.[6] Once a person was acquitted or discharged of any criminal offence, there was no necessity of disclosing the same to the voters. Information regarding the assets of the candidate was not to be disseminated at the time of election, but to be disclosed to the Speaker of the House *after* a candidate was elected. While the spirit of the Supreme Court judgement had been to equip the voter with maximum information to enable him/her to exercise the vote judiciously, the amended Act preferred to inform the voter only selectively.

The amended Act was challenged in the Supreme Court by the People's Union for Civil Liberties (PUCL), Lok Satta and ADR. In its judgement delivered on 13 March 2003, in the case *People's Union for Civil Liberties & Another v. Union of India & Another*, the Supreme Court declared the amendment null and void. In the process of delivering the judgement the Supreme Court revisited the relative powers of the Election Commission and Parliament, examined the scope of the legislative powers that Parliament claimed with the insertion of Article 33B in the amended Act and reaffirmed the right to information as an integral part of the democratic right to vote. Striking down the newly inserted Article 33B as invalid, the judges reasserted the premises of the earlier judgement holding that the right to know the antecedents of a candidate was a fundamental right of the voter 'independent of statutory rights under the election law':

> The attempt of courts should be to expand the reach and ambit of the fundamental rights by a process of judicial interpretation. There cannot be any distinction between the fundamental rights mentioned in Chapter III of the Constitution and the declaration of such rights on the basis of the judgments rendered by the Supreme Court.[7]

EXTRAORDINARY LAWS AND THE SUPREME COURT: POLITICS BY OTHER MEANS

Identification of 'extraordinary' situations and their rectification through a separate set of laws justified as *necessary* exceptions to the rule of law has a long history in India. It is assumed that in exceptional circumstances 'normal' legal procedures may be set aside and citizens' rights curtailed. Notions of 'public order' and 'morality' figure prominently in the Constitution as grounds for waiving the fundamental rights of citizens. Yet the waiving of rights of citizens has to take place within a framework of safeguards that the Constitution provides. Thus, when the Constitution provides for preventive detention under Article 22(7), it also lays down the precise procedural framework setting the conditions in which detention can take place. While the Constitution envisages extraordinary powers as exceptions, to be used sparingly and in the last resort, they have been used by successive governments against political dissent of all hues through preventive detention acts (like the Preventive Detention Act, 1950, National Security Act, 1980 and the various Disturbed Areas Acts) and substantive acts like the AFSPA, TADA and POTA whose provisions allow/allowed long durations of imprisonment without charges being drawn. The Supreme Court has upheld the constitutionality of each of these acts, validating the power of the executive to decide that an extraordinary situation in fact exists, and citing 'security of the state' as a compelling condition necessitating the curtailment of the rights of citizens. This section will show how the Supreme Court judgements upholding the validity of AFSPA, TADA and POTA, respectively, affirmed the contests and ideological shifts that were taking place in the state and politics in India. This affirmation may be seen to have occurred in the following two ways.

Procedural Contours of the Exception and Adversarial Politics

In its judgements in TADA cases and its validation of TADA, AFSPA[8] and later POTA, the Supreme Court in particular and the judiciary in general meticulously reinforced the legal and procedural contours of the exception. In specific cases tried under TADA and POTA the Supreme Court managed to present the most precise othering and 'legal excision' of communities and groups from the national-political, buttressed by the projection of a need to protect the 'us' under threat from the 'enemy within'. Simultaneously, the Court also reinforced notions of the hegemonic nation state, giving perhaps the most emphatic endorsement to the spectre of 'national security' as a persuasive reason for suspending rights and delimiting the boundaries of acceptable political activity. In the process it confirmed the Schmittian proposition that the 'exception' is the *only* condition where the political is fully manifested, not only because it requires the assertion and affirmation of sovereign authority, but also because it assumes the existence of fundamental and intense antagonism of the nature of 'existential negation' between political entities, which compels/precipitates such assertion.[9]

Writing about the fate of personal liberty in India after independence, K. G. Kannabiran has argued that 'in the matter of personal liberty the courts have by and large, as a matter of policy, validated the conferment of vast powers to the executive' (2003: 50). It is not surprising, therefore, that while the Supreme Court defended the 'right to know' of the citizen-voter, buttressing procedural/electoral democracy, by upholding the constitutional validity of extraordinary laws like POTA, it effectively curtailed the right to freedom of expression, to organise, mobilise and collectively express ideological/political dissent or struggle for the institutionalisation and recognition of socio-economic and cultural rights of groups/communities. In the history of extraordinary laws, this was made evident more recently in the case of now repealed POTA. Chapter III (Sections 18 to 22) of POTA dealing with banning of 'terrorist organisations' imposed stringent curbs on political activity by organisations declared 'terrorist' and notified as such in the schedule of the Act. Immediately after the promulgation of POTO on 24 October 2001, the government announced a list of twenty-three banned organisations,[10] which for the first time included groups from Jammu and Kashmir. Several of these banned organisations were associated with political movements. Section 21 of POTA made it an offence to 'invite support for a terrorist organisation', and to 'arrange, manage, or assist in arranging or managing a meeting which is to support a terrorist organisation'. Significantly, for the purposes of this section, the expression 'meeting' meant 'a meeting of *three or more persons* whether or not the public are admitted' (emphasis added). The invocation of this section against the Marumalarchi Dravida Munnetra Kazhagam (MDMK) leader V. Gopalasamy *aka* Vaiko, a member of Parliament and an ally of the BJP-led ruling coalition in the Centre, for making a speech supporting the Liberation Tigers of Tamil Eelam (LTTE), an organisation banned in 1991 under the Unlawful Activities Prevention Act, 1967, was contested by Vaiko in the Supreme Court.

Vaiko's petition was clubbed with *PUCL v. the Union of India,* which put before the Supreme Court the question of constitutional validity of POTA.[11] The Supreme Court upheld the constitutional validity of POTA and its extraordinary provisions on the ground that 'the crime' (terrorism) referred to under POTA was of an 'aggravated' nature, requiring provisions that departed from the ordinary law, which was 'inadequate and not sufficiently effective'. Section 21 was contemplated as one such provision to deal with new challenges.[12]

What is significant for our purposes is that the Supreme Court, by upholding the provisions pertaining to banning of terrorist organisations, including Section 21 which put a curb on meetings, not merely endorsed a subjective criterion for declaring/notifying such an organisation, it also gave the political executive absolute powers to determine the procedures for notification as well as denotification within the framework of the Act (POTA), removing both the processes out of the purview of judicial review or scrutiny.

Much of the Supreme Court's position on POTA is indicative of the 'new discursivity' around the rule of law, which, as Upendra Baxi points out, exhibits an unprecedented explosion in the reconfigured post-9/11 world order. Much of this, he argues, remains 'unexamined' and is *assumed* to be a 'good thing' (Baxi 2004). All extraordinary laws embody procedures which legitimise exceptions in investigation and trial. The legitimacy of procedural exceptions derives from political decisions identifying and affirming the existence of a state of emergency, which, it is assumed, make such exceptions imperative. These exceptions inject ambivalence in the rule of law that gets deepened with each specific exercise of state sovereignty in deciding the exception. While the decision on identification of exceptional conditions is deeply political and states of exception are indicative of a specific kind of politics, the latter ultimately envisages a society which is thoroughly depoliticised, evened out of cultural and ideological plurality, and deeply conformist.

The response of the Supreme Court is significant insofar as it has garnered legal-constitutional support for extraordinary laws by upholding the competence of the legislature to legislate on matters pertaining to 'public order'. It has, moreover, reinforced/validated Parliament's claims to the existence of a clear and present danger to national security, and sought to address concerns of arbitrariness merely by providing procedural 'safeguards' and guidelines to make them 'safe from abuse'. It is interesting how Supreme Court judgements, which have come in the 1990s, upholding the constitutional validity of TADA, AFSPA and later POTA have followed almost a similar pattern. The constitutional validity of all such laws was questioned in the Supreme Court by civil rights groups (Naga People's Movement for Human Rights [NPMHR] in the case of AFSPA and PUCL in the case of POTA). In TADA the appellant's case was argued by lawyers who were active in the struggle against extraordinary laws (Rajinder Sachar and Ram Jethmalani, among others). It was, however, in the judgement on AFSPA (*NPMHR v. Union of India*, decided on 27 November 1997) that the criminalisation and depoliticisation of people's struggles, in this case nationality struggles, became most evident. The petitioners contended that the conditions that obtained in the region were akin to an armed rebellion, which fell in the ambit of the emergency powers (Articles 352 to 360) of the Constitution, and were therefore outside the legislative authority of Parliament and that emergency provisions of Article 352 carried certain safeguards which were bypassed when the government brought in the AFSPA. Countering these arguments the judges concluded that there was 'no material on the record' which showed that 'the disturbed conditions' in the states in which AFSPA had been extended were in fact due to an 'armed rebellion'; even if the disturbance was indeed the result of armed rebellion by a section of the people, it was not of such a magnitude 'as to pose a threat to the security of the country or part thereof so as to call for invocation of the emergency powers under Article 352'. The Court therefore saw no ground to invoke the 'drastic power under Article 352', if the situation could be handled by the deployment of armed forces in the disturbed areas buttressed by the conferment of certain powers.[13] Significantly, while rejecting the petitioner's argument that what was being proclaimed by the government as a problem of public order in a disturbed area was in fact a 'rebellion', the judges effectively dismissed the contention that what was being construed as a 'disturbance' was indeed a political struggle being waged by a people resisting the hegemonic rule of the Indian state, and that AFSPA was one of the instruments for sustaining this rule.

The Supreme Court's affirmation of TADA was similarly replete with legal formalism. The Court validated the provisions of TADA and ruled that since terrorism was not an enumerated category in any of the three lists in the Seventh Schedule, it fell within the residuary powers belonging to Parliament.[14] More substantially, however, the Supreme Court steered clear of the crucial question of primacy of fundamental rights in the Constitution, by treating violation of rights as episodic cases of 'abuse' emerging not from the content of the law, but from the manner of its implementation. Thus, while upholding confessions in TADA, the Court addressed the issue of the rights of the accused by inserting procedural safeguards and review procedures.[15] A similar question of abuse arose out of the immunity from criminal prosecution enjoyed by the armed forces under AFSPA. In its judgement delivered in the *NPMHR. v. Union of India* case, the Supreme Court addressed the question of 'impunity' to armed forces under the Act and cases of human rights abuses, by reiterating the attorney general's (appearing for the Union of India) recipe of *dos and don'ts* which the army was ostensibly following.

Similarly, the admissibility of confession before a police officer under Section 15 of TADA was upheld by the Supreme Court in *Kartar Singh v. State of Punjab* as an 'overwhelming need'.[16] Subscribing to what may be called the *principle of legislative classification and rule of differentiation,* the judges affirmed the existence of 'terrorists and disruptionists' as a *distinct class of offenders,* who could not be tried under 'normal' laws, and 'terrorism' as a *distinct category of offence,* requiring the special provision of Section 15. Starting from this premise, the Supreme Court held that the provisions of Section 15 were 'non-discriminatory', and 'in the circumstances' *not* 'unjust, unfair or oppressive' (*Kartar Singh v. State of Punjab*: para 218).

By pushing the principle of legislative competence and the rule of differentiation within the framework of 'need', the Supreme Court relinquished the responsibility of addressing the question of harshness of provisions. In the process the Court revised the principles of fair and just trial. With the acceptance of the prosecution's assertion that '*a fair trial has two objectives*: it must be fair to the accused and also to the prosecution', rights of the prosecution protecting and representing the 'victim' were recognised as co-equal with those of the accused, modifying thereby the basic principle of a fair trial, viz., the assumption of innocence. It needs to be emphasised that the case against Section 15 of TADA pertaining to confessions was being built not only on the ground of its redundancy in the context of a pending presentation before the magistrate, but also on account of the scope it provided for torture and abuse of the accused.

Procedural Rupture, Contests Within, and the Permanence of the Temporary

As seen in the discussions earlier, the Supreme Court not only endorsed extraordinary procedures on the rationale of supreme necessity not covered by regular law, it also accepted and upheld the executive's delineation of necessity. While affirming the constitutional validity of extraordinary laws, the Supreme Court invariably focussed on the question of 'legislative competence', choosing not to interrogate the 'need' for such a law on the ground that it was a 'policy matter', and therefore not subject to judicial review. In the process, the Supreme Court expanded the legislative authority of the executive, giving it an overreach, to bridge the gap between what the state perceived as necessary power, and what the law actually makes available. Simultaneously, the judiciary eroded its specific overseeing function of judicial review, while aligning itself with the political class in the domain of policy-making.

Extraordinary laws may, however, be seen as occupying a domain of contest where the law-making, law-enforcing and adjudicating structures of the state traverse shifting/reconfiguring/realigning fields of convergences and divergences. Thus, even when the Supreme Court affirmed 'legal' responses of the state to people's movements, the judgements were often layered, and interspersed with dissenting notes. It is the points of convergence, however, which have had an enduring impact on notions of procedural and substantive justice and rights, and the structure of the criminal justice system. It is important, therefore, to identify how in these moments of convergence the judiciary became complicit in the 'violence of jurisprudence' (Hillyard 1993) and the law became an integral part of the organisation of state violence.[17]

Significantly, the history of judicial dissent may be traced to the Preventive Detention Act of 1950 when Justice Vivian Bose differed from his colleagues to adhere to an understanding of the Constitution which prioritised the people and their struggles:

> Look past the mere verbiage of the words & penetrate deep into the heart and spirit of the Constitution. ... I cannot bring myself to believe that the framers of our Constitution intended that the liberties guaranteed should be illusory and meaningless or that they should be toyed with by this person or that...
>
> I am not hampered here by the consideration of war necessity or emergency legislation where some authorities hold that the canons of construction are different and that allowance must be made in favour of the State for imperfections of language used in legislation which had to be drafted and enacted in a desperate hurry with the State in dire and immediate peril. I am construing a Constitution which was hammered out solemnly and deliberately after the most mature consideration and with the most anxious care... After all, who framed the constitution and for whose benefit was it made? Not just for those in brief authority, not only for lawyers and dialecticians but for the common people of India. ...To my mind, the whole concept of the Constitution is that after years of bitter struggle the citizens of India are assured that certain liberties shall be guaranteed to them and these liberties cannot be curtailed beyond limits... [18]

The dissenting judgement by Justice Shah in the TADA case *Devender Pal Singh v. State of NCT of Delhi and Another* focussed on the admissibility of confession as evidence, refusing to consider the confession valid solely on its merits as an act of morality. Justice Shah's note of dissent focussed on restoring the legal and procedural norms that the majority judgement had disregarded as mere 'irregularities'. The dissenting judgements by Justices K. Ramaswamy and R. M. Sahai, two out of the five judges in *Kartar Singh v. State of Punjab* which lay down the guidelines for procedural safeguards, may also be recalled here. Starting from the premise that 'one of the established rules or norms established everywhere is that custodial confession is presumed to be tainted', the judges sought to emphasise that both consistency with constitutional provisions and procedural logic were important considerations. Questioning the principles of legislative wisdom and legislative competence that was so central to the majority judgement, the dissenting judges pointed out that 'the mere fact that the Legislature was competent to make law' did not automatically mean that it was also 'empowered to curtail or erode a person of his fundamental rights'. The scope of legislative competence was determined by the limits put by the Constitution itself:

> Making a provision that has the effect of forcing a person to admit his guilt amounts to denial of liberty. The class of offences dealt by TADA Act may be different than any other offences but the offender under TADA Act is as much entitled to protection of Articles 20 and 21 as any other (Judgement: paras 456 and 460).[19]

The judgement of the Supreme Court in the Parliament Attack case, delivered on 4 August 2005, similarly distanced itself from the position on confessions articulated in judgements in the same case by the Special POTA Court and the Delhi High Court. Perhaps the most significant part of the judgement is its appraisal of Section 32 of POTA as upheld by the Supreme Court in the People's Union for Civil Liberties case:

> But as we see Section 32, a formidable doubt lingers in our minds despite the pronouncement in Kartar Singh's case.... *the evils which the framers of the Indian Evidence Act had in mind to exclude confessions to the police, are still prevalent though not in the same degree... In this scenario, we have serious doubts whether it would be safe to concede the power of recording confessions to the police officers to be used in evidence against the accused making the confession and the co-accused...*[20]

The judges subsequently set aside the confessional statement made by two of the accused for not having followed procedural safeguards which made their truthfulness suspect.

Despite the trajectory of dissent, substantive liberty, holding out the promise of weaving rights into legal formalism, and substantive notions of the rule of law, where procedures protect specific rights integral to fair trial, remain inadequately realised. This has largely been the result of another aspect of the Indian legal system, which, as Upendra Baxi (1982: 30–31) has argued, has existed ever since the enactment of the Preventive Detention Act in 1950. The Indian legal system, he argues, has managed the coexistence of the Preventive Detention System (PDS), an institution authorised by the Constitution of India itself, which has been used increasingly not just to deny fundamental rights to political opposition but also as a parallel legal system in aid of the Criminal Justice System (CJS). The most striking distinctions between the two systems pertain to the object, models of justice and patterns of power-sharing that they espouse. The CJS is based on the assumption of primacy of social defence as the object of law, the maximisation and optimisation of due process as its strategy, and the pre-eminence of courts that are legalistic and pro-accused in their disposition. The PDS, on the other hand, is primarily geared towards repressing (primarily political and ideological) opposition, thrives on minimal due process and gives pre-eminence to executive decision-making and 'satisfaction' in the initiation and affirmation of extraordinary proceedings. The prioritisation of the executive becomes instrumental in relegating the pro-libertarian aspects of adjudication, and the subsequent predomination of a 'jurisdiction of suspicion' (Ibid.).

Yet, an integration of the two systems may also be seen in a distinctive pattern of concurrence and interlocking that has emerged in recent years between the extraordinary and ordinary. POTA and TADA judgements that have come after 9/11, as well as the Report of the Committee on Reforms of Criminal Justice System (the Malimath Committee) submitted in April 2003, show the development of a complex and interlocking system of laws, so that laws pertaining to 'ordinary crimes' and those claiming to deal with extraordinary contexts intertwine and come to traverse common grounds, leading to permanence of the temporary (Singh 2004, 2007). Anti-terror laws may, moreover, amend specific statutes of the ordinary law or there may be a mutual sharing of provisions between the ordinary and extraordinary laws. As a result of this symbiosis between ordinary criminal law and emergency legislation, there occurs a general tightening up throughout the statutory law (Hillyard 1993: 263). This standardisation of law becomes symptomatic of 'an insidious circular process in which draconian laws soften us up to similar laws which become the desired standard for further measure' (Sim and Thomas 1983: 75). There are two specific constituents of this mutual sharing or interlocking. As mentioned at the outset, TADA gave evidentiary value to confessions before police officers. This judicial validation of an exception constituted a rupture in criminal jurisprudence, which persisted in POTA. Specific provisions of POTA, after it was repealed, percolated into an existing (ordinary/normal) law (Unlawful Activities Prevention Act [UAPA] 1967), giving extraordinary provisions a hitherto elusive permanence.

This erosion of boundaries between the ordinary and extraordinary has become a preferred official policy, as evident in the recommendations of the Malimath Committee (2003) and the Second Administrative Reforms Commission (2007). The Malimath Committee had recommended the dislodging of what it termed 'the well recognised fundamental principles of criminal jurisprudence', i.e., the 'presumption of innocence' and 'the right to silence of the accused' and the 'burden of proof on the prosecution'. Arguing for a dynamic 'quest for truth' (Ministry of Home Affairs 2003: 6, 29, 266), the Committee favoured abbreviating the 'right to silence' of the accused which, the Committee felt, was an impediment in the quest for truth. In the search for truth, the judge was bound to tap the accused as a source of information. This 'tapping' was envisaged by the Committee as *a non-coercive* exercise despite the fact that failure to answer in a convincing way was to be construed as evidence of guilt. The Committee sought to facilitate this by following Section 27 of POTA that authorised the Special Court to take from the accused finger prints, foot prints, photographs, blood, saliva, semen, hair, voice of any accused person, and refusal to give such samples would allow the court to 'draw adverse inference against accused' (Ibid.: 276). The aforementioned has moreover become part of a trend whereby the law feeds on the body of the accused to draw evidence of guilt, often by creating conditions, as in narco-analysis or the administration of the so-called truth serum, where the accused is deprived of control over his/her self.

Irrespective of the changes in criminal jurisprudence, the courts through the 1990s and onwards have not resisted the gradual 'piling up of laws' that have, through devious and deceptive labelling, targeted specific communities in some cases and political/intellectual dissent in others. Thus, if the Maharashtra Control of Organised Crime Act (MCOCA), which came in 1999 to deal with organised crime, became a precursor and model for POTA, the Chhattisgarh Public Security Act achieved in the state what GUJCOCA in Gujarat, or a similar Bill being proposed in Uttar Pradesh, seek to attain.

The two sets of judgements examined in this essay show that in the domain of formal/electoral politics, the Supreme Court substantiated political rights by making an emphatic case for citizens' right to know within the broad ambit of freedom of speech and expression. Clearly, in a context where the relative functional boundaries of two constitutional bodies are to be determined, the Supreme Court functions as a regulatory institution by putting a check on the legislature's attempt to limit the reservoir of the Election Commission's sphere of constitutional authority. In the process it not only affirmed the residuary powers of the Election Commission, but also expanded the domain of autonomy of the citizen-voter, by making his/her act of voting an outcome of informed rational-choice. Yet, if this judgement is seen in tandem with those that have come in matters pertaining to the constitutional validity of extraordinary laws, such as AFSPA, TADA and POTA, all of which give exceptional powers to the political executive and enhance the coercive powers of the state, it may be suggested that the Supreme Court's notion of the 'political' is by and large enframed by a notion of procedural democracy. Moreover, unlike the judgement in the case of electoral reforms, where the Court insisted on a purging of the electoral domain by eliminating criminals, intervening thereby in the constitution of the elected/representative body, while upholding extraordinary laws, it clearly takes up a position of legal-formalism and a notion of politics where political rights and civil liberties may be dispensed with in the face of what it considers more pressing concerns of security of the state. The fact that almost always the target of such laws are people's movements, which have been raising issues of identity, autonomy, access to resources and rights of minority communities, is considered irrelevant in favour of regime-sustenance. Almost inadvertently, it endorses a politics that seeks to institutionalise exceptions in law, freeing itself of the constraints of due process, burden of proof and reasoned assessment of possible alternatives.

The political gets constrained and occluded where questions of ideological pluralism are concerned, so much so that the court does not hesitate in becoming complicit with the state in its neo-liberal agenda and a willing partner in the hegemonic nationalist project, excluding people's movements, and ushering in a jurisprudence of suspicion around communities and groups. By and large there seems to be a continuing trajectory of the Supreme Court's location within liberal democratic jurisprudence where the court is apprehensive of collective action—of social and political movements—that may dismantle existing socio-economic and political structures.

NOTES

1. The shifts had set in the late 1980s in the social-ideological domain of the state—the emergence of aggressive Hindutva forces, caste competitiveness in the electoral sphere, the assertion of nationality aspirations; in the economic sphere—the commencement of the liberalisation process; and the political realm with the onset of coalition politics at the Centre and the federalisation of national political parties.
2. Iris Marion Young (2007) draws an analogy between the legitimation of inequality in the family and practices of the security state which emerged after 9/11 in the US and elsewhere. Such legitimation practices invoke the necessity for masculine protection eliciting thereby the consent and willing submission to state dictates.
3. These are the Armed Forces Special Powers Act (AFSPA, 1958) and the Disturbed Areas Acts, lapsed or repealed anti-terror laws like Terrorist Affected Areas (Special Courts) Act (1984), Terrorist and Disruptive Activities (Prevention) Act (TADA, 1985, 1987) and Prevention of Terrorism Act (POTO, 2001, POTA, 2002), under which cases continue to be tried, the Unlawful Activities Prevention Act (UAPA, 1967, 2004, 2008), which has been amended to incorporate extraordinary provisions of repealed POTA, and Maharashtra Control of Organised Crime Act (MCOCA, 1999) and other public safety acts brought in by specific states (such as the Chhattisgarh Public Safety Act, 2005).
4. The expression refers to the dynamism which the electoral process witnessed in the period, characterised by a hitherto unprecedented upsurge in the electoral participation of the socially underprivileged, so that the likelihood of a very poor person casting his/her vote not only became more pronounced, it became more than one-and-a-half times higher than his/her upper-class counterpart (Yadav 1997: 177–207).
5. For details and context of the Supreme Court judgement, see *Union of India v. Association for Democratic Reforms & Anr* (SC 249/2002).
6. Section 33B inserted in the amended Act lay down: 'Notwithstanding anything contained in any judgment, decree or order of any court or any direction, order or any other instruction issued by the Election Commission, no candidate shall be liable to disclose or furnish any such information, in respect of his election which is not required to be disclosed or furnished under this Act or the rules made thereunder.'
7. *People's Union for Civil Liberties (PUCL) & Another v. Union of India and Another*, in *Judgment Today*, 2 (10), 20 March 2003, SC 529–533.

8. The AFSPA was enacted in 1958, giving special powers to the armed forces in the 'disturbed areas' of Assam and the then Union Territory of Manipur. The Act was amended in 1972 and 1986, and was extended to the whole of Assam and Manipur, and also to Arunachal Pradesh, Meghalaya, Mizoram, Nagaland and Tripura. In 1990, the Act was extended to Jammu and Kashmir.
9. In his work, *The Concept of the Political* (1932, trans. 1976) coinciding with the disintegration of the Weimar Republic, Schmitt proposes that in a state of emergency, the state is faced with an imperiling condition, threatening its existence, which makes the ordinary law and order mechanisms ineffective. The nature of politics that such a response espouses is embedded in a fundamental distinction between friend and enemy where the basis of distinction, viz., race, religion, ethnicity, class, is not important as much as the intensity of difference. The distinction arises when one political entity regards the other as its 'existential negation' so that the appropriate response can only be one which brings about the death of the enemy. See, for details, David Dyzenhaus (2001: 21–38).
10. Ten of the twenty-three groups—the United Liberation Front of Assam (ULFA), the National Democratic Front of Bodoland (NDFB), the People's Liberation Army (PLA), the United National Liberation Front (UNLF), the People's Revolutionary Party of Kangleipak (PREPAK), Kangleipak Communist Party (KCP), the Kanglei Yaol Kanba Lup (KYKL), the Manipur People's Liberation Front (MPLF), the All Tripura Tiger Force and the National Liberation Front of Tripura (NLFT)—were from the North-East. The other organisations were: the Liberation Tigers of Tamil Eelam (LTTE), the Students Islamic Movement of India (SIMI), the Deendar Anjuman, the Babbar Khalsa International, the Khalistan Commando Force, the Khalistan Zindabad Force, and the International Sikh Youth Foundation. On 5 December 2001, the Communist Party of India (Marxist Leninist) People's War and Maoist Communist Centre (MCC) along with all their 'Formations and Front Organisations' were added to the list. Several other organisations were added later and by 21 July 2002, the number of banned organisations had reached thirty-two. Later, Al Badr, Jamait-Ul-Mujahideen, Al-Qaida, Dukhtaran-E-Millat (DEM), Tamil Nadu Liberation Army (TNLA), Tamil National Retrieval Troops (TNRT) and Akhil Bharatiya Nepali Ekta Samaj (ABNES) were added.
11. Three petitions by PUCL, the All India Human Rights and Social Justice Front, and Vaiko, respectively, were admitted in the Supreme Court on 13 January 2003.
12. *People's Union for Civil Liberties & Anr v. Union of India*, paras 48–50, *Scale*, No. 10, 2003, pp. 967–98.
13. *Naga People's Movement for Human Rights v. Union of India* (1998) 2 SCC 109 at page 35.
14. The Lists contained in the Seventh Schedule to the Constitution of India separate the powers of legislation over subjects between the Union and the states. List I enumerates the subjects over which the Union may legislate, List II—the subjects over which the states may legislate, and List III—the subjects over which both the

Union and the states may legislate. If an item is not mentioned in any of the Lists, the power to legislate over that subject matter lies with the Union.

15. While looking at the constitutional validity of the Act, in the case *Kartar Singh v. State of Punjab* (1994), the Constitution Bench of the Supreme Court suggested that a 'higher level of scrutiny and applicability of TADA' should be ensured by setting up a screening or review committee. *Kartar Singh v. State of Punjab* (1994) 3 SCC 569, at page 683.
16. *Kartar Singh v. State of Punjab* Writ petition no. 1833 of 1984 (decided on 11 March 1994)—SCC 569, 1994, pp. 569–791.
17. The 'violence of jurisprudence' approach identifies with a position that refuses to see law as an antithesis to power and violence. In his work, Paddy Hillyard (1993: 263) examines 'the awesome, physical force that law deploys' and the '*effects* of legal force', showing the ways in which law becomes an integral part of the organisation of state violence, eroding rights and institutions that are entrusted with the responsibility to guard and restore them (emphasis added).
18. *S. Krishnan and Others v. The State Of Madras* AIR 1951 SC 301 at para 43.
19. *Kartar Singh v. State of Punjab* (1994) 3 SCC 569 at page 763 (para 456) and 767 (para 460).
20. Supreme Court judgement in the Parliament Attack Case (Criminal Appeal nos 373–381). Emphasis added. *State (National Capital Territory of Delhi) v. Navjot Sandhu and Others* (2005) 11 SCC 600, at page 677.

REFERENCES

Baxi, Upendra. 1982. *The Crisis of the Indian Legal System*. New Delhi: Vikas.

———. 2002. 'The (Im)possibility of Constitutional Justice: Seismographic Notes on Indian Constitutionalism'. In *India's Living Constitution: Ideas, Practices, Controversies*, eds Zoya Hasan, E. Sridharan and R. Sudarshan, 31–63. New Delhi: Permanent Black.

———. 2004. 'Rule of Law in India: Theory and Practice'. In *Asian Discourses of Rule of Law: Theories and Implementation of Rule of Law in Twelve Asian Countries, France and the US*, ed. Randall Peerenboom, 318–39. London and New York: Routledge.

Chatterjee, Partha. 2004. *The Politics of the Governed*. New Delhi: Permanent Black.

Dyzenhaus, David. 2001. 'The Permanence of the Temporary: Can Emergency Powers be Normalised'. In *The Security of Freedom: Essays on Canada's Anti-Terrorism Bill*, eds Ronald J. Daniels, Patrick Macklem and Kent Roach, 21–37. Toronto: University of Toronto Press.

Hillyard, Paddy. 1993. *Suspect Community: People's Experience of Terrorism Acts in Britain*. London: Pluto Press.

Kannabiran, K. G. 2003. *Wages of Impunity: Power, Justice and Human Rights.* Hyderabad: Orient Longman.

Kapur, Devesh, and Pratap Bhanu Mehta. 2005. *Public Institutions in India: Performance and Design.* New Delhi: Oxford University Press.

Ministry of Home Affairs. 2003. Report of the Committee on Reforms of Criminal Justice System. Vol. I, March. Delhi: Ministry of Home Affairs, Government of India. Available at http://mha.nic.in/pdfs/criminal_justice_system.pdf. Accessed on 13 August, 2013

Report of the Second Administrative Reforms Commission on Public Order. 2007. Delhi: Government of India, June.

Schmitt, Carl. 1996. *The Concept of the Political.* Trans. George Schwab. London: University of Chicago Press.

Sim, J., and P. A. Thomas. 1983. 'The Prevention of Terrorism Act: Normalising the Politics of Repression'. *Journal of Law and Society,* 10 (1): 71–84.

Singh, Ujjwal Kumar. 2004. 'State and the Emerging Interlocking Legal Systems in India: Permanence of the Temporary'. *Economic and Political Weekly,* 39 (2): 149–54.

———.2007. *The State, Democracy and Anti-terror Laws in India.* New Delhi: Sage.

Yadav, Yogendra. 1997. 'Reconfiguration in Indian Politics: State Assembly Elections 1993–1995'. In *State and Politics in India,* ed. Partha Chatterjee, 177–207. New Delhi: Oxford University Press.

Young, Iris Marion. 2007. 'The Logic of Masculinist Protection: Reflections on the Current Security State'. In *Global Challenges, War, Self Determination and Responsibility for Justice,* Iris Marion Young, 117–40. Cambridge: Polity Press.

Notes on Contributors

Upendra Baxi is Professor Emeritus, University of Warwick, UK and Professor Emeritus, University of Delhi.

Philippe Cullet is Professor of International and Environmental Law at SOAS, University of London, the Convener of the International Environmental Law Research Centre (IELRC) and a Senior Visiting Fellow at the Centre for Policy Research, Delhi.

Varun Gauri is Head of the Global Insights Initiative (GINI) and Senior Economist with the Development Research Group of the World Bank.

Madhav Khosla is currently pursuing his PhD in political theory at Harvard University.

Sudhir Krishnaswamy is a Professor of Law at Azim Premji University, Bangalore and the Dr B. R. Ambedkar Visiting Professor of Indian Constitutional Law, Columbia Law School, New York.

Nivedita Menon is Professor at the Centre for Comparative Politics and Political Theory, Jawaharlal Nehru University.

Siddharth Narrain is a lawyer, and Research Associate at Sarai-Centre for the Study of Developing Societies (CSDS), Delhi.

Aditya Nigam is Professor at Centre for the Study of Developing Societies, Delhi.

Usha Ramanathan works on the jurisprudence of law, poverty and rights. She writes and speaks on issues that include the Bhopal Gas Disaster, mass displacement, eminent domain, civil liberties, beggary, criminal law, custodial institutions, the death penalty, the environment, and judicial process.

Mayur Suresh is a Lecturer at the School of Oriental and African Studies (SOAS), University of London.

Ujjwal Kumar Singh is Professor in the Department of Political Science, University of Delhi.

Arun K. Thiruvengadam is an Associate Professor at the School of Policy and Governance, Azim Premji University (APU), Bangalore.

Index